Virgil

UNDERSTANDING CLASSICS

Richard Stoneman (University of Exeter)

When the great Roman poets of the Augustan Age – Ovid, Virgil and Horace – composed their odes, love poetry and lyrical verse, could they have imagined that their works would one day form a cornerstone of Western civilization, or serve as the basis of study for generations of schoolchildren learning Latin? Could Aeschylus or Euripides have envisaged the remarkable popularity of contemporary stagings of their tragedies? The legacy and continuing resonance of Homer's *Iliad* and *Odyssey* – Greek poetical epics written many millennia ago – again testify to the capacity of the classics to cross the divide of thousands of years and speak powerfully and relevantly to audiences quite different from those to which they were originally addressed.

Understanding Classics is a specially commissioned series which aims to introduce the outstanding authors and thinkers of antiquity to a wide audience of appreciative modern readers, whether undergraduate students of classics, literature, philosophy and ancient history or generalists interested in the classical world. Each volume – written by leading figures internationally – will examine the historical significance of the writer or writers in question; their social, political and cultural contexts; their use of language, literature and mythology; extracts from their major works; and their reception in later European literature, art, music and culture. *Understanding Classics* will build a library of readable, authoritative introductions offering fresh and elegant surveys of the greatest literatures, philosophies and poetries of the ancient world.

Cicero, Gesine Manuwald
Euripides, Isabelle Torrance
Eusebius, Aaron P. Johnson
Homer, Jonathan S. Burgess
Horace, Paul Allen Miller
Latin Love Poetry, Denise McCoskey & Zara Torlone

Virgil

Alison Keith

UNDERSTANDING CLASSICS SERIES EDITOR:
RICHARD STONEMAN

BLOOMSBURY ACADEMIC
LONDON • NEW YORK • OXFORD • NEW DELHI • SYDNEY

BLOOMSBURY ACADEMIC
Bloomsbury Publishing Plc
50 Bedford Square, London, WC1B 3DP, UK
1385 Broadway, New York, NY 10018, USA

BLOOMSBURY, BLOOMSBURY ACADEMIC and the Diana logo are
trademarks of Bloomsbury Publishing Plc

First published in Great Britain 2020

Cover design and illustration: www.simonlevyassociates.co.uk

A catalogue record for this book is available from the British Library.

Library of Congress Control Number 2019949582.

ISBN: HB: 978-1-8488-5919-7
        PB: 978-1-8488-5920-3
        ePDF: 978-1-3501-1435-7
        eBook: 978-1-3501-1436-4

Series: Understanding Classics

Typeset by RefineCatch Limited, Bungay, Suffolk
Printed and bound in Great Britain

To find out more about our authors and books visit www.bloomsbury.com
and sign up for our newsletters.

D.M.

R.E.F.
A.G.K.

Contents

Preface

I am grateful to Richard Stoneman and Alex Wright, who first commissioned this volume for I.B. Tauris, and to Alice Wright and Lily Mac Mahon, who have seen it through to publication for Bloomsbury Academic. The changes in press and personnel bear witness to the slow pace at which I worked, as I moved from the chair of Classics into the directorship of the Jackman Humanities Institute at the University of Toronto. I am truly obliged to my editors, my colleagues and my students for their patience and forbearance along the way.

Anyone who writes a book about Virgil comes quickly to see how greatly they stand in the debt of their predecessors, ancient and modern, creative and critical. It has been sheer pleasure to spend time with the Roman poet and his literary and scholarly acolytes, though my notes cannot do justice to them all. I have presented parts of the discussions in this volume in various scholarly venues: the Classical Association of Canada, the University of British Columbia workshop on Virgil's translators, the conference on 'Flavian Campania' in Naples, *Symposium Cumanum* at the Villa Vergiliana in Italy, the 11th *Trends in Classics* conference on 'Intratextuality and Roman literature' in Thessaloniki, the University of Manitoba and Western University. I am grateful to my interlocutors on those occasions and especially to friends and colleagues who read part or all of the manuscript: Lorenza Bennardo, †Elaine Fantham, Stephen Hinds, Sharon James, Sarah McCallum, Jim O'Hara and Stephen Rupp. They have all tried to talk some sense into me as I have wrestled with the philosophical infrastructure of Virgil's verse. Marion Durand, Nathan Gilbert and John MacCormick have been especially helpful with this material, as have several generations of Toronto graduate students, among whom I thank in particular Chiara Graf, Laura Harris, Caitlin Hines and Samantha Mazzilli.

This book was conceived and written not for professional scholars but for amateur students of the classics and the general reader, the first and best of whom was exemplified for me by my father. His wide reading and catholic taste were an inspiration and a challenge to me in my own student days, and I would like to think that this book is some small testimony to his love of learning and literature. My other dedicatee was one of the foremost professional classicists of her, or any other, generation, but she was also a leading voice in the dissemination of knowledge about the ancient world beyond the academy, and it is in memory of her personal and professional generosity that I offer the present work.

Life and Times

Publius Vergilius Maro (70–19 BCE) was the most celebrated poet of his time and so he remains today: the most famous classical Latin poet, author of the *Aeneid* and conduit of classical epic and pastoral verse to Europe and the western artistic tradition. His poetry was widely read and immensely popular already in his own lifetime, when he was acclaimed the Roman Homer, and interest in his life and habits was intense and continuing. As a result, we possess a good deal of contemporary anecdotal evidence about his life as well as a number of ancient biographies, most of them probably derived from the lost *Life of Virgil* by Suetonius (*c.* 70–130 CE, biographer and imperial bureaucrat), which was included in the section 'On Poets' in his *Lives* 'Of Famous Men' and probably formed the basis of the life appended to Donatus' (lost) commentary on Virgil's complete works.[1] We thus have richer and more abundant evidence for Virgil's life than for any other Latin poet of classical antiquity.[2]

Classical scholars have shown, however, that ancient biographers had different standards of evidence and historical accuracy than we do today and so we cannot always take the claims of the ancient biographies at face value.[3] Much of the material preserved in the ancient *Lives* is obviously based on inferences drawn from biographical reading of Virgil's poetry – not only of his pastoral collection *Bucolica* (often called *Eclogues* after the individual selections) and his four-book disquisition on farming entitled *Georgica*, but also of a host of works collected in the *Appendix Vergiliana*, which scholars no longer consider authentically Virgilian. This interpretive strategy was current in antiquity at least as early as the Hellenistic period, when Aristotle's students and the scholars working in the Mouseion in Alexandria began to compile biographies of the archaic and classical Greek poets.[4] Modern scepticism concerning the validity of this procedure notwithstanding, Virgil and his earliest readers will have been schooled in the ancient literary critical convention of deducing the details of an author's life from his textual corpus.[5] Indeed, Virgil manifestly invites autobiographical interpretation at various points in *B.* (Ch. 2.2) and *G.* (Ch. 3.2). By testing the ancient biographers' statements with scrupulous care against quotations both from Virgil's own works and from surviving non-Virgilian texts and documents, we can often confirm, contextualize and/or discount the information our poet and his biographers provide.[6]

Virgil lived through the final series of military and political crises that brought an end to nearly 500 years of republican government in ancient Rome. The period of Julius Caesar's dominance, from his embattled consulship of 59 BCE and subsequent tenure of a provincial military command in Gaul (58–50), culminated in the civil wars of 49–46, in which he crushed his republican opponents, and ended in his dictatorship (46–44) and assassination on the Ides of March 44. Caesar's murder sparked the renewal of civil war between the republican forces (led by the tyrannicides, Cassius and Brutus) and his heirs (the triumvirs Marc Antony, Octavian and Lepidus), which resulted in the defeat of the republican army at Philippi in 42. But another decade of civil war ensued as the triumvirs campaigned not only against the remnants of the republican party (who rallied in Sicily under Pompey's son Sextus, until his defeat at Naulochus in 36), but also against one another (Battle of Mutina, 43; Perusine War, 41; Pact of Brundisium, 40; Treaty of Tarentum, 37; etc.). Octavian and Marc Antony finally broke off relations in 32 and confronted one another at the Battle of Actium in September 31. After his defeat of Antony and Cleopatra there, Octavian invaded and annexed Egypt, before returning to Rome and celebrating a triple triumph in August 29, commemorating his conquest of Illyricum, victory at Actium and annexation of Egypt. Even after his 'restoration' of the republic and receipt of the title 'Augustus' in 27, there remained residual resistance to his supremacy, as evidenced by the abortive conspiracy of Varro Murena in 23, among others.[7] Virgil was an eyewitness to much of the conflict, having lived in Rome for about a decade from the mid-50s to the mid-40s BCE, and then perhaps losing his family estate in the confiscations after the Battle of Philippi at the end of the 40s, when he met some of Octavian's most prominent political operatives. He composed his first two collections of poetry, *Bucolica* and *Georgica*, during the uncertainty and upheaval of the triumviral period, completing the *Georgica* shortly after the Battle of Actium, and he worked on the *Aeneid* throughout the 20s. Nor did he live long enough to see Caesar's ruthless great-nephew Octavian transform himself fully into the accomplished elder statesman Augustus, who celebrated the renewal of the state in the 'Secular Games' of 17.

The ancient lives agree that Virgil was born on the Ides (15th) of October in the year 70 BCE. Donatus (*VSD* 3) reports that the poet was born in a small village called Andes, near Mantua, to parents of humble background. The biographers record the name of Virgil's mother as Polla Magia, while the conventions of Roman nomenclature confirm that his father's family name was Vergilius. The Latin spelling of Vergilius, with an initial 'e', was changed in the Christian middle ages to 'Virgilius' as a pun on his 'virginal' character (see below), and English orthography traditionally retains the initial 'i'. The ancient biographers report that Virgil's father was of lower social status than his mother, but modern scholars have been sceptical of these reports of his humble background, in part because lowly origins are a conventional feature of ancient biographies.[8] A more substantive indicator of Virgil's class background can be found in the detail of his *cognomen*, Maro, which is the name of an Etruscan magistracy.[9] Virgil's *cognomen* implies that an ancestor (or ancestors) had held this important elective office at Mantua, with the further implication that his family possessed sufficient wealth to qualify them for local politics. The conclusion seems inescapable, therefore, that Virgil belonged to the rank of municipal equestrians and came from a leading family of Mantua.

Virgil's privileged class background is confirmed by the ancient accounts of his elite educational attainments. He studied at Cremona until he assumed the 'adult toga' either in 55 or 53, 'on the very day that the poet Lucretius died' (*VSD* 6). Biographical syncretism is a conventional feature of ancient lives,[10] and modern scholars are rightly sceptical of the coincidence of Virgil's assumption of the adult toga on the very day of the death of T. Lucretius Carus (*c.* 99 – *c.* 55 BCE), the author of a six-book didactic poem on Epicurean physics, 'On the nature of the universe' (*De rerum natura*). We may interpret the biographical syncretism that links Virgil's coming of age to Lucretius' death, however, as an index of the breadth and depth of Virgil's imitations of his admired elder contemporary's great Epicurean manifesto.

In his *Chronica*, the church father Jerome specifies the year 53 as the date of Virgil's removal first to Milan and then, soon after, to Rome, where the biographer Probus explicitly places Virgil's studies 'with the most learned exponents of rhetoric', when civil war broke out between Octavian and Marc Antony at Mutina in April 43. Although Probus' text is confused and lacunose at this point, he seems to date the end of Virgil's rhetorical studies to the renewal of civil war in the aftermath of Caesar's assassination. Our poet's study at Rome is therefore best put in the decade 53–44 BCE. In this period, a formal education served as the foundation for entry into a legal or political career in the forum and senate, and Donatus reports that Virgil pleaded a single case in a court of law (*VSD* 15).

Virgil himself, however, appears to have preferred philosophy to rhetoric. Donatus (*VSD* 15) records his interests in medicine and mathematics, both branches of the study of philosophy in antiquity, and Servius' reference to his studies at Naples also implies philosophical pursuits, for Naples and Campania more generally were storied bastions in Italy of Greek culture, especially philosophical study. The ancient biographies attest Virgil's study with the Epicurean teacher Siro at Naples in the 40s. A comparatively obscure figure today, Siro is known to us only from two poems in the *Appendix Vergiliana*, a papyrus fragment from Herculaneum (*P.Herc.* 312) and a reference in the second book of Cicero's treatise 'On the ends of goods and evils' (*De finibus bonorum et malorum*), where the speaker Torquatus yields to the authority of the Epicurean teachers Siro and Philodemos, 'both excellent fellows and very learned men' (Cic. *Fin.* 2.119).[11]

We are better informed about Siro's friend and associate Philodemos, the leader of an Epicurean community near Naples, at Herculaneum.[12] There he apparently lived in the patronage of L. Calpurnius Piso Caesoninus (Julius Caesar's father-in-law), from approximately the late 70s to the late 40s or early 30s, when he is thought to have died. Ongoing excavations at the Villa of the Papyri in Herculaneum – a town buried by Vesuvius along with Pompeii in 79 CE – have yielded over 1,100 charred papyrus rolls, of which Philodemos is the author of the greatest number. Three papyrus fragments are of particular interest, because they document Virgil as one of the four addressees of Philodemos' work 'On Flattery', part of his major work *On Vices and their Corresponding Virtues* dated to the middle of the first century BCE.[13] A papyrus fragment names Philodemos' four Roman addressees as Plotius, Varius, Virgil and Quintilius (*P.Herc. Paris.* 2; cf. *P.Herc.* 1082). Virgil is here addressed in the company of the very Epicurean comrades with whom the biographer Probus reports that 'he lived for many years in wealthy leisure, as a follower of the sect of [the Athenian philosopher] Epicurus [341–270 BCE],[14] enjoying outstanding harmony and friendship'.

Both the ancient biographies and contemporary anecdotes confirm the importance of these friends, not only in Virgil's Epicurean community but also for his literary career. Donatus identifies Varius and Plotius as Virgil's literary executors, in his report of his death on 21 September 19 BCE (*VSD* 37). Varius is of particular interest as the literary executor who took the lead in editing Virgil's unfinished *Aeneid*. He is commonly agreed to be L. Varius Rufus, the author of a Latin epic poem 'On Death', written between 44 and 39, on a favourite Epicurean theme (cf. Philodemos, 'On Death'; Lucretius, *De rerum natura* Book 3).[15] The poet Horace (Q. Horatius Flaccus, 69–8 BCE), Virgil's friend and contemporary, lauds Varius as the foremost exponent of Latin epic

(*Sat.* 1.10.43–4) in the mid-30s BCE, while in the ninth eclogue Virgil himself praises Varius, together with C. Helvius Cinna (d. 44 BCE),[16] a poet and politician of the preceding generation (*B.* 9.35–6).

Horace's first book of *Satires* (put into circulation as a collection in 35 BCE, but containing poems composed somewhat earlier in the decade) is a rich source of evidence for Virgil's life during the early 30s.[17] In *Satire* 1.10 Horace mentions Virgil alongside Plotius, Varius and C. Cilnius Maecenas (68–8 BCE), Octavian's wealthy Etruscan friend and a generous patron to many contemporary poets, in a passage listing the discriminating critics to whom he entrusts his verse (*Sat.* 1.10.81–90): 'may Plotius and Varius, Maecenas and Virgil, Valgius and Octavius approve these poems, and the excellent Fuscus'. Virgil, Varius and Plotius also appear together in *Satire* 1.5, which describes a trip to Brindisi with their patron Maecenas on a diplomatic mission in 38 or 37. Horace recalls that while travelling with Maecenas he met these friends at Sinuessa (*Sat.* 1.5.39–40), which lay on the Gulf of Caieta, just north of the Bay of Naples, where the Epicurean communities of Siro and Philodemos were located in the 40s, and where we may assume Virgil and his Epicurean intimates continued to live in the 30s. Horace's reference to his close relationship with the three friends (*Sat.* 1.5.41–4) is couched in specifically Epicurean terms, and recalls Torquatus' translation of Epicurus' teaching of the bliss of friendship (*KD* 27) in Cicero's *De finibus* (1.65). Elsewhere in his first book of *Satires*, Horace credits Virgil and Varius with having introduced him to Maecenas (*Sat.* 1.6.54–5). While we do not know the circumstances that led to Virgil's meeting with Maecenas in the late 40s, his relations with this wealthy patron of the arts and long-time associate of Octavian were close enough for him to recommend Horace to him in the early 30s, and clearly remained so throughout the rest of the decade, when Donatus reports (*VSD* 20, 25) that Virgil was at work on the *Georgics*, dedicated to Maecenas (*G.* 1.2, 2.41, 3.41, 4.2).[18]

Quintilius Varus, the last of Virgil's three Epicurean friends mentioned by Probus and fellow dedicatee of Philodemos' 'On Flattery', is also well attested, named by both Horace (*Ars* 438–44) and the late antique grammarian Servius in his discussion of *B.* 6.13–15: 'the youths Chromis and Mnasyllos saw Silenus lying asleep in a glade, sleeping off yesterday's wine, as always'. Servius sets this passage in the context of Virgil's studies with his friends under Siro in Naples and explains: 'He urges the Muses to recall the song that Silenus sang to the boys: for he means to follow the Epicurean sect, which Virgil (like Varus) had learned under Siro's tutelage. And he introduces Siro as if in the *persona* of Silenus, but Chromis and Mnasyllos he means to be identified as himself and Varus'. We shall return to the Epicurean colour of these lines in the next chapter (Ch. 2.3); here we should note that Virgil's Epicurean comrade Varus has been persuasively identified with Horace's literary companion Quintilius, described in the *Ars Poetica* as a true friend and discriminating critic who, in commenting on a friend's poetry, offers not false flattery but honest criticism. Horace's late antique commentator Porphyry identifies this man as Quintilius Varus of Cremona, and his provenance suggests long acquaintance with Virgil.[19]

Why would Philodemos address a treatise 'On Flattery' to the four friends? David Sider has argued that Philodemos and his addressees 'shared a common interest not only in poetry and philosophy but more particularly in the relationship between poetry and philosophy'.[20] He has therefore suggested that Philodemos makes the same point in his treatise 'On Flattery' as Horace does at this point in his *Ars Poetica* – 'namely that people truly interested in philosophy would never flatter their friends'.[21] In light of the evidence of the Herculaneum papyri, Horace's contemporary witness to Virgil's Epicurean friendships, and Probus' explicit testimony in his biography of our poet, there can be no reason to doubt Virgil's serious and sustained study of Epicurean philosophy, and we shall try to remain open to its resonances when reading his poetry.[22]

The political turbulence provoked by Julius Caesar's murder seems to have interrupted Virgil's philosophical studies. A persistent biographical tradition reports the loss of his patrimony during the civil wars and violent dispossessions of the triumvirate, which was established in November 43 BCE after Octavian and Antony joined forces in the aftermath of the Battle of Mutina (April 43) and were appointed, together with Lepidus, by a law of the Senate as a 'commission of three for the ordering of the state' for a five-year term, later renewed (43–33 BCE). The biographers are lacunose, confused and confusing on the issue, no doubt because several of the characters in the *Bucolics* have suffered just such dispossession (Ch. 2.2). All, however, mention the triumvirs' settlement of their veterans in the territory around Cremona and Mantua in northern Italy, which we know began in the late 40s, after the defeat of the republican forces led by Cassius and Brutus at Philippi in October 42.[23]

Virgil's early experience of civil war and the possible diminution of his patrimony find suggestive parallels in those of his contemporaries, the poets Horace, Propertius and Tibullus, whose familial estates were also purportedly diminished in the civil wars of their youth (or even earlier, in Horace's case).[24] It was during this period that Virgil met the powerful Roman magnates C. Asinius Pollio (75 BCE–4 CE, *cos.* 40 BCE), dedicatee of *B.* 3, 4 and 8; P. Alfenus Varus (*fl.* second half of the first century BCE, governor of Cisalpine Gaul 41, *suff. cos.* 39), dedicatee of *B.* 6 and 9; and C. Cornelius Gallus (70–26 BCE, first prefect of Egypt 29–27), dedicatee of *B.* 10 and honorand of *B.* 6.[25] All three of them are connected not only by Virgil's biographers but also by ancient historians with the supervision of the land confiscations in northern Italy after Philippi, at the end of the 40s BCE (Don. *VSD* 19; Appian, *BC* 5.2.12–13; Dio 48.6–12).

The ancient biographers date Virgil's composition of the *Bucolics* to three years, starting from his twenty-eighth year (42–39 BCE), and they credit Pollio both with proposing the theme to him and with his earliest patronage. Virgil also met his future patron Maecenas around this time, though it is not known exactly how or when. While Donatus and Probus assert that Virgil retained his family farm as a result of the intervention of these politicians, Servius assumes that Virgil's loss was permanent. Whatever the outcome, Virgil never returned to his ancestral estate. Donatus reports that he lived most of his adulthood in southern Italy (*VSD* 13): 'he possessed nearly ten million sesterces [ten times the census qualification for senatorial rank] as a result of the generosity of his friends and he had a house at Rome on the Esquiline near the Gardens of Maecenas, although he generally lived in retirement in Campania and Sicily'. Virgil's preference for the retired life in southern Italy implies a continuing commitment to Epicurean tranquillity and the philosophical life,[26] for Donatus' phrasing recalls not only the retreat from society characteristic of Epicurean communities in Athens and southern Italy, but also the Epicurean dictum 'live unknown'.[27] The biographer attributes Virgil's determination to live out of the limelight to his modest character, and adduces as evidence our poet's habit of ducking into the nearest doorway to hide from the crowds of adoring fans who followed him through the city on those rare occasions when he visited Rome (*VSD* 11), an attitude consistent with Epicurean principle.

Donatus provides abundant evidence of Virgil's abiding interest in philosophical study all the way to the end of his life, in his report (*VSD* 35) that 'in his fifty-second year, wishing to give the final touches to the *Aeneid*, he determined to go away to Greece and Asia, and after devoting three entire years to the sole work of improving his poem, to give up the rest of his life wholly to philosophy'. Virgil fell ill on the trip to Greece and died after returning to Brindisi in the company of Augustus, on 21 September 19 BCE. The poet's lasting commitment to Naples, the ground of Greek philosophy in Italy, is also attested in the report that he was buried on the road to Puteoli (modern Pozzuoli), outside Naples (*VSD* 35–6).

The ancient biographers relate that Virgil began to compose poetry while still at the grammarian's school (*VSD* 17), and Irene Peirano has shown that the poems collected in the *Appendix Vergiliana* supplement the works of his maturity by furnishing him with a corpus of juvenilia.[28] While some of the poems preserved in the *Catalepton* may be genuine (5 and 8 have been accepted by many scholars, while 7, addressed to Varius, is another favoured candidate for authenticity), we are on altogether firmer ground with the composition of the canonical works: *Bucolica*, *Georgica*, *Aeneis*. Probus reports that Virgil began *B*. at the age of 28, taking the Hellenistic Greek poet Theocritus (*c.* 300–260 BCE) as his model, and Donatus (*VSD* 19) explains his purpose in writing bucolic poetry as praise of Octavian's land surveyors Asinius Pollio, Alfenus Varus and Cornelius Gallus. The biographers concur that the work was completed and corrected within three years (42–39 BCE), though many modern scholars have preferred to down-date both the composition of individual poems and the circulation of the completed collection further into the 30s. All we can say with assurance is that his bucolic verse made him famous. Donatus (*VSD* 26) reports that *B.* were published to such acclaim that individual eclogues were frequently performed on stage by singers, presumably presented as mimes or pantomimes, both newly popular forms of stage production in Virgil's day.[29]

The ancient biographers assert that Virgil wrote his next poem, *Georgica*, for Maecenas, as the recurrent dedications in each book of the poem confirm (*G.* 1.2, 2.41, 3.41, 4.2). Servius credits Maecenas with the suggestion of the georgic theme to Virgil, as Pollio had proposed bucolic poetry, but Donatus (*VSD* 20) explains the dedication as a result of Maecenas' assistance to the poet after a violent quarrel with a veteran, an explanation that retrojects the hostility towards resettled army veterans expressed by some of the pastoral speakers in *B.* (Ch. 2.2) onto Virgil's biography. Servius and Donatus (*VSD* 25) agree that Virgil devoted seven years to the composition of *G.* (37–30 BCE), and Probus adds the detail that his literary models were the archaic Greek didactic poet Hesiod (*c.* 700 BCE), author of a didactic poem on farming entitled *Works and Days*, and the late republican polymath M. Terentius Varro (116–27), whose three-book prose treatise on farming, *De re rustica*, appeared in 37 (Ch. 3.1). Like *B.*, *G.* were accorded canonical status immediately upon publication: Suetonius reports that when Q. Caecilius Epirota opened up a school in the mid-20s BCE, after the death of his patron Gallus (Virgil's friend, the dedicatee of *B.* 10), he instituted the practice of reading and commenting on 'Virgil and the other new poets' (*De gramm.* 16).

Donatus (*VSD* 22) preserves two anecdotes about Virgil's composition and recitation of *G.*, respectively. In the first, he reports the tradition that Virgil dictated several lines of verse every morning and then devoted the rest of the day to reducing them to very few, 'saying not without reason that he delivered his poem like a she-bear and gradually licked it into shape'.[30] In the second, he credits Virgil with a command performance of the finished poem, over four days in August 29, for Octavian (delayed at Atella with a sore throat on his return to the peninsula), with Maecenas picking up the recitation when Virgil's voice failed.[31] Here Donatus adds the detail that the poet Julius Montanus, a younger contemporary of Virgil and bosom friend of the future emperor Tiberius (Sen. Rhet. *Contr.* 7.1.27), used to say that he would have stolen some of Virgil's lines if he could also have stolen 'his voice, expression, and dramatic power – for the same verses sounded well when Virgil recited them himself, but were empty and dumb without him' (*VSD* 28–9). The specificity of the recollection has encouraged scholars to accept Montanus' testimony as that of an eyewitness.[32]

The ancient biographers unanimously attribute the inspiration of *Aeneis* to Augustus. Probus explains that Virgil embarked on the project when Octavian initiated the Cantabrian War in Spain (29–19 BCE), after the *princeps* had honoured him with a gift of one million sesterces (i.e. senatorial rank). Both Servius and Donatus (*VSD* 39–41) credit Augustus with preserving the unfinished poem, and Donatus relates several anecdotes that testify vividly to contemporary excitement about Virgil's new project: in the mid-20s, Propertius hailed the poem as 'something greater than the *Iliad*' (*VSD* 31, quoting Prop. 2.34.66), while Augustus is reported to have demanded 'in entreating and jocularly threatening letters, that he be sent something from the *Aeneid* – in his own words, either a first draft of the poem or any passage [Virgil] liked' (*VSD* 31). The correspondence between *princeps* and poet has been convincingly dated to the years Augustus spent in Gaul and Spain prosecuting the Cantabrian War (May/June 27–June 24 BCE).[33] Macrobius preserves some fragments from Virgil's reply, which testifies to a series of letters from the emperor (*Saturn.* 1.24.11; cf. Suet. *Aug.* 89). Our poet responds that he would happily send the emperor something if he had anything worthy, 'but the subject I've begun is so large that I almost seem to have embarked on such a huge project in a moment of madness, especially since, as you know, I attempt other and much more valuable studies for it as well'. The sterile scholarly debate concerning the degree of imperial pressure brought to bear on the Augustan poets arises in part from Donatus' report of Augustus' interest.[34] Virgil responds to the emperor's urgent requests for a preview with both self-deprecatory tact and charming familiarity.

The ancient biographers agree that Virgil's purpose in writing *Aeneis* (*A.*) was to praise Augustus, and as Augustus' personal intervention saved the poem from the flames (*VSD* 41), it may be assumed that he thought likewise. Donatus records a few more anecdotes about imperial interest in the epic: long after he began the poem, Virgil recited three books (2, 4 and 6) to Augustus (*VSD* 32), and the emperor's sister Octavia fainted when the poet reached the lines in Book 6 (860–86) that memorialize the premature death of her son Marcellus (*VSD* 33). But although Virgil recited his poetry to others as well, he did so rarely and only, Donatus claims, to solicit critical opinion on passages on which he was then at work (*VSD* 33) – a detail that coheres with Horace's representation of the attitude of their mutual friend Quintilius Varus towards literary recital in the *Ars Poetica*.[35] Donatus offers the fullest account of our poet's aims in composing *A.* (*VSD* 21): 'at last, he began work on the *Aeneid*, a varied and complex theme, as if modelled on both of Homer's poems, moreover with Greek and Latin names and history in common, and in which – as he especially desired – were contained together the origins of the city of Rome and of Augustus'. No wonder our sources attribute the preservation of the poem to the authority of the emperor himself (*VSD* 37; cf. *VSD* 41).

Beyond Probus' report of Virgil's harmonious life with his Epicurean friends Quintilius, Plotius and Varius, the ancient biographers record little detail about Virgil's adult life. Donatus (*VSD* 14) mentions that two younger brothers by the same parents predeceased him, though modern scholars have deemed both fictitious.[36] He was survived by a half-brother (by another father), Valerius Proculus (*VSD* 37). The ancient biographers credit him with neither wife nor mistress, although

Donatus (*VSD* 9) reports the rumour of an affair with a woman named Plotia Hieria, implying that she was Varius' wife (since he supposedly offered to share her with our poet) and Plotius' sister.[37] Even in antiquity, however, the rumour earned little credence, and Donatus records the woman's denial (*VSD* 10), reported by Cicero's early imperial commentator Q. Asconius Pedianus (9 BCE–76 CE), in his work rebutting the charges of Virgil's detractors (Ch. 5). Donatus (*VSD* 9) asserts that Virgil preferred boys to women and he preserves the names of two youths whom our poet 'especially loved', Cebes and Alexander, both purportedly given to him by Pollio and the latter supposedly memorialized under the name of Alexis in *B*. 2.[38] In general, however, the ancient biographers insist on Virgil's modesty and moderation,[39] deriving his nickname *Parthenias* ('Maiden') from this aspect of his character, though modern scholars have preferred to explain the name (if they accept its authenticity) by reference to the poet's choice of Naples in which to make his home, since the Greek city was also called Parthenope (*G*. 4.564; cf. *VSD* 36).

The details of Virgil's will were apparently well known, as both Probus and Donatus report them, though not in testamentary language. He died a wealthy man, the owner of a house in Rome and an estate in southern Italy, with the financial resources of a senator (*VSD* 13). The primary heirs were his half-brother Valerius Proculus, to whom he left half of his estate; the emperor Augustus, who received a quarter; and his long-standing friend and patron Maecenas, who inherited a twelfth. To his old Epicurean comrades Varius and Tucca fell the rest of his estate (presumably another twelfth each), including his writings; and on Augustus' authority they edited *A*. for publication. The poem was released into general circulation a couple of years later, in 17 BCE.

The turbulent times in which Virgil lived, as well as his philosophical interests, have offered his readers two compelling avenues of approach to his poetry, and both political history and philosophy will figure largely in the chapters that follow. But ancient criticism of Virgil's Homeric 'thefts' (Ch. 5) opens up a third line of discussion that has proven the most powerful spur to the interpretation of his poetry in the last two millennia. Both his critics and his proponents have focused attention on the relationship of his poetry to classical models, and we too shall devote considerable discussion to his distillation of diverse traditions of classical literature and myth in *B.*, *G.* and *A.* Virgil came of age in a period of great literary experimentation and technical innovation in Latin literature, and almost every line of his verse betrays the impact of the pre-eminent poets of the final generation of the republic, Catullus and Lucretius. We have already had occasion to consider the impact of Lucretius and Epicurean philosophy on our poet's philosophical formation, and we shall see evidence of Virgil's thorough study of the *De rerum natura* from beginning to end of his literary career.

Lucretius' contemporary C. Valerius Catullus (*c.* 84–54 BCE) was the leading figure in a group of self-consciously modern poets active in the mid-50s BCE, which included the Cinna mentioned by Virgil at *B.* 9.35, several times named by Catullus in his verse (*c.* 10.29–30, 95, 113); C. Licinius Calvus (b. 28 May 82 BCE, dead by 47 BCE), repeatedly addressed by Catullus (*c.* 14, 50, 53, 96);[40] and Asinius Pollio, Virgil's earliest patron and the dedicatee of *B.* 3, 4 and 8, whom Catullus praises for his wit in comparison with a brother who lacked his social finesse (*c.* 12), and Horace for his tragedies and critical acumen (*Sat.* 1.10.42–3, *Carm.* 2.1.9–12). Virgil's patron and friend Cornelius Gallus also seems to have been on friendly terms with the surviving members of the coterie after Catullus' death around 54, for the earliest extant reference to him appears in a letter by Asinius Pollio to Cicero in June 43 BCE (*ad Fam.* 10.32; cf. 10.31).[41]

The 'new poets' ('Neoterics') focused their creative energies on the composition of short, elegant, learned and witty poetry in a variety of metres that were new to Rome but long-established in Greece: lyric (iambics, sapphics, hendecasyllabics), elegy and short epic (sometimes called 'epyllion'). Catullus himself seems to have especially admired the archaic lyric poet Sappho (*c.* 610–*c.* 570 BCE) and the Hellenistic poet Callimachus (*c.* 305–*c.* 240 BCE), both of whom he names in his verse (Sappho, *c.* 35.16; Callimachus, *c.* 65.16, 116.2). He essays poems in metres associated closely with each of them (*c*. 11 and 51 in 'Sapphics'; *c*. 69–116 in elegiac epigrams, in the tradition of Callimachus' famous book of *Epigrams*); adapts at least one poem by each (*c*. 51 ~ Sappho fr. 31; *c*. 66 ~ Call. *Aetia* 4.1); and calls his mistress by a pseudonym derived from Sappho's island of Lesbos. In theme, as in form, the new poets revolutionized Latin poetry, taking as their subjects such highly subjective themes as their amatory, poetic and political commitments. In their hexameter verse, they disdained the familiar martial themes of grand epic to explore instead the psychopathology of love in myths combining doomed erotic passion with exotic metamorphoses and recondite geographical settings.

Virgil's friendship with Pollio and Gallus, along with his praise of the dead Cinna, constitutes ample testimony to his admiration of the new poets. In addition, almost every line of his verse attests to their lasting formal and thematic impact. Although he eschewed any metre but dactylic hexameter, abandoning the metrical experimentation of the new poets to refine the Lucretian hexameter, his themes are recognizably 'neoteric': the doomed love of Dido for Aeneas (*A*. 4), Orpheus for Eurydice (*G*. 4), Corydon for Alexis (*B*. 2), Gallus for Lycoris (*B*. 10); the metamorphoses of mythological heroines (*B*. 6), the Trojan prince Polydorus (*A*. 3) and the Trojan ships (*A*. 9); the contemporary political commitments enunciated by the pastoral speakers of *B*. and the mythological characters of *A*.; the statements of poetics in elaborate programmatic passages (*B*. 6, *G*. 3, *A*. 1 and 7); and the ethnographic, geographic, historical, mythological and philosophical erudition on display throughout his poetry. In the following chapters, we shall explore the intersection of Virgil's poetic, political and philosophical interests in each of the canonical works.

Bucolica

Virgil's collection of pastoral poetry circulated under the title *Bucolica* ('cattle-herding songs') in antiquity, while individual poems were called 'eclogues', literally 'extracts' from the collection.[1] The thematic significance of the collection's title is underlined in the first poem's opening exchange (*B.* 1.1–10):

> *Meliboeus* – Tityrus, reclining beneath the canopy of a spreading beech, you practise woodland music on a slender oaten straw; we are leaving the bounds of our fatherland and our sweet fields. We are going into exile from our fatherland; you, Tityrus, relaxing in the shade, are teaching the woods to re-echo 'Beautiful Amaryllis'.
> *Tityrus* – O Meliboeus, a god gave us this leisure. For he will always be a god to me, and a tender lamb from our sheepfold will often stain his altar. He allowed my cattle to roam, as you see, and me to play what I wished on the rustic pipe.

Meliboeus bears a speaking name derived from the Greek words for 'herding' (*melô*) and 'cow' (*bous*, cognate with Latin *bos*); the first element of his name also puns on the Greek word for 'song' (*melos*). Meliboeus' name thus encapsulates the thematic focus of Virgil's collection in its collocation of cattle-herding and -song. His interlocutor Tityrus, moreover, has been granted permission to 'pasture his cattle and play what he wants on his rustic pipe' (9–10) by a youthful god who has instructed him to 'pasture cattle as before, and raise plough oxen' (45).[2] Virgil thereby marks his adherence to the Greek bucolic tradition and its most celebrated exponent, Theocritus, whose characters use the verb 'bucolicize', literally 'play the cowherd', to describe their music making and song exchange (*Id.* 5.60, 7.36), and the adjectival phrases 'bucolic music/songs' (*Id.* 1.20, 7.49–51) to describe the songs themselves.

2.1 *Theocritean Bucolic*

We know little about the collection and circulation of Theocritus' poems, not even whether he produced a collected edition of his own work as his Alexandrian contemporary Callimachus, for example, seems to have done.[3] The grammarian Artemidoros prepared an edition of Theocritus' poetry in the first half of the first century BCE, and the prefatory epigram to his collection is preserved in the Palatine Anthology (*AP* 9.205): 'The Bucolic Muses, once scattered, now are all together in one fold, in one flock'. The epigram implies that this Theocritean collection went by the title *Boukolika* and its appearance may have been a factor in the inspiration of Virgil's own *Bucolica*.[4] Servius reports (on *B.* 3) that Virgil wrote 'only seven purely rustic eclogues, Theocritus ten', which has been thought to imply that a ten-poem collection of Theocritean bucolic (as distinct from his urban mimes)[5] circulated in antiquity, whether in conjunction with his other poetry or not we cannot say. Nonetheless, the ten bucolic idylls circulating under Theocritus' name (1, 3–11) seem to have provided inspiration for the number of poems in Virgil's *B.*, which in turn set the fashion for collections of ten poems by Virgil's contemporaries Horace (*Satires* 1) and Tibullus (*Elegies* 1).[6]

Certainly Virgil's debt to Theocritus is everywhere apparent, from the names of his characters to the themes of their songs, from the country settings and pastoral activities of the herdsmen to their song exchanges and artistic rivalries. The opening line of every eclogue contains a Greek name, normally Theocritean (*B.* 1, 2, 3, 7, 8; cf. 5.4, 9.2)[7] or associated with Theocritus' homeland of Sicily (*B.* 4.1, 6.1, 10.1),[8] the setting *par excellence* of Greek pastoral.[9] The first eclogue's Tityrus is not only Theocritean (*Id.* 3.2–4, 7.72–82), but also a 'speaking' name: Servius reports that the word *tityrus* meant the herd-leading billy-goat in the Spartan dialect, while Athenaeus preserves the information that in Italian Doric the diminutive *titurinos* denoted the single reed pipe played by rustics (*Deipn.* 4.1.82d). Thus, like the name Meliboeus, that of Tityrus encodes the activities of herding and music central to Theocritean bucolic.

From the start of *B.*, Virgil sounds a self-consciously Theocritean and Sicilian note. The opening line of the first eclogue (*Tityre, tu patulae recubans sub tegmine fagi*) reproduces the setting, sound effects and musicality of the first lines of the idyll that seems to have opened all ancient collections of Theocritus' poetry (*Id.* 1.1–3): 'Something sweet, goatherd, the whispering which that pine by the spring sings, and sweet too your syrinx-piping' (*hadu ti to psithurisma kai ha pitus, aipole, têna,/ ha poti tais pagaisi, melisdetai, hadu de kai tû/ surisdes*). The opening verses of both poems are onomatopoeic, evocative not only of the clear notes of the syrinx or pan-pipe in the repetition of the vowel tones 'i' and 'ü',[10] but also of the rustle of foliage in the alliterative succession of stops ('p' in Theocritus, 't' in Virgil) and sibilants. The 'figure of echo' resonates throughout the collection.[11] On the most basic level, the pastoral landscape is alive with music even before the herdsmen sing – the rustle of foliage (*Id.* 1.1, 7.135; *B.* 1.5, 2.5, etc.), the whisper of breezes (*Id.* 1.1; *B.* 9.58), the hum of bees (*Id.* 7.145; *B.* 1.53–5, 7.13), the call of wood pigeon and turtle-dove (*Id.* 7.141; *B.* 1.57–8), the song of the cicada (*Id.* 7.138–9; *B.* 2.13). Yet Virgil's herdsmen's songs are not only rustic snatches of song redolent of the music of the natural world but also highly crafted interventions into the sophisticated Greek tradition of pastoral poetry. The woods' echo of Tityrus' song (*B.* 1.5) is 'learned', and obliquely hints at Virgil's own literary learning, apparent in the intricately allusive play of his language and metre, themes and imagery, with those of Theocritus and his bucolic successors Bion (*c.* 325–*c.* 255 BCE) and Moschus (*fl. c.* 150 BCE).[12]

Within Virgil's collection too, characters, settings and verses repeatedly re-echo earlier pastoral poetry, including his own as the collection proceeds. The Latin poet repeats words, phrases and half lines throughout the collection,[13] a convention of pastoral poetry especially notable in the herdsmen's musical exchanges, known as amoebean song, often performed in singing contests. Two eclogues feature such singing matches, *B.* 3 and 7, and well illustrate the echoic effects of imitation and rivalry, constitutive features both within individual poems and across the tradition of bucolic verse.[14] *B.* 3 in particular draws heavily on Theocritus,[15] and dramatizes Virgil's inheritance of Theocritean bucolic to articulate an ambitious challenge to the Greek tradition of pastoral poetry.[16]

The eclogue opens with a boisterous exchange of insults between the herdsmen Menalcas and Damoetas (3.1–6):

> *M.* Tell me, Damoetas, whose herd? Meliboeus'?
> *D.* No, rather Aegon's; recently Aegon handed it over to me.
> *M.* O wretched flock of sheep, always unlucky! While he cuddles Neaera and worries that she prefers me to him, this stranger milks his sheep twice an hour, stealing vital sap from the flock and milk from the lambs.

Both herdsmen bear Theocritean names and play important roles in the Theocritean bucolic collection available to Virgil, having competed in song with Daphnis, the cowherd and bucolic culture hero of *Idylls* 1, 6 and 8. Both thus symbolize the Theocritean pastoral tradition writ large. Yet both are also, already, Virgilian herdsmen, for they appear in the preceding eclogue: Damoetas is the master singer who gave his syrinx to Corydon (the singer of *B.* 2 and the name of a character in *Idyll* 8); Menalcas is the youth Corydon had previously loved. It has therefore been suggested that the elder, Damoetas, represents the Theocritean tradition while the younger, Menalcas (whose characterization here differs substantively from that in *Idyll* 8), represents the Virgilian voice of youthful challenge.[17]

The opening exchange between Virgil's herdsmen closely reworks the opening of Theocritus' fourth idyll, where Battos accuses Korydon of stealing another herdman's cattle and milk (*Id.* 4.1–3, 13):

B. Tell me, Korydon, whose are the cattle? Philondas'?

K. No, rather Aegon's. He gave them to me to pasture.

B. And you, maybe, milk them all on the sly in the evening? ...
      They're wretched, as they've found a bad cowherd.

Virgil translates Battos' 'cattle' (*boes*, *Id.* 4.1) as a 'herd' (*pecus*, *B.* 3.1) in another programmatic gesture towards Theocritean 'bucolic', even though Meliboeus specifies the animals in Damoetas' keeping as sheep (3.3).[18] When upbraiding Damoetas in *B.* 3.1, Menalcas echoes both the wording and the syntax of Battos' insult, and Damoetas follows suit in his reply, which not only reproduces the wording and grammar of Korydon's response to Battos, but also recycles the name of the herdsman Aegon, whose herd his Greek counterpart pastures. Virgil's close imitation – almost translation – of Theocritus continues in Menalcas' riposte, pitying the sheep their bad herdsman and insinuating his rival's theft of their milk, before Menalcas goes on to level further accusations about Damoetas' thieving ways (3.16–20):

M. What should masters do when thieves dare such things? Didn't I
      see you, rogue, snaring Damon's goat with trickery, while Lycisca
      barked her head off? And when I called, 'Where's he running now?
      Tityrus, round up the flock', you were hiding behind the sedge.

Their exchange of abuse culminates in mutual insults about one another's musical prowess, when Damoetas flatly denies the charge of theft (21–2): 'Beaten in the singing match, didn't he fail to give back to me the goat which my pipe had earned with its songs?'

With the introduction of the theme of the song contest, Virgil's eclogue moves away from the model of Theocritus' fourth *Idyll* to that of the fifth, which also opens with a charge of theft in Komatas' accusation that Lakon has stolen his goatskin but moves thence into a singing contest (*Id.* 5.1–7):

K. Goats, get away from that shepherd, the Sybarite, Lakon, the one
      who stole my goatskin yesterday.

L. Get away from the spring, lambs. Don't you see Komatas? The day
      before yesterday he stole my pipe.

K. What pipe was that? Have you, Sibyrta's slave, ever come by a pipe? Why aren't you content any more to tootle away on a straw pipe with Korydon?

Virgil's herdsmen's accusations and counteraccusations of theft (*B.* 3.1–6, 16–20) are thus themselves 'stolen' from Theocritus (*Id.* 4.1–3, 5.1–7), and thereby dramatize Virgilian bucolic as 'thefts' from the Greek pastoral tradition; for 'theft' (i.e. plagiarism) was a frequent metaphor for literary allusion and generic alignment in ancient Rome. Virgil includes a number of very close imitations, sometimes almost word-for-word translations, of Theocritean material in *B.* 3, as in Menalcas' jibe about Damoetas' vulgar playing (*B.* 3.25–7): 'You beat him in singing? Did you ever have a pipe of reeds joined with wax? Didn't you used to murder a wretched song on a shrill cornstalk at the crossroads?' Menalcas' insults closely rework Komatas' derisive dismissal of Lakon's piping (*Id.* 5.5–7), as the 'pipe of reeds joined with wax' (*B.* 3.25–6) picks up Komatas' syrinx (*Id.* 5.6) and the 'shrill cornstalk' (*B.* 3.27) his reed (*Id.* 5.7).

Like the exchange of insults and the ensuing singing match, the herdsmen's wagers are drawn from Theocritus. On proposing the contest, Damoetas stakes a heifer (another glance at the tradition of Theocritean 'bucolic'). Menalcas, however, is not of age and so cannot wager an animal, because the herd he pastures belongs to his father. Instead, he stakes two marvellous beech-wood cups, the work of the artist Alcimedon 'on which he added the curling vine with a turn of the lathe and covered the spreading clusters of pale ivy' (*B.* 3.38–9). The description of Alcimedon's cups stands in a long line of ecphrastic emblems of poetic artistry, from Homer's Shield of Achilles in *Iliad* 18 to Theocritus' ivy cup in *Idyll* 1. Menalcas' cups clearly take the latter as their point of reference, but their material of beech-wood distinguishes them from Theocritus' ivy cup and recalls instead the beech tree under which Tityrus pipes at the opening of Virgil's collection (*B.* 1.1); they thus symbolize Virgilian innovation within the tradition of Theocritean pastoral.[19] Damoetas dismisses the wager of cups, however, because he has his own pair, also of Alcimedon's workmanship (*B.* 3.45–6): 'around the handles soft ivy embraces them, and he placed Orpheus in the middle with the woods following him'. The details of their decoration imply Damoetas' status as a master singer, in the tradition of Orpheus, the inventor of song, whose music charmed the natural world.

On Menalcas' cups, by contrast, Alcimedon has crafted two embossed figures among the vines (40–2): 'Conon and – who was the other, who delimited with his rod the whole celestial orb for all people, what seasons belonged to the reaper, what to the stooped ploughman?' These finely wrought figures evoke the cultural sophistication of Ptolemaic Alexandria and the poetic artistry of Theocritus, but are specifically non-pastoral: the third-century BCE Alexandrian court astronomer Conon and another unnamed astronomer. Their inclusion on the cups widens the ambit of the youthful singer of bucolic to the related arena of farming and beyond, to the rival realm of astronomy, and may hint at Virgil's admiration for both Hesiod's *Works and Days* (which supplies the model for the *Georgics*, Ch. 3.1) and also Hellenistic Greek and neoteric Latin astronomical poetry,[20] such as Callimachus' poem about the translation of a lock of the Ptolemaic queen Berenice's hair into the constellation discovered by Conon (*Aetia* 4.1 Pf.), adapted into Latin by Catullus (*c.* 66); and the *Phaenomena*, a didactic poem on heavenly bodies by Aratus (*c.* 315–240/239 BCE), adapted into Latin by Cicero.

In both *B.* 3 and *Idyll* 5, a fellow herder adjudicates the herdsmen's competition in a refereed singing match, but only in Virgil's poem does the arbitrator, Palaemon, reflect on the transformative power of poetry. As the herdsmen take their places, he transmutes their comically[21] aggressive charges of theft into amoebean song (*B.* 3.55–9):

> P. Sing, seeing that we're sitting together on the soft grass. Now every field bears crops, now every tree fruit, now the woods grow green with foliage, now is the most beautiful time of the year. Begin, Damoetas; you then follow, Menalcas. Sing in alternation: the rustic Muses love alternating verses.

Palaemon invokes the beauty of the *locus amoenus* landscape, or 'pleasance',[22] as the setting for the exchange of songs, deftly setting the scene for the singing match that follows, in which the rival herdsmen take up in alternation such conventional pastoral themes as rustic piety and unrequited love. Their efforts to cap one another's verses figure both echo and theft, as successive snatches of verse replay and repurpose earlier words, images and themes.

In the end, Palaemon declares both singers worthy of the heifer they stake. The conflict between the herdsmen, transmuted to the plane of poetry, offers an idealized view of both the countryside and the bucolic genre in which it features so centrally. The indeterminacy of the outcome reflects the polysemy of the songs, and adumbrates the success of both Theocritean pastoral and its Latin challenger, Virgilian bucolic. The extraordinary depth and richness of the eclogue's literary texture 'turns the poem into a kind of echoing chamber of poetic allusion',[23] as Virgil's extensive echoes of Greek pastoral, and many other literary texts, contribute to the aesthetic polish and erudition of the eclogue. His herdsmen's insults have sometimes seemed incongruous by comparison with the sophisticated literary allusions and astronomical lore encoded in their descriptions of Alcimedon's marvellous cups and the learned riddles that conclude the exchange. A further inconcinnity has been seen in the overt compliment to Virgil's patron Pollio in the herdsmen's songs (*B.* 3.84–91), since Theocritean pastoral neither compliments a named patron nor records historical events among the country songs and rustic activities celebrated in the genre.[24] Virgil admits contemporary politics to 'the green cabinet'[25] of his *Bucolics*, in a radical break with Greek pastoral convention.

2.2 *History and Politics*

If the first two lines of *B.* 1 sound a distinctly Theocritean note, the next two lines rupture pastoral convention by introducing contemporary history and politics into the collection.[26] There is no echo of Theocritus or the Greek pastoral tradition in these lines.[27] Meliboeus' exile from the pastoral landscape offers a bleak contrast to Tityrus' relaxed leisure and secure tenure of his smallholding, and the former generously congratulates the latter on his good fortune (46–7, 51–2): 'Fortunate old man, your farm will remain, and large enough for you ... Fortunate old man, here amid familiar rivers and sacred springs you will enjoy cool shade'. The Sicilian locale implied by Meliboeus' reference in the following lines to 'Hyblaean bees' (54) gestures to the conventional setting of Theocritean pastoral, but the historical events the herdsmen discuss have a specific referent in the Italian dispossessions entailed by the triumvirs' settlement of their veterans in 41 BCE, after their victory at Philippi. Suetonius reports (*Aug.* 13) that Marc Antony, then the senior partner as the undisputed victor of Philippi, took the eastern empire as his share of triumviral rule and left to Octavian the difficult and unpopular task of supervising the distribution of Italian land to their veterans. The process continued for over a decade and met from the start with the concerted resistance of the dispossessed, who banded together in 41 to march on Rome and demand redress from Octavian along with a fairer allocation of land.[28]

The first eclogue characterizes Meliboeus as one of the displaced landholders, evicted and going into exile at the borders of the empire (*B.* 1.64–6): 'But some of us will go hence to the thirsty Africans, others will reach Scythia and the rapid stream of the chalky Oaxes, and far away the Britons separated from the whole world'. His rehearsal of possible destinations adumbrates the extent of Rome's empire by the four points of the compass, but is historically unrealistic, for the majority of the dispossessed landowners went to Sicily, the ostensible location of the eclogue, where they swelled Sextus Pompey's republican ranks and worked to overthrow triumviral authority.[29] Virgil's geographical erudition underwrites the literary quality of the eclogue, but has been criticized as incongrous in the mouth of a rustic herdsman and as an implicit statement of partisan support for the triumvirs in its aestheticization of Roman political conflict.[30] Meliboeus suppresses the details of the Italian upheavals in his bitter reproach to his countrymen for their propensity for civil war, which has resulted in displacement and dispossession on such a scale (70–2): 'An impious soldier will own these fallow fields, so well cultivated, and these crops. Look where civil war has led our wretched citizens: we have sown our fields for these soldiers!' The emotive contrast between soldier and farmer, barbarian and citizen, underlines the impiety of civil war, which has reduced citizen-farmers to exiles and made rough soldiers denizens of the pastoral landscape. With acerbic melancholy, Meliboeus exhorts himself to graft pears and dress vines for these interlopers (73). Although he can apparently take what remains of his devastated flock with him into exile, he will sing no more songs (74–8). The loss of his smallholding, with its *locus amoenus* setting conducive to cattle-song, has exiled him from the bucolic genre altogether.

The unhappily dispossessed Meliboeus contrasts his sorry plight with Tityrus' great good fortune, graciously asking how his friend managed to retain his estate amid 'such disruption everywhere, in all the fields' (11–12). This upheaval in the countryside is another pointed reference to the settlement of the veterans in Italy after Philippi, and Meliboeus is curious about the identity of the god to whom Tityrus owes his farm (18): 'this god of yours, Tityrus, tell us who he is'. Tityrus responds at first obliquely, contrasting Rome with the local market town, and Meliboeus, not unnaturally, inquires why Tityrus went to Rome in the first place (26): 'and what was so important that it caused you to see Rome?' Tityrus' response characterizes him as a slave who has gained his freedom as a result of his petition to the youthful god (27–32): 'Freedom, which though late nonetheless looked back at an idle man, after my beard fell whiter at the barber's, nonetheless she looked back at me and came a long time later, after Amaryllis took us on and Galatea left, for (yes, I will confess it) while Galatea held me, I had neither hope of freedom nor concern for my allowance'. The slave's interest in his freedom has a political valence here, for both slavery and freedom were contemporary political metaphors deployed for rhetorical effect in the propaganda campaigns of a long line of republican strongmen.[31] The slogan 'freedom' was the rallying cry of Octavian and his faction.[32] Virgil condenses the political and socio-legal meanings of slavery and freedom in these lines to characterize the former slave

Tityrus as a successful petitioner of triumviral authority, granted a reprieve from dispossession by the youthful god whom Servius identifies as Octavian. Already in the *Philippics*, Cicero had called him 'divine youth' (*Phil.* 5.43) and after Caesar's deification in 42 BCE Octavian styled himself 'son of a god'. Virgil thus sets a signal compliment to the young Octavian in the mouth of his character Tityrus, whom Servius (on *B.* 1.1) views as the mouthpiece of Virgil himself here.

Virgil seems to invite the identification with Tityrus on at least two occasions, the first soon after, in the dedicatory preface to the sixth eclogue. There the poet speaks in the first person of Apollo's epiphany to him at the very moment of composition (*B.* 6.3–5): 'when I would sing of kings and battles, [Apollo] Cynthius plucked my ear and warned: "it behooves a shepherd to pasture fat sheep, Tityrus, but to sing a slender song"'. Addressed to the 'singer of the eclogues'[33] under the name of his character Tityrus, Apollo's words adapt into Latin the god's own earlier advice to the Alexandrian poet Callimachus (*Aetia* Prologue, fr. 1.21–4): 'For when I first set a writing tablet on my knees, Apollo the Lycian said to me: "[it is fitting], poet, to rear the sacrificial beast as fat as possible, but the Muse, my good fellow, [keep her] slender"'. Callimachus articulates his poetic principles in response to the censure of his critics, and Virgil's lines likewise form part of a longer meditation on his poetic programme in *B.*, for his is the first attempt to render Theocritus' Sicilian bucolic into Latin verse (6.1–2). Virgil dedicates *B.* 6 to the politician P. Alfenus Varus (Ch. 1), whose deeds, he predicts, will earn epic praise (6.6–7) – but not from him. Instead, the eclogue-singer determines to continue with the project inaugurated in *B.* 1, styling the poetic ego of *B.* 6 as Tityrus and characterizing his verse as 'country music practised on a slender reed' (6.8) in an echo of the opening of *B.* 1.

Many years later, in the sphragis to *G.*, Virgil contrasts his poetic labours with the military projects of Octavian, by 30 BCE a seasoned military campaigner and the victor of Actium, in phrasing that, again, invites the identification of the bucolic poet with Tityrus (*G.* 4.563–6): 'At that time, sweet Naples nourished me, flourishing in the pursuits of indolent leisure – Virgil, who sported shepherds' songs and, in my youth, boldly sang of you Tityrus, beneath the canopy of a spreading beech tree'. Here Virgil reclaims for himself, *qua* poet, the posture of pastoral leisure that distinguished Tityrus in the opening lines of the first eclogue. The self-citation confirms Virgilian authorship of both *G.* and *B.* (if such were needed), and retrospectively invites the identification of the bucolic poet with his pastoral alter-ego. It is worth noting, however, that in *B.* 1 the poet nowhere explicitly assumes the persona of Tityrus; indeed, the dramatic format of the dialogue leaves the fortunate smallholder's debt to the divine youth in striking and unresolved contrast with the unhappy fate of his interlocutor. Lacking authorial resolution of the relative claims of landholders (whether of long-standing or new possession) and the dispossessed, *B.* 1 presents two starkly opposing, indeed irreconcilable, views of the Roman political landscape after Philippi.

Elsewhere in the collection, the eclogue-poet speaks in his own voice in praise of his consular patron (*B.* 4.1–3): 'Sicilian Muses, let us sing songs a little grander! Orchards and humble tamarisks do not please everyone; if we sing of woods, let the woods be worthy of a consul'. The consul honoured here is explicitly addressed as Pollio (11–13), whom we know to have held the office in 40 BCE. The eclogue-singer proclaims the birth of a child who will usher in a new golden age (4–10):

> Already the last age of Cumaean prophecy has come; the great order of the centuries is reborn anew. Now the Maiden returns, Saturn's kingdoms return, now a new line is sent down from high heaven. May you, chaste Lucina, honour the boy at his birth, when the iron age will first yield and the golden race arise in the whole world: now may your brother Apollo rule.

Virgil here combines Hesiod's myth of the races of men with the astronomical concept of the 'great year'. Hesiod (*fl.* 700 BCE) offers a characteristically pessimistic account of the races of men in his didactic *Works and Days*, which traces man's deterioration from a golden race that enjoyed contact with the gods through silver and bronze races to his own race of iron, with a brief reversal of decline in the race of heroes which preceded his (*Op*. 109–201). The astronomers' 'great year' stands in uneasy tension with the Hesiodic myth of races, for the former was held to be the length of time between each recurrence of the same arrangement of celestial phenomena (Cic. *Rep.* 6.24). In Stoic philosophy, the astronomical concept was further redefined as the period between successive dissolutions of the universe into the original 'creative fire' out of which it was repeatedly born anew (Cic. *Nat. D.* 2.41, 118).

In formulating this complex amalgam, Virgil draws extensively on Roman traditions of religious lore and Greek traditions of Sibylline prophecy, both of which Julius Caesar had overseen as Pontifex Maximus for almost two decades, until his death in 44 BCE. When Caesar reformed the Roman calendar as Dictator in 46 there may already have been speculation that he intended to inaugurate a new era by celebrating 'Secular Games', last held in 146 BCE on the occasion of Rome's destruction of her Mediterranean rivals Carthage and Corinth. In the event, his assassination on the Ides of March 44 forestalled any such plans, but the appearance of a comet, the so-called 'Julian star' in July 44,[34] during Octavian's funerary games in his adoptive father's honour, was interpreted as evidence of Caesar's translation to heaven as a god and no doubt spurred further expectation of the announcement of a new era.[35] Servius (on *B.* 9.46) records the interpretation of the comet by a contemporary Etruscan diviner as a portent of the inauguration of Rome's tenth (and therefore, in Etruscan religious tradition, last) era. Oversight of foreign cult practice in Rome was the responsibility of a Board of Fifteen Men, who held the official collection of the oracles of the Cumaean Sibyl, and this body would normally be charged with consultation of the Sibylline books at a time of crisis such as the appearance of a comet.[36] Both the optimism of the eclogue and its compliment to the poet's patron militate against a pessimistic explanation of the new era, since Virgil explicitly celebrates the new age as a return to gold from iron.

Virgil's encomiastic interpretation, and literary memorial, of the momentous political events of 40 BCE are confirmed in the eclogue's divergence from its primary models – Hesiod's myth of the races of men and Catullus' account of the heroic age in his *Peleus and Thetis* (*c.* 64).[37] Both Hesiod and Catullus emphasize the deterioration of men's character over time, Hesiod in the devaluation of the metal characterizing each successive age and Catullus in the despairing conclusion of his epyllion, where he draws a Hesiodic contrast between the Olympian gods' regular interaction with mankind in the age of heroes (*c.* 64.385–7) and their abandonment of a debased humanity to its own iniquity (64.398–407), a state of affairs that continues in the poet's own day (64.408–9). Catullus follows Hesiod (and Aratus) by marking the Olympians' break with humankind on the occasion of the withdrawal of a personified goddess of Justice from the earth (Hes. *Op.* 197–201, Arat. *Phaen.* 105–36, Catull. *c.* 64.399). Virgil, by contrast, proclaims the Maiden Justice's return in the same breath as that of Saturn's golden age, along with the advent of the birth of a mysterious child who will preside over a new era and witness the mingling of gods and heroes once again. In this brave new world, *B.* 4 refutes the pessimistic conclusions of Hesiod and Catullus point for point: instead of departing, the personified goddess returns; instead of further degeneration, the iron race will die out and a golden race be born anew; instead of the continued separation of gods and men, in the new age of heroes men will mingle with gods once more. The fourth eclogue thus endows the proclamation of a new era with the authority of Sibylline oracular prophecy in its optimistic description of the renewal of the golden age on earth.

   B. 4 became by far the most famous poem in the collection as a result of the later allegorical identification of the child with Christ (Ch. 5).[38] But in Virgil's own day the identification was unimaginable. Given the propensity in classical antiquity to interpret literature biographically, however, it should not surprise that speculation about the child's identity began early. Servius reports that Pollio's son Asinius Gallus (b. 41, *cos.* 8 BCE) boasted of being the child, though Servius preferred to identify the child as his fictitious younger brother Asinius Saloninus.[39] Modern consensus sees in the prophecy rather the hope of a child from the marriage between Antony and Octavian's sister Octavia, concluded in the fall of 40 BCE to cement the Pact of Brundisium between the uneasy allies. In the event, Antony sired two daughters with Octavia (Antoniae Maior and Minor, b. 39 and 37 BCE). Octavian too celebrated a marriage in the summer of 40, with Scribonia, the sister of Sextus Pompey's father-in-law and staunch ally, Scribonius Libo. The following year, she too bore her new husband a daughter, his only child Julia, and was summarily divorced in order to free him for marriage with the pregnant Livia Drusilla (Suet. *Aug.* 52.2).[40] It is easy, in hindsight, to see in Virgil's miraculous child the symbol of a new era of long-hoped-for peace and prosperity after decades of unrelenting constitutional crises and civil war. But although neither the rapprochement of Octavian with Sextus Pompey nor the Pact of Brundisium between Antony and Octavian in Pollio's year of office brought a lasting peace, there is no reason to question the optimism expressed in the eclogue. Twenty years later, Virgil could imply the fulfilment of the eclogue's aspirations in the *pax Augusta*, fulsomely praised as a golden age by the emperor's remote Trojan ancestor, Anchises (*A.* 6.792–5; Ch. 4.2).

Like the fourth eclogue, *B.* 5 sounds an optimistic and encomiastic political note. Two herders, Menalcas and Mopsus, compliment one another on their musical prowess (1–19) and then exchange songs. Mopsus sings first (20–44), on the Theocritean theme of the death of the cowherd and bucolic culture hero Daphnis (*Id.* 1).[41] Menalcas follows his lead but transforms the conventional theme of pastoral lament into an encomium of the dead hero's deification (56–7): 'Bright Daphnis wonders at the unaccustomed threshold of Olympus, and sees the clouds and stars beneath his feet'. All the inhabitants of the countryside rejoice in his apotheosis (58–9); predators spare their prey (60–1); and every feature of the pastoral landscape celebrates Daphnis' translation to heaven (62–4). The reminiscence of *B.* 1.6–7 (quoted above) in 5.64 ('He's a god, a god, Menalcas!') connects the divine youth of the first eclogue with the divinized Daphnis of the fifth: just as the former will receive monthly sacrifice from Tityrus every year (1.42–3), so the latter will receive two altars (5.66), semi-annual libations of milk

(67), olive oil (5.68) and wine (69–71), along with performances of song and dance (72–3) in the rural cult of the Ambarvalia (75).[42]

Menalcas' encomium, like his promises of bucolic worship, is certainly appropriate to the divinized hero of bucolic song. But many critics have also seen in these lines an invitation to interpret Daphnis' untimely death and astral deification as historical allegory, not least because of the revelation at the end of the song exchange that Menalcas is a mouthpiece for Virgil himself (85–7): 'We shall grant you first this delicate stalk of hemlock: this reed taught us "Corydon was burning for beautiful Alexis", and the same reed taught "Whose herd? Meliboeus'?"' In making Mopsus a gift of his pastoral pipe, Menalcas mentions two other songs he has played on it, quoting the opening lines of *B.* 2 (5.86) and 3 (5.87) respectively. Servius noted that some ancient critics saw in the account of Daphnis' death and divinization here an allegorical treatment of the assassination and deification of Caesar, though he himself interpreted the eclogue as a lament for a fictitious brother of Virgil named Flaccus. Modern consensus, however, accepts the identification of the dead Daphnis with Caesar,[43] on the basis of the implied catasterism of Daphnis and its evocation of the 'Julian star', the comet that appeared during the celebration of Caesar's funeral games in July 44 BCE. Again, we may note Virgil's implied qualification of the new god's praise by setting it in the mouth of a herdsman, even if that herdsman takes credit for Virgil's own bucolic songs.

The political optimism of *B.* 1, 4 and 5 does not continue in the second half of the collection. Virgil declines to sing Varus' praises in epic verse in *B.* 6, and the picture is darker still in *B.* 9, where two herdsmen rehearse snatches of bucolic song while they walk into town. The situation recalls that of the first eclogue, except that here the dispossessed herder, Moeris, has remained as a tenant on his former holding, which he farms for the military veteran who now owns it but lives in town (2–6). Lycidas apparently retains his own holding and is more optimistic than Moeris, having heard that the famed singer Menalcas (a Virgilian *persona*)[44] had saved his land (7–10). But Moeris denies it and, worse still, he reports that both he and Menalcas nearly lost their lives in a quarrel with the new owners (14–16). These lines probably gave rise to the story Donatus reports (*VSD* 20) about Virgil's debt to Maecenas for having saved him from an altercation with a veteran, in accordance with ancient habits of biographical interpretation.[45]

We need not see Virgilian autobiography in the report of Menalcas' quarrel to recognize that the incursion of civil war into the Italian countryside dramatizes the incursion of history and politics into the bucolic landscape and thereby hints at the threat to poetry in the aftermath of Philippi (27–9): 'Varus, only let our Mantua survive – Mantua alas too close to wretched Cremona – and singing swans will bear your name aloft to the stars'. Moeris recalls an unfinished song by Menalcas (26) that relocates pastoral verse from the conventional Sicilian setting to the troubled site of Mantua in the aftermath of the triumviral dispossessions. There are no reminiscences of Theocritean pastoral in these lines, which also lack not only the generic herdsmen but even the conventional Greek names. There is no place for either encomium or bucolic in the context of the triumviral land confiscations. The snatches of Menalcan song the herdsmen rehearse are therefore tentative and fragmentary, overwhelmed by the brute facts of recent history and contemporary politics. Even the star of Caesar, which in the fifth eclogue seemed an optimistic portent, proves ill-omened here (46–50): 'Daphnis, why do you look up at the old constellations? Look, the star of Venus' Caesar has come forth, a star by which crops may rejoice with corn and the grape take on colour in the sunny hills. Graft your pears, Daphnis: your grandchildren will harvest your fruit'. Comets were traditionally ill-omened at Rome,[46] and for all the golden age imagery of these lines, the final verse of the song recalls Meliboeus' dispossession in the first eclogue (1.73) and thereby confirms it as a negative portent here. Certainly that is how Moeris takes it (9.51): 'Time carries all things off, even memory'. He has forgotten 'so many songs' (53) that 'even his voice has fled' (53–4). His words bear poignant witness to the conquest of poetry by politics in the context of the triumviral depredations of the Italian countryside. Although Lycidas wishes to continue their exchange (59–65), Moeris advises him to wait until the return of Menalcas (55), and the poem ends with the indefinite deferral of bucolic song (66–7): 'Leave off singing more songs, boy, and let's get on with what's pressing now; we shall better sing songs then, when he himself has come'.

2.3 *Epicurean Music and Leisure*

Like Meliboeus in the first eclogue, the herdsmen of *B.* 9 lack the leisure with which the youthful god endows Tityrus, and in its absence bucolic song fades away. Leisure would thus seem to be necessary for both the herdsmen's engagement in amoebean song and the poet's composition of bucolic verse. Thomas Rosenmeyer drew attention to the Epicurean quality of Theocritean bucolic, especially in its celebration of leisure.[47] Although we lack information about Theocritus' philosophical commitments, we have extensive evidence linking Virgil with the Epicurean communities of Siro and Philodemos on the Bay of Naples from the mid-40s BCE (Ch. 1). It should therefore occasion no surprise that nearly every line of *B.* is shot through with Epicurean sentiment and Lucretian reminiscence.[48]

The first eclogue is especially rich in Lucretian phraseology.[49] It has long been recognized that Virgil owes Meliboeus' description of Tityrus' 'woodland music' (1.2, *siluestrem musam*) to Lucretius' explanation of popular belief in musical woodland deities arising from widespread misunderstanding of the acoustical phenomenon of echo (*DRN* 4.586–9): 'And the race of farmers perceives the sounds from afar when Pan, shaking the piney veils of his half-wild head, often blows through the open reeds with his lip curled, lest his pipe cease to pour forth woodland music' (*siluestrem musam*, 4.589). Meliboeus' definition of pastoral poetry thus 'echoes' Lucretius' discussion of echo, and Virgil's later programmatic definition of pastoral poetry as 'country music' (6.8, *agrestem musam*) also echoes Lucretius in his association of song with the invention of agriculture (*DRN* 5.1398): 'for at that time country music (*agrestis musa*) was flourishing'. The specificity of Virgil's programmatic citations of Lucretius' poem in *B.* 1.2 and 6.8 hints at the importance of Epicurean philosophy to the bucolic collection, for neither phrase occurs anywhere else in either poet's oeuvre. Taken together, both Lucretian passages supply an important contextual framework for Virgil's bucolic programme, since they constitute the earliest extant instances of Latin bucolic poetry.[50] In the former passage, Lucretius attributes popular belief in Pan and other woodland gods to the widespread misinterpretation of the acoustical phenomenon of echo, for which he provides a materialist explanation. Virgil's literary echo thus draws precisely on the sylvan context of the Epicurean poet's account of the physics of echo. In the latter passage, Lucretius brings together evolutionary accounts of the origins of agriculture and music in the idealizing context of the bucolic landscape, which he identifies as the locus of true pleasure, linking Epicurean pleasure with bucolic song and the *locus amoenus* landscape. Epicurus himself is reported to have said that 'the wise man will love the countryside' (D.L. 10.120) and his school was popularly known as 'the Garden', so called from its location on his extra-urban Athenian estate.[51] Lucretius' idyllic picture of true Epicurean pleasure in the countryside, in conjunction with the sect's idealization of the garden, thus adds an additional philosophical aspect to Virgil's interest in bucolic poetry.

Further evidence of Virgil's philosophical and literary debts to Lucretius can be found in Tityrus' programmatic reply to Meliboeus in *B.* 1.6–7 (quoted above), since the 'leisure' (*otia*, 1.6), in which Tityrus lives has overtones of the tranquillity sought by the Epicureans.[52] The way the fortunate herdsman phrases his debt to the unnamed god for the gift of leisure in these lines also alludes specifically to the proem of Lucretius' fifth book, where the didactic poet invokes Epicurus as 'that god ... who by his skill rescued life from such tempests and such darkness, and set it in such calm ... and bright light' (*DRN* 5.8, 10–12). Peter Bing has suggested that Tityrus' god, 'who "created for us [this peace]" ... reads almost as a gloss on Lucretius' conception of a deity who set life [in such calm]'.[53] Just as Lucretius asserts his personal belief in Epicurus' divinity (*DRN* 5.19), so Virgil's herdsman proclaims that the youth 'will always be a god to me' (*B.* 1.7). Tityrus' 'leisure' (1.6) has a precise referent in Lucretius' phrase 'divine leisure' (*otia dia, DRN* 5.1387) in his account of the origins of music. Even the detail of Tityrus' altars smoking every month for the god (*B.* 1.42–3) may have Epicurean point, if we recall their tradition of a shared monthly meal in memory of Epicurus.[54] Commentators have preferred to compare the monthly celebration of the king's birthday in Hellenistic ruler cult,[55] but Epicurus made provision in his will for his own monthly commemoration in cult and his adherents duly followed the practice for centuries after his death.

If there is an Epicurean valence in Virgil's use of *deus* and *otium* here, he has left it implicit by withholding the name of the god Tityrus worships, even though Meliboeus specifically inquires into the god's identity (1.18, quoted above). Moreover, as we have seen, a tradition as old as Servius identified the unnamed god as Octavian and this identification is widely accepted today.[56] Scholars have therefore preferred to interpret this passage in the light of triumviral history rather than Epicurean philosophy. However, we may be able to unite historical allegory with philosophical interpretation if we give due weight to Tityrus' emphasis on the god's youth (*iuuenem*, 1.42). The polymath Varro, Cicero's contemporary and the author of a treatise on farming from which Virgil drew extensively in *G.*, seems to have derived this noun from the verb 'help' (*iuuo*) in his study of Latin etymologies, *De lingua latina* (45/44 BCE), and Virgil himself draws attention to the etymology, again in connection with the youth Octavian, in *G.* 1, when he entreats the gods to let 'this youth help' the present generation of Italians, overwhelmed by the catastrophe of civil war (*G.* 1.500; Ch. 3.1). As Isidore, the seventh-century CE Bishop of Seville, explains (*Orig.* 11.2.16): 'a youth (*iuuenis*) is so called because he is starting to be able to help (*iuuare*)'.[57] This is precisely the same etymology as that of the Greek noun *epikouros* ('helper'), the name of the founder of Epicureanism.[58] Thus Tityrus' unnamed deity enters the collection doubly marked, by Lucretian allusion and his youth, as an Epicurean saviour.

Scholars may have been reluctant to see political point in the Epicurean colour of the divine youth's representation in *B.* 1, because Epicurus notoriously advised his followers to avoid politics (D.L. 10.119).[59] But there is increasing recognition that Epicurus himself allowed for exceptions to the rule, and we also have strong evidence of Epicurean philosophical engagement among Roman politicians of Virgil's day.[60] In addition to Piso (*cos.* 58 BCE), Caesar's father-in-law and Philodemos' patron, Caesar's assassin Cassius (*quaest.* 53, *trib.* 49, *pr.* 44, d. 42 BCE) was a prominent Roman adherent of the sect, whose conversion to Epicureanism (probably in 48) Cicero deprecated in a series of letters expressing his objections to Epicurean doctrine (*ad Fam.* 5.16–19).[61] Cicero's correspondence amply shows that philosophically engaged senators were accustomed to formulate their political decisions, at least in part, according to their ethical commitments.[62] It is by no means anachronistic, therefore, to see a similar political significance in the Epicurean tonality of Tityrus' response to Meliboeus, for his language draws on a complex of Epicurean concepts and Lucretian phrases to characterize the deity (the triumvir Octavian) as a contemporary Roman Epicurean saviour and the bucolic singer (Tityrus-Virgil) as a committed Epicurean.

The Epicurean valence of *B.* 1 finds a suggestive parallel in the fifth eclogue, where Menalcas hymns the apotheosis of Daphnis.[63] We have already considered Daphnis' catasterism in relation to the Julian star and interpreted the divinized bucolic herdsman as a historical allegory for the apotheosed Roman dictator Caesar, who – like his adoptive son Octavian in *B.* 1 – has earned multiple altars and annual sacrifice from a grateful bucolic community. But, like Tityrus, Menalcas also articulates specifically Epicurean principles in his song. Daphnis' apotheosis is a source of pleasure to the pastoral landscape and its inhabitants (58–9): 'and so keen pleasure took hold of the woods and the rest of the countryside, as well as Pan, the herders, and dryad maidens'. Epicurus and his followers were notorious in antiquity for making pleasure the aim of the philosophical life (D.L. 10.128; cf. Lucr. *DRN* 1.1),[64] and Virgil frames the pleasure Daphnis' apotheosis brings the pastoral landscape

(5.57–8) with a reminiscence of Lucretius' eulogy of Epicurus in the proem to *De rerum natura* 3 (27–8).[65] The Epicurean pleasure that grips the countryside at Daphnis' catasterism is further marked by a pervasive leisure (*B.* 5.61: 'good Daphnis loves leisure'), as the divinized bucolic culture hero assumes an Epicurean profile in his love of tranquillity. All nature resounds with his worship (62–4): 'The wooded mountains themselves vaunted their words to the stars with happiness; now the very rocks, the very orchards re-echo: "He is a god, a god, Menalcas!"' Thus, the natural world hails the divinized Daphnis in the very words with which we have seen Lucretius invoke Epicurus as a god (*DRN* 5.8, quoted above).

Critics have noted the care with which Virgil attends to the responsion of his herdsmen's songs in *B.* 5: Menalcas' celebration of Daphnis' apotheosis corresponds in numerous details to Mopsus' lament for the dead culture hero.[66] But we may wonder how the Epicurean colour of Menalcas' song relates to Mopsus' Theocritean threnody, in which all nature succumbs to grief. In his study of Virgil's interrelation of philosophical and poetic themes in *B.*, Gregson Davis draws attention to the Epicurean doctrine of pleasure as the aim of the blessed life, and the implication that the initiate should therefore focus on pleasure rather than misfortune, on felicity and happiness rather than pain and grief (cf. Cic. *Tusc.* 3.15.33, 31.76). He therefore interprets Menalcas' consolatory song of the pleasure attendant on Daphnis' apotheosis by reference to Epicurus' well-known therapeutic remedy for the expression of pain (*VS* 66): 'We show our feelings for friends not by lamentation [at their funerals] but by meditating [on their lives]'. On an Epicurean interpretation, Menalcas 'corrects' Mopsus by celebrating, rather than lamenting, Daphnis' passing.[67]

The herdsmen's exchange of gifts, at the conclusion of the fifth eclogue, marks the integration of philosophical tranquillity, poetic composition and political commitment. Menalcas bestows upon the younger poet the hemlock-stalk pipe on which he played *B.* 2 and 3. The detail of the pipe's material (5.85, *hac fragili cicuta*; cf. 2.36–7) is ultimately derived from Lucretius' account of the origin of music (*DRN*

5.1382–3):[68] 'And it was the whistling of the zephyr in the cavities of reeds that first taught country folk to blow into hollow hemlock stalks' (*cicutas*). Menalcas endows Mopsus, the singer of traditional bucolic lament, with an Epicurean instrument in an implicit invitation to deepen the philosophical contours of his song. In response, Mopsus gives Menalcas a shepherd's staff (5.88–90), a gift reminiscent not only of Theocritean bucolic (Lycidas' gift of a staff to Simichidas in *Id.* 7.128), but also of Hesiodic didactic (the Muses' gift of a laurel rod to Hesiod, *Theog.* 29–34). As in *B.* 1, the integration of bucolic song and Epicurean philosophy implies the existence of a political order amenable to the composition of pastoral verse.

In the light of Virgil's widespread reminiscences of Lucretius, scholars have investigated individual eclogues for evidence of Epicurean doctrine.[69] Gregson Davis, for example, has explored the significance of the Epicurean values enunciated in *B.* 2.[70] There the shepherd Corydon, burning with unrequited passion for the beautiful Alexis, sings of his passion in the thick shade of a stand of beeches (2.1–5), while the rest of the pastoral world seeks respite from the searing heat (2.8–13). In Epicurean thought, excess of any kind troubles the tranquillity that is the philosopher's goal, and sexual obsession was a particular focus of Epicurean therapy.[71] Epicurus counsels sex as an antidote to the mental disturbance of erotic passion (*VS* 51; cf. D.L. 10.136–7), while Lucretius denounces men's propensity for amatory obsession in a memorable diatribe against love (*DRN* 4.1030–1287).

Corydon's opening words show that his passion for Alexis falls into the category of pathological love (*B.* 2.6–7): 'O cruel Alexis, do you care nothing for my songs? Do you pity me not at all? Do you compel me, then, to die?' His song is modelled on the Cyclops' song in Theocritus' *Idyll* 11, which the Greek poet introduces with a dedication to his friend, the famous physician Nikias (*Id.* 11.1–18); but he implicitly proposes the greater efficacy of song than medicine in curing erotic obsession (*Id.* 11.17–18, 80–1). In championing the view of Theocritus' verse as Epicurean in orientation, Rosenmeyer adduced the emotional detachment of Theocritean bucolic in partial support of his thesis.[72]

The focus of *Idyll* 11 is on the Cyclops' account of 'the ghastly wound under his breast' (15), a negative image of erotic passion that recurs in Lucretius' diatribe against love, which is figured as a 'wound' (*DRN* 4.1049, 1070) and ulcerous 'sore' (*DRN* 4.1068). Theocritus' characterization of song as a 'mild' and 'sweet' (*hadu-*) cure for love is couched in the language of Epicurean therapy, for the Greek noun meaning 'pleasure', *hêdonê*, is cognate with the adjective 'sweet' (*hêdu-/hadu-*), while the adjective 'mild' sums up the Epicurean distaste for strong emotion that unsettles the mental tranquillity that is the goal of the philosophical sage.

Corydon's love, like the Cyclops', burns out of control, but he too finds a cure in the course of his song, eventually realizing that 'his own pleasure draws each man on' (*B.* 2.65). Corydon echoes Lucretius' crucial connection of free will with pleasure (*DRN* 2.257–8): 'What, I ask, is the source of this power of will wrested from destiny, which enables each of us to advance where pleasure leads us?' If Corydon reverts to his passion immediately afterwards, at least he recognizes the necessity of setting a limit to it (68): 'Yet love burns me: for what limit can be set to love?' Corydon echoes the Theocritean Cyclops (*Id.* 11.73) in recognizing his erotic obsession (*B.* 2.69: 'Ah, Corydon, Corydon, what madness has possessed you!') and ruefully acknowledges that there are other things to do besides wallowing in unrequited passion, such as pruning vines or plaiting a basket for use on the farm (70–2). His song even ends on a note of Epicurean illumination, in his reflection that there are other lovers to be found if Alexis disdains him (2.73). His insight can be paralleled in the contemporary teaching of Philodemos, whom Horace reports to have said, 'his type of girl was the one who neither set a great price nor delayed to come when bidden' (*Sat.* 1.2.121–2), i.e. was both available and willing at the lover's convenience. This sentiment coheres with the Epicurean prescription of 'natural' sexual release to cure erotic madness.[73] In Corydon's song, Virgil combines the pleasure of bucolic song with that of Epicurean principle to set a limit to erotic obsession.

Another passage that repays attention in the context of Epicurean philosophy occurs in *B.* 6. We have seen that Servius interprets the poem as an elaborate Epicurean masque (Ch. 1), with Silenus representing Siro; Chromis and Mnasyllos, Virgil and his Epicurean comrade Quintilius Varus; and the nymph Aegle, Epicurean pleasure.[74] Whether or not we accept his proposed identifications, there is clearly something of the philosopher in the figure of Silenus, who recalls Plato's characterization of Socrates in the *Symposium* and sings a marvellous song combining scientific erudition with mythological and aetiological lore, to which pastoral figures dance in Lucretian rhythm (27) while the trees sway as if to Orphic song (28, 30).[75] The old satyr begins his recital with a cosmogony couched in Lucretian language (31–40):

> For he sang how, through the great void, the seeds of earth, wind, sea and pure fire had been driven at the same time; how from these first principles,[76] all things and even the tender globe of the world itself cohered; then the land began to harden and to shut Nereus off in the sea, and little by little to take on the shapes of things; and now the lands marvel that the new sun grows bright, and the rains fall from the clouds that have risen higher, when first the woods begin to rise and a few living creatures wander through the mountains that know them not.

Silenus here recites a condensed Epicurean cosmogony in Lucretian language. The void is central to the atomists' physics and Virgil owes the phrase 'through the great void' to Lucretian precedent. Lucretius regularly denotes the atoms that move through the void by the phrases 'seeds of things', 'first bodies' and 'primary elements' (*DRN* 1.54–61), which combine to become 'the beginnings of the great universe, of land, sea and heaven, and the race of living creatures' (*DRN* 2.1062–3). The fiery ether (*B.* 6.33; cf. Lucr. 6.205) surrounding a spherical world was an Epicurean concept (D.L. 10.88, Lucr. 5.495–508), as much as Stoic, and Lucretius (*DRN* 5.465–71) explains the process by which the globe of the universe grew together before hardening into solid form in language distinctly similar to Virgil here. Lucretius also describes the process that separates sea from land and the maternal earth that witnessed the creation of human and animal races 'sporting everywhere on the great mountains' (*DRN* 5.824).[77]

As Silenus' song continues, his focus shifts from Lucretian cosmogony to neoteric themes of pathological love and fantastic metamorphosis (6.43–63, 74–81). Scholars have seen in this shift evidence of Virgil's disinclination to maintain an Epicurean doctrinal line, even though he continues to echo Lucretian language throughout.[78] Yet, if the lurid myths that Virgil recounts in the body of Silenus' song come from the Callimachean-Neoteric tradition, the erotic delusions on display in those very myths signally validate Epicurean doctrine about the perils of amatory passion. Indeed, when Virgil comes to the poetic investiture of Gallus (64–73) at the climax of the eclogue, he implicitly endorses aetiological rather than amatory verse, urging on Gallus an aetiological theme (72): 'on these pipes, let the origin of the Grynean grove be sung'.

2.4 *Virgil's Poetry Book*

The sixth eclogue is often interpreted as a new beginning for the collection because of the programmatic opening lines (1–12), which rehearse the polemic of Callimachus' *Aetia* Prologue and decline to celebrate the dedicatee in grand epic. The 'proem in the middle' is a characteristically Virgilian site for the negotiation of literary programme (cf. Ch. 3.3, 4.1),[79] and the rest of the eclogue articulates a sophisticated statement of bucolic poetics in support of his rejection of martial epic. In its place, Virgil sets scientific poetry (cosmogony) and Alexandrian learning (obscure erotic and metamorphic myths).[80] A two-line transition from cosmogony to myth contrasts the golden age of Saturn's reign with the loss of innocence in the ensuing age of deceit (41–2). The myths that follow belong to the heroic age, implicitly characterized as morally dubious by their introduction after Prometheus' theft of fire, and combine erotic obsession with lurid metamorphosis: Hercules' loss of his squire Hylas, ravished by water nymphs and transformed into echo (43–4), a myth related by both Theocritus (*Id.* 13) and Apollonius (*Arg.* 1.1207–355); Pasiphaë's lust for a bull (45–7, 52–60), with the inset contrast of the Proetides' hallucination of their own transformation into cows (48–51); Atalanta's desire for the golden apples of the Hesperides and the youth who threw them during their footrace (61), a neoteric subject (Cat. *c.* 2.11–13) drawn from Hellenistic epic (Ap. Rhod. *Arg.* 4.611–18); and the metamorphosis of Phaethon's sisters, the Heliades, into alders (62–3).

Pasiphaë claims Silenus' attention most prominently, and rightly so in a bucolic collection, as Virgil embellishes a myth already featuring Minos' bull (46, 58), with the addition of herds (45), cattle (49), cows (60) and cow hallucinations (48–51). Particularly striking is the singer's sympathy for Pasiphaë in her erotic madness (6.45–7): 'And he consoles Paisphaë, fortunate if there had never been herds, for her love of a snow-white bullock. Ah, unhappy maiden, what madness possessed you!' She too might have enjoyed happiness had Minos not reneged on his vow to sacrifice to the sea-god the beautiful white bull he had sent. Silenus suppresses the backstory of her husband's impiety and the god's resulting vengeance to focus on the lovelorn Pasiphaë, but interrupts his own song to comfort her with words borrowed from Calvus' epyllion *Io* (fr. 20, Hollis: 'Ah, unlucky maiden, you will pasture on bitter grasses!') and Virgil's own Corydon (*B.* 2.69, quoted above). Unlike Corydon, who discovers a cure for love in pastoral labour at the end of his song, Pasiphaë seems doomed to erotic obsession. For like Calvus' Io, transformed into a heifer and maddened by the gadfly's sting, Pasiphaë wanders on the mountains tracking an elusive, not to say delusory, love. The play of cow myths continues in Silenus' allusive account of the daughters of Proetus, who insulted Hera and were maddened by her with the hallucination that they had been transformed into cows. The technique of embedding one myth in another was typical of both the Alexandrian and Neoteric poets,[81] and there is presumably much of the Calvan intertext here that is lost to us because his *Io* is no longer extant.

The bucolic myths give way abruptly with the introduction of Virgil's friend and contemporary Gallus, who was already a renowned elegiac poet and Caesarian politician. In a symbolically charged landscape reminiscent of Hesiod's poetic investiture (*Theog.* 26–8), as invoked by

Callimachus at the outset of his *Aetia* (fr. 2), Gallus encounters the Muses (*B.* 6.64–6) and the divine shepherd Linus, who commissions him in an initiation scene that transforms the love elegist into an Orphic bard (69–71): 'The Muses give you these reeds (look, take them), which they gave before to the old man of Ascra [i.e. Hesiod], with which he used to lead the stiff oaks down from the mountains with his singing'. Linus also proposes a new theme for Gallus' poetry, the origin of the Grynean Grove (72, quoted above). Virgil may here allude to Gallus' current poetic project, inspired by his Greek mentor Parthenios of Nicea (first century BCE)[82] and two other Greek poets of obscure learning, Callimachus (Ch. 1) and Euphorion of Chalcis (b. *c.* 275 BCE). Gallus' ascent of Mount Helicon in the company of a Muse (65) and the full chorus' homage to him (66) signal the literary ambition of his new theme, for aetiological poetry was a Hesiodic (i.e. didactic epic) mode that stood above amatory elegy in the classical hierarchy of genres.

In Virgil's compliment to his friend and literary mentor Gallus, we may also discern the tentative adumbration of his own developing interest in Hesiodic didactic, from which his next poetry book will spring (Ch. 3.1). For the moment, he remains in the humbler hexameter mode of bucolic, and sketches three further subjects of Silenus' song: the transformation of Nisus' daughter Scylla, whom he conflates with the eponymous sea-monster who harassed Ulysses and his crew on their return from Troy to Ithaca, anticipates the Homeric themes of *A.* (74–7); the transformation of Tereus, Procne and Philomela into the hoopoe, swallow and nightingale (78–81), another Homeric subject (*Od.* 19.518–23) briefly treated by Catullus (*c.* 65.13–14); and Apollo's lament for his lover Hyacinthus, whom he accidentally killed on the shore of the Spartan river Eurotas (82–3).[83] Silenus' song closes with the familiar bucolic 'sympathy figure' as Eurotas bids the laurel trees on his banks learn Apollo's song and his own song re-echoes to the stars (84). The final image sounds a note of pride in Virgil's own achievement in pastoral verse, if we recall Tityrus teaching the woods to re-echo his Amaryllis song at the outset of the first eclogue.

The tenth eclogue, also addressed to Gallus, is a pendant to the sixth and functions as an epilogue to the book as a whole. The eclogue-singer asks the Sicilian spring Arethusa, once a Nereid whom the Arcadian river god Alpheus pursued, to inspire one final bucolic 'labour' for Gallus, such that his friend's elegiac girlfriend Lycoris might read (1–3). Virgil thus implies that the subject of his final selection will be a confrontation between Gallan love elegy and his own bucolic verse (6–7): 'Let us sing of Gallus' troubled love, while the snub-nosed goats crop the tender shoots'.[84] The assurance with which the bucolic poet affirms the responsion of the natural world (8: 'we sing not to the deaf, the woods re-echo all') implies his confidence in the ultimate victory of his own genre over Gallus'.

Taking Theocritus' description of the dying Daphnis (*Id.* 1.66–75) as his model, Virgil presents Gallus dying of love in Arcadia (*B.* 10.9–10): 'What groves or glades held you, Naiads, when Gallus was perishing of unworthy love?' In a return of the sympathy figure, all nature laments – from the Greek mountain ranges of Parnassus and Pindus (11) to Mt Helicon's spring Aganippe (12, a line with a number of exotic Greek sound effects), along with the trees characteristic of the pastoral landscape (laurels, tamarisk and the pine, sacred to Pan, 13–14), and the Arcadian mountains of Maenalus and Lycaeus (15). Virgil locates Gallus in Arcadia, the mythical home of Hermes and his son Pan, both tutelary deities of herders and the latter the inventor of their instrument, the pan-pipe, and patron of their songs (cf. *B.* 7.4, where the rival herdsmen are 'Arcadians both'). Virgil's relocation of the genre from Theocritus' Sicily to his own symbolic Arcadia was to prove a momentous intervention in the pastoral tradition, for 'Arcady' became the home of European pastoral (Ch. 5).[85]

Not only the natural world but all the creatures of the bucolic landscape attend Gallus in his agony: sheep (16) and their herders, including the sixth eclogue's divine poet Linus (17); the shepherd Adonis (18), lamented in Bion's great pastoral dirge; unnamed shepherds and swineherds (19); and the Virgilian Menalcas himself (20), perhaps a stand-in for the eclogue-singer in his own poem. The pastoral gods

come too: Apollo, Silvanus and Pan (21–7). Apollo takes a particular
interest in Gallus' erotic mania (22), for Gallus' mistress bears a name
derived from the god's obscure cult-title Lykoreus, first attested in
Callimachus' poetry (22–3):[86] 'Your girlfriend Lycoris has followed
another through snow and brutal army camps'. Scholars have seen in
Apollo's words a quotation from Gallus' own love poetry,[87] four books
of elegies detailing the highs, and especially the lows, of an affair with a
faithless mistress whose defection to a frigid army camp on the northern
frontier (cf. *B.* 10.46–9) is tantamount to her rejection of elegiac
urbanity. Pan frames Gallus' resulting dilemma in Epicurean terms
(28): 'What limit will there be?' Presented, like Corydon, with the
Epicurean problem of setting a limit to erotic obsession (cf. 2.68, quoted
above), the Virgilian Gallus recasts his amatory song in the bucolic
mode (10.33–4): 'O how softly would my bones then lie, if once your
pipe should recite my love!' He dreams of pastoral promiscuity, enjoying
'Phyllis or Amyntas, or some other passion' (37–8), all apparently
interchangeable, in approved Epicurean fashion. His transposition into
the bucolic landscape, however, can neither mask nor ameliorate his
elegiac erotic passion: the generic bucolic beloveds Phyllis and Amyntas
hold his attention for no more than five lines (37–41) before he reverts
to his erotic obsession with Lycoris (42–8), even, according to Servius,
reciting lines from his love elegies (46–9).

Virgil depicts the suffering love poet attempting to free himself from
erotic madness through a transposition into the bucolic mode, following
the models of the learned Greek poets Euphorion and Parthenios.
Quintilian interpreted Gallus' proposal to rehearse Chalcidean verse on
the pastoral pipe (50–1) as a reference to his interest in the poetry of
Euphorion of Chalcis (*Inst. Or.* 10.1.56), whose abstruse mythological
learning and obscurity of expression were derided by Cicero (*Tusc.*
3.45; *ad Att.* 7.2.1) but admired by the Neoterics. Gallus redirects
pastoral music into elegiac channels, however, imagining himself
inscribing his 'loves' (both the name of his beloved and the lines of his
verse) on the trees symbolic of the bucolic landscape, thus overwriting
pastoral with elegy (52–4).[88] His proposal to hunt in 'Parthenian glades'

(57) is widely agreed to imply his literary allegiance to Parthenios, a contemporary exponent of Callimachean poetics whom Cinna had brought to Rome. Reputedly Virgil's Greek teacher, Parthenios dedicated to Gallus a still extant compendium of myths on the theme of pathological love for his use in poetic composition. Gallus finds no cure for love in these activities, because they nourish both his erotic obsession and his elegiac verse. The experiment ends with his renunciation of bucolic song (10.62–3,69): 'now neither the Hamadyrads nor their very songs please me; you very woods yield ... Love conquers all things: and so let us yield to Love'.

The final poem of Virgil's first collection closes with the singer of the eclogue also yielding to love (72–4): 'Muses, you will make these greatest verses for Gallus – for Gallus, love of whom increases so much in me every hour as the green alder grows tall in early spring'. He puts an end to bucolic composition (70) in a symbolically charged description of his poetic practice as 'plaiting a slight basket of slender mallow' (71): the Callimachean resonances can be heard in both the small size of the object and its humble materials. His self-exhortation to rise (75) suggests a desire to leave humble pastoral behind and essay a higher genre. *B.* 10 closes with nightfall and the return of the poet's well-fed flock (his completed poetry book) to the fold (cf. *AP* 9.205, quoted above).

Between the two eclogues in which Gallus figures so prominently, Virgil follows bucolic convention more closely. *B.* 7 like *B.* 3 features a song contest, in this case between Corydon and Thyrsis, presided over by Daphnis and recalled by Meliboeus. The herders' names are richly evocative of both Theocritean and Virgilian pastoral: Corydon and Daphnis we have met in *Idylls* 4 (Korydon), 8 and 9 (Daphnis), while Thyrsis is the name of the herdsman who hears the goatherd's song about the death of Daphnis in *Idyll* 1. All but Thyrsis have also appeared in Virgilian bucolic: Meliboeus in the opening eclogue, Corydon in the second and the dead Daphnis in the fifth. The song exchange between Corydon and Thyrsis rehearses several themes from *B.* 3 – love, rustic piety and herding (cf. above, 2.1) – but adapts, steals and/or echoes far fewer Theocritean themes and images. Virgil thus strikes a self-consciously proprietary note in his recapitulation of his own earlier bucolic. Meliboeus does not report Daphnis' decision in the contest, pre-empting his official judgement to declare Corydon victorious (70: 'since that time it's been Corydon, Corydon, with us'), in an unmistakable echo of Corydon's own song (2.69, quoted above) that implies the wide renown of Virgil's bucolic poetry.

B. 8 also recapitulates and expands material from the first half of the collection, especially Corydon's love song, but doubles the number of singers and introduces the city as a rival setting to the countryside. Dedicated to Pollio, the poem reports the song exchange of Damon and Alphesiboeus, whose name, meaning 'producing a good yield of oxen', makes him another exemplary bucolic figure. Instead of singing in alternating (i.e. amoebean) verse, they each sing a single long song on the theme of love, articulating their songs with a repeated refrain that invests their verses with magical efficacy. Damon laments his beloved Nysa's marriage to Mopsus (17–60), while Alphesiboeus reports the spell chanted by Daphnis' lover to bring him home from the city (64–108). Damon's song conforms to the generic conventions of pastoral in its rehearsal of the posture of the dying Daphnis (though a Daphnis dying of love rather than in opposition to it). But Alphesiboeus' song strains at the limits of Virgilian bucolic in multiple ways, for he introduces (and impersonates) a female singer of bucolic song; conflates magic incantation with bucolic verse; and thereby introduces the newly popular genres of mime and/or pantomime into the generic palette of bucolic. In Alphesiboeus' innovations, Virgil also pays tribute to the breadth of Theocritean poetry, which included not only bucolic selections but also urban mimes; indeed, Theocritus' second *Idyll* is the model for Alphesiboeus' song here.

The care with which Virgil has crafted each individual eclogue is reflected in that with which he arranged the collection, and the complex design of the book has prompted numerous studies.[89] Odd numbered pieces are dialogic and often feature song exchange, while even numbered pieces are monologues (even if sometimes shared, as in *B*. 8, between Damon and Alphesiboeus, or in *B.* 10, between 'Gallus' and the eclogue-singer). The restatement of bucolic programme in *B.* 6 has been seen as dividing the book into two halves: 1–5 and 6–10. The statements of literary programme in *B.* 1 and 6 are balanced by Virgil's use of Theocritus' dying Daphnis as a model for *B.* 5 and 10. *B.* 1 and 5 are united in their focus on political allegory, 6 and 10 in their focus on Gallus and his poetry. However, the optimistic tone of 1–5 finds a pessimistic counterpart in 6–10. Individual eclogues within the two halves of the collection have also been seen as reflecting one another in concentric circles around *B.* 5, which emerges as the central poem, with 10 set apart as an epilogue. On this interpretation, 1 and 9 treat the political upheavals of the dispossessions, 2 and 8 are set in dialogue as love songs, 3 and 7 as song contests, and 4 and 6 as oracular songs that strain at the limits of the pastoral genre. The collection has also been read as a series of three triads, again with 10 as a pendant to the collection: 1–3 set out Virgil's emulative challenge to Theocritean pastoral; 4–6 expand the horizons of the genre to universal history, oracular song and recent politics; and 7–9 pull back to present Virgil's achievement in the genre. The individual pieces of Virgil's collection thus combine to form a poetry book of the utmost literary sophistication in its exploration of contemporary politics, philosophical principle and poetic programme.

3

Georgica

Already in *B.*, Virgil occasionally widens his ambit to include glimpses of a fuller range of farming activities than herding. In *B.* 1, for example, Meliboeus laments the loss of his 'fields' (1.1) and congratulates Tityrus on the retention of his own (1.46). However poor Tityrus' land, which Meliboeus describes as marsh and rocky ground (1.47–8), it offers sufficient fodder for herds (1.49–50), as well as good pasturage for bees (1.53–5), and it even seems to include an orchard (1.56–8; cf. 1.80–1). Elsewhere in the collection, Menalcas boasts that his marvellous cups are embossed with the figure of an unnamed astronomer 'who diagrammed the cycle of the seasons, the times for the reaper and the bent ploughman' (3.41–2, Ch. 2.1). In *B.* 9, Lycidas recites a snatch of Menalcan song (47–50, Ch. 2.2) that casts the 'Julian star' as an omen for crops, vines and fruit trees. All these passages look forward, in brief compass, to the agricultural themes of *G.*: crops (Book 1), fruit trees and viticulture (Book 2), animal husbandry (Book 3) and bee-keeping (Book 4). The subjects of the second half of *G.* constitute the conventional features of the bucolic landscape, where the pasturage of flocks lies always on the margins of the herders' songs (e.g. *B.* 3.92–103) and the hum of bees is programmatic (*B.* 1.53–5, Ch. 2.1). In addition, we have seen that in *B.* 6 (64–73, Ch. 2.4) Virgil inscribes his friend Gallus, the elegiac poet, in a genealogy of exemplary poets that descends, under the auspices of Apollo, from the legendary singer Linus to the archaic Greek poet Hesiod, 'the old man of Ascra', whose *Works and Days* were the fountainhead not only of georgic verse, but also, more broadly, of didactic poetry.

3.1 *The Didactic Tradition*

Virgil explicitly acknowledges his transplantation of Hesiodic didactic
into the Roman soil of *G.* in a famous line from the second book (2.176):
'I sing an Ascraean song through Roman towns'.[1] He thus makes good
on his intention to raise the poetic level of his song ('let us rise', *B.*10.75),
as he moves from composition in the pastoral mode to that of didactic.
Like bucolic, didactic verse was conventionally composed in the dactylic
hexameters of epic poetry, and stood below only the cosmological and
martial modes of epic in the classical hierarchy of genres. In ancient
criticism, Homer was the source of all genres, both verse and prose, and
his martial epics, *Iliad* and *Odyssey*, were deemed the earliest and
greatest works of the classical tradition. In the Hellenistic period, there
also seems to have been a vogue for Hesiodic verse and the didactic
mode. Callimachus, the great Alexandrian court bibliographer and
arbiter of literary taste, reworked the scene of Hesiod's initiation
(refashioned by Virgil in *B.* 6, Ch. 2.4) early in his *Aetia* (fr. 2), a quasi-
didactic poem composed like *G.* in four books. In his *Epigrams*,
Callimachus praises the Macedonian poet Aratus' versification of
Eudoxus' treatise on celestial bodies, *Phaenomena*, as 'Hesiodic in theme
and manner' (Callim. *Epigr.* 27 Pf. [= *AP* 9.507]). Many titles of didactic
works are reported from the Hellenistic period, including not only
Aratus' *Phaenomena*, but also Nicander's lost *Georgika* ('farming
matters'), which supplied Virgil's title, and the latter's two extant poems,
Theriaka (on venomous creatures) and *Alexipharmaka* (on poisons and
their antidotes).[2] In Latin literature, the didactic tradition was newly
represented in Virgil's day by an early work of Cicero's, commonly
called *Aratea*, that adapted Aratus' *Phaenomena* into Latin verse;[3] and
by Lucretius' slightly later *De rerum natura*, the six-book treatise on
Epicurean physics that exerted such a profound influence on all of
Virgil's poetry.[4] His choice of the didactic mode for *G.* thus advertises
the grander pretensions to which his new work lays claim.

   G. opens with an outline of their contents, introduced according to
the order of the books in which they are treated (1.1–5): 'What makes

crops fertile, under what star it is fitting to turn the earth, Maecenas, and join vines to elms, what may constitute the care of cattle, what tending for keeping a herd, how great the skill for thrifty bees – from here I shall begin to sing'. Despite the rhetorical differentiation of *G.* from *B.* as interpersonal poetry, indicated by the address to the poet's new patron, Maecenas, and the generic differentiation of pastoral from didactic hexameter modes announced here, Virgil emphasizes continuity between the two works, just as he foreshadows *G.* in *B.* Thus, animal husbandry is introduced, already at the outset of *G.*, under the sign of cattle (1.3), as if to emphasize the new project's literary succession from *B.* (Ch. 2.1).[5]

Embedded in the 'table of contents' is a dedication to the poet's patron Maecenas, the wealthy Etruscan magnate, close friend and political advisor of the triumvir Octavian, named in the second line of the poem and again in the second line of the last book, as well as in the forty-first lines of the two central books. The symmetry of the addresses bespeaks Virgil's careful arrangement of every aspect of *G.* and underlines the interpersonal dimension of didactic poetry, with its speaking 'I' and listening 'you'. While the audience of the eclogues 'overhears' the herders as they sing and interact with one another, apparently oblivious to us listening in on their songs, the audience of *G.* is directly addressed, through the second-person forms that proliferate throughout the poem, and we are thereby exhorted to 'play the farmer', in Philip Thibodeau's pregnant phrase.[6]

In the prayer that follows the outline of the poem's contents, Virgil invokes the tutelary gods of the Italian countryside (1.5–23) in distinctly bucolic guise.[7] The celestial bodies which govern the seasons head the list (1.5–6), and Lucretian precedent confirms their identity as Sun and Moon (*DRN* 5.1436–8). Virgil signals a tight connection between agronomy and astronomy already in Menalcas' description of Alcimedon's cup (*B.* 3.41–2, Ch. 2.1), where the celestial globe plots the farmer's seasonal cycle. As the opening prayer continues, the tutelary deities of *B.* return by name, Father Liber (i.e. Bacchus) and generous Ceres (*G.* 1.7; cf. *B.* 5.79–80). The subsequent invocation of Fauns, the 'attending divinities of countrymen', and the Dryads (*G.* 1.10–11) is especially resonant of the eclogues, where these rustic deities appear frequently (e.g. *B.* 5.59), often in the company of their Greek analogues Pan and the Nymphs (e.g. 2.31–3), whom the poet next invokes (*G.* 1.16–20). Pan is the special deity of bucolic, invoked by the singer of Theocritus' first *Idyll* (123–4), and repeatedly petitioned by the herders of Virgilian pastoral, once even together with the old Italian woodland deity Silvanus (*B.* 10.24–6), who accompanies him here (*G.* 1.20). Between the two sets of archetypal country gods, the poet-*praeceptor* invokes the father of the horse, Neptune (1.12–14), and the 'herdsman of Ceos' groves', Aristaeus, 'for whom three hundred white bullocks shear the island's shrubs' (1.14–15). Unnamed here, Aristaeus will feature prominently in the final book as a bee-keeper (Ch. 3.3), but Virgil's learned periphrasis aligns him with *B.*'s herdsmen, who pass their days singing in shady groves while pasturing their flocks. The implied characterization of Aristaeus as a cowherd recalls the etymological connection of bucolic with cattle and also accords with Hesiod's representation of Aristaeus as the patron of herdsmen (*Cat.* fr. 217 M–W).

Virgil closes the invocation of the gods and goddesses of the countryside with a summary trio of lines about their oversight of the cultivation of the fields (1.21–3). But the opening prayer is far from over, as the invocation continues with an address to a single, indeed singular, deity, named Caesar, on whom the focus remains for the next nineteen lines as he is invited to consider which cosmic realm he might wish to rule – earth, sea, or even, following in his adoptive father's wake as a new star, heaven (1.24–39). The proem concludes with his invocation as the tutelary deity of the poet's new project (1.40–2): 'Grant an easy course and inspire my bold undertaking; and, pitying with me the countrymen ignorant of their path, embark and accustom yourself, now already, to be entreated in my prayers'. Scholarly consensus agrees that the Caesar addressed here is not the dead and deified Julius Caesar, commemorated as Daphnis in *B.* 5, but his adoptive son and heir Octavian, the young god marked out as an Epicurean saviour in *B.* 1

(Ch. 2.3). At the end of *G*. 1 too, Virgil underlines the salvific potential of the youthful Caesar, when he begs the gods not to prevent the divine youth from assisting mortals in troubled times (1.500, Ch. 2.3). The poet-*praeceptor*'s valedictory prayer thus concludes *G*. 1 in ring composition with the opening prayer to Octavian and the Italian divinities, while its Epicurean tonality reprises the complex of philosophical and political ideals set in play in *B*. 1. We may thus hear a continuing political valence in the Epicurean contours in which the young Caesar reappears in *G*. 1, as a contemporary saviour in whom the poet invests the hopes and prayers of Italian farmers.[8]

The poem proper begins with the farmer's labours early in the spring, with oxen put to the plough (1.45–6): 'already then let my bull begin to groan at the deep pressure of the plough'. The poet signals his commitment to didactic georgic with the personal pronoun ('my', 1.45), juxtaposed to his programmatic plough-ox, and he concludes his opening precept, in ring composition, with the return of the farmer's plough-oxen from the fields (1.63–6). Virgil introduces the overarching theme of his didactic poem, 'work' (*labor*), in close conjunction with the farmer's plough-oxen (1.118–24):[9]

> Nor nevertheless, after all that the work (*labores*) of men and oxen has achieved in turning the earth, does the wicked goose do no mischief, or the Strymonian cranes, or the endive with its bitter fibres; or the shade is harmful. The heavenly father himself has willed that the path of cultivation should be by no means easy – he who first moved the fields with skill, piercing mortals' hearts with cares, nor suffering his realm to languish in heavy lassitude.

In the phrase 'the work of men and oxen', Virgil conjoins quotations of Homer (*Od*. 10.98) and Hesiod (*Op*. 46), in an exemplary instance of 'combinatorial' allusion.[10] Hesiod's programmatic use of the phrase 'the work of oxen' early in the *Works and Days* confirms its thematic primacy for Virgil's didactic project. For in setting out the theme of his poem to his addressee, Perses, Hesiod bitterly observes that the fields worked by plough-oxen and sturdy mules would run to waste if man could sustain

himself for a year on a day's work (*Op.* 42–6). Indeed, the argument of
Hesiod's poem is precisely that the farmer can do no such thing, that he
must rather engage the unremitting toil of plough-oxen and sturdy
mules, as well as his own, to sustain himself. Virgil recuperates Hesiod's
didactic programme along with his agricultural lexicon in the
introduction of his own controlling theme of the constant work (*labor*)
required of georgic life (*G.* 1.145–6): 'relentless toil has overwhelmed
everything, and pressing need in harsh circumstances'.[11] Virgil's
emphasis at the outset on the primacy of toil – both that of oxen and of
men – functions not only intertextually, as an extended programmatic
allusion to Hesiod, in the Greek poet's role as the founder of didactic
georgic in the *Works and Days*, but also intratextually, conjoining the
work of oxen with the labour of man in the leitmotif of his own didactic
agricultural poem.

A programmatic concern with textual models and literary forms is
clearly at issue in Virgil's repetition of the Hesiodic phrase 'the work of
oxen' again later in the first book (1.324–6): 'High heaven bursts and
washes away the fertile crops and work of oxen in the huge downpour'.
Although this description of the storm is indebted to Homeric simile
(*Il.* 16.384–92) and Lucretian physics (*DRN* 1.271–6, 6.253–61), in
addition to Hesiod's didactic treatment of the effects of storm on
cultivation (*Op.* 507–16), the repetition of the Hesiodic motif specifically
confirms the *Works and Days* as the 'code' (i.e. generic)[12] model for
Virgil's didactic poem on farming, as it simultaneously reinforces the
thematic focus on toil and cattle husbandry in his georgic continuation
of *B.* So too, when Virgil instructs his reader about the best time to
break oxen to the plough, he draws on specifically Hesiodic style and
precept in his reiteration of the importance of the task (1.284–6): 'The
seventeenth is lucky for planting the vine, for yoking and breaking in
oxen, and for adding loops to the warp. The ninth is better for the
runaway but opposed to the thief'. These instructions come at the close
of Virgil's 'Days' (1.276–86), a passage that opens with the first attested
reference in Latin to the title of Hesiod's poem (1.276–7): 'The moon
herself has allotted some days favourable for work'. Richard Thomas

has observed the 'ostentatiously Hesiodic' character of the passage, which pointedly recalls Hesiod's 'Days' (*Op.* 765–828), 'from which at first sight V. appears to give a straightforward translation, apparently excerpting 802–13, treating the fifth, seventeenth, and nin(eteen)th [days]'.[13]

A similar concern to signal his poem's formal generic alignment with Hesiodic georgic animates Virgil's disavowal of the fire-breathing bulls of martial epic, as distinct from the plough-oxen of didactic georgic, in a passage singing the 'praises of Italy' (*G.* 2.140–2): 'Fire-snorting bulls have not ploughed these fields with the sown teeth of a great dragon, nor has a crop of men's helmets and serried lances bristled here'. Virgil caps this implied rejection of the heroic themes of Apollonius' epic *Argonautica* (about the voyage of the Argonauts, including the hero Jason's yoking of fire-breathing bulls at Colchis) with a ringing endorsement of his distinctively Hesiodic didactic programme in the closing lines of the passage (2.176, quoted above).[14]

The closing movement of *G.* 2 likewise reflects Virgil's programmatic alignment of his 'poem of the earth'[15] with Hesiodic didactic (as opposed to Homeric martial epic) in its famous praise of the farmer and farming life (2.458–60, 467–70, 513–15):

> O farmers, happy (*fortunatos*) beyond measure, could they but know their blessings! For them, far from the clash of arms, most righteous Earth pours forth from her soil an easy living … And they have leisure free from anxiety, a life free of deceit and rich in a variety of resources. Nor do they lack the peace of broad holdings, caverns, and natural lakes, cool valleys, and the lowing of oxen, and soft slumbers beneath the trees … The farmer has parted the earth with his curved plough; here is his year's work, hence he sustains his country and small grandsons, hence his herds of cattle and deserving bullocks.

In drawing the idyllic contours of the farming life, Virgil underlines the farmer's distance from the world of war (2.459), his georgic poem from martial epic; and he emphasizes the countryman's close relation, in the work and produce of the farm, to his plough-oxen (2.513–15), and thereby his own literary commitment to didactic georgic. The two sets of 'praises' in *G*. 2 – of Italy and of the farmer – confirm Virgil's new generic allegiance to Hesiodic georgic, in their contrasting presentation of the heroic bulls of martial epic and the farmer's plough-oxen of didactic epic.

Virgil adapts multiple models of didactic verse in style, structure and theme to underline his poem's generic alignment with this hexameter mode, and his first book invokes a particularly diverse array of didactic predecessors.[16] The famous precept 'naked plough; sow naked' (1.299), with its archaic Latin phrasing, closely translates (as it reverses) Hesiod's similarly abrupt injunction 'naked to sow, and naked to plough' (*Op.* 381). This adaptation of Hesiod's 'Days' is set within a larger treatment of the seasons and weather-signs in the second half of *G*. 1, where Virgil's focus on the constellations (1.257–8) looks as much or more in its overall structure to Aratus' *Phaenomena*.[17] The opening line of Virgil's 'Days' (1.351, 'And that we might learn these things from sure signs' [*signis*]; cf. 1.354, 'by what sign [*signo*] the South Winds fall') quotes Aratus' first word in his treatment of weather-'signs' (*sêma*, *Phaen.* 909).[18] Virgil also adapts the first four lines of Aratus' passage at the outset of his own (1.356–9): 'Immediately, when the wind comes up, either the straits of the sea begin to swell, churned up, and a dry crash is heard on the high mountains, or the shores, re-echoing far and wide, join in the confusion and the rumble of the glades grows more frequent'. Like Aratus – who mentions the swelling sea, waves breaking on the beach, echoing headlands, and the moaning wind on the mountains (*Phaen.* 909–12) – Virgil describes four signs of the impending gale. Of special interest is his adaptation of Aratus' 'echoing' headlands (*Phaen.* 911) as 're-echoing' shores (*G*. 1.358), for here Virgil offers self-conscious comment on his literary 'imitation' of Aratus. Late in his treatment of weather-signs, the Latin poet similarly annotates his debt to Aratus in a parenthetical reference to 'the surest authority' (*certissimus auctor*)[19] for the interpretation of weather, a punning compliment to the Hellenistic poet of celestial phenomena (1.432).[20]

Joseph Farrell has discussed in detail Virgil's artful restructuring of Aratus' presentation of weather-signs in his own treatment of the phenomenon.[21] The Latin poet begins with windy weather, closely following his Greek model (1.351–69 ~ *Phaen.* 909–32), before proceeding to signs of rain (1.370–92 ~ *Phaen.* 933–87) and scattering throughout signs of fair weather (1.351–423 ~ *Phaen.* 999–1141). But these terrestrial weather-signs belong to the second part of Aratus' discussion, which opens with the celestial phenomena that predict the weather (*Phaen.* 778–891), and Virgil has reversed these signs in his exposition in order to conclude *G.* 1 with a lengthy list of the signs of cosmic unrest that presaged Caesar's assassination in 44 BCE and the Battle of Philippi in 42 BCE (1.424–514).[22] Virgil emphasizes the reliability of celestial portents in a world out-of-joint (1.463–92), as his depiction of cosmic collapse culminates, at the end of the book, in the prayer to the gods to keep Octavian safe (1.500, quoted Ch. 2.3).

Virgil's decision to turn to a georgic theme after the eclogues has often been interpreted in the context of the dire political situation to which successive Roman strong men had reduced the republic in a series of disastrous civil wars. It has been posited that Italian farming was devastated by the twin forces of dislocation (of farmers) and resettlement (of veterans) driven by the triumvirs in the aftermath of Philippi, and then by Sextus Pompey's ruinous blockade of Italy in the early 30s, which caused or contributed to widespread famine in the peninsula before Octavian's general Agrippa defeated him in a sea battle at Naulochus (3 September 36 BCE). It is certainly possible that the conjunction of land redistribution and widespread famine inspired, or confirmed, Virgil's interest in composing georgic didactic, especially in the light of his background in the landed provincial elite and his continuing ownership of extensive holdings in southern Italy.

There may also have been a more immediate inspiration in the publication in 37 BCE of a treatise on farming by the polymath M. Terentius Varro (116–27 BCE), which constituted an indispensable source for much of Virgil's poem.[23] In addition to the verse tradition of didactic, there was by Virgil's day an extensive prose literature on farming and property management, the most famous that of the Carthaginian Mago, which was translated from Punic into Latin on the order of the Senate after the fall of Carthage in 146 BCE. The Roman tradition of farming treatises began still earlier, however, with the elder Cato's *De agricultura* (*c.* 160 BCE), which inaugurated a long line of georgic handbooks, amongst them Varro's *De re rustica*. Varro's work was the product of his retirement from active politics, in the aftermath of Pompey's death in 48 and the subsequent defeat of the republican forces under Brutus and Cassius at Philippi in 42. In composing a work on farming at this critical juncture, Varro has been interpreted as engaging with the Greek philosophical tradition that conflated the administration of an agricultural estate with the management of the state, in order to propound an anti-Caesarian politics in a far safer forum than an Italian political arena now more akin to Greek tyranny than Roman republican governance.[24]

3.2 *The Philosophical Tradition*

Xenophon's *Oeconomicus* (? after 362 BCE) furnishes an early, and exceedingly famous, instance of this philosophical tradition, and the form of the treatise reveals its author's pretensions to far more than merely technical agricultural knowledge. Presented in the manner of a Socratic dialogue, familiar from the works of Plato, the *Oeconomicus* stages a discussion between Socrates and Critoboulus, a wealthy Athenian profligate, about the views of the rich landowner Ischomachus concerning property management, a subject that Xenophon elsewhere represents as an allegory for political rule (*Oec.* 13–14; cf. *Mem.* 3.4.12, 4.2.11) and that the Greek philosophical tradition consistently imbues with ethical, as well as practical, implications.[25] Xenophon's example was followed by a member of Aristotle's school in an extant treatise of the same name that Philodemos attributes to Theophrastos, Aristotle's successor as the head of the Lyceum. Like Xenophon, Theophrastos considers property management not only a technical skill, but also both an analogy for political rule (Arist. [*Oec.*] 1343a1–16) and an ethical template for virtuous living (Arist. [*Oec.*] 1345a13–14; cf. Xen.

Oec. 20.14). Indeed, Theophrastos identifies agriculture and farming as the best, and most virtuous, source of income; and like Xenophon, he views the acquisition and preservation of wealth as integral to the art of property management. Although only the treatises of Xenophon and Theophrastos are still extant, it is clear that there continued in the Hellenistic period a lively philosophical debate about the art of administering property, especially in its ethical and political dimensions,[26] on which Philodemos appears to draw in his own treatise on property management, *De oeconomia* (*P.Herc.* 1424).[27]

In the extant portion of the text, Philodemos first quotes and critiques Xenophon and Theophrastos (*De oec.* colls. A–11), and then sets out his own views on 'what attitude one must take up ... with regard to the acquisition and the preservation of wealth, concerning which property management and the property-management expert are in fact conceived specifically ... [and] discussing the acquisition (of property) that is appropriate for the philosopher, [not] for just anyone' (col. 12).[28] Philodemos particularly censures his predecessors for their assumption that the acquisition of wealth is a virtue in and of itself, noting (col. 17) that 'there is an empirical practice and ability specially related ... to money-making, of which a good man will not have a share, nor will he watch the opportunities in combination with which even this kind of ability could be useful. For all these things characterize the person who loves money'. Voula Tsouna has suggested that 'it is plausible to think that the love of money is the vice standing opposite to the virtue exhibited by the good property manager ... [which] is, precisely, the disposition to administer one's property well, namely, to administer it according to the principles of the Epicurean philosophical life'.[29]

How, then, might one administer property according to Epicurean principle?[30] Philodemos concedes that the Cynics and the Epicureans agreed that the happy life was free from toil and care, but disagreed about how to attain such a life, especially in regard to the acquisition and management of property. The Cynics rejected property out of hand and advocated a life of mendicancy, because they viewed wealth as troublesome and therefore a source of cares. In his rejection of the

Cynics' position, Philodemos advances the Epicurean argument that 'a peaceful and happy life is obtained not by avoiding all toils and efforts but by opting for things that may involve a certain amount of trouble at present but relieve us of much greater concerns in the future',[31] such as health, wealth and friendship (col. 13). Thus, he accepts the Epicurean premise that, while the acquisition and management of wealth entail continuous mental attention and often physical labour (i.e. care and toil), rational calculation according to the Epicurean hedonistic calculus nonetheless suggests that the possession and administration of wealth enable one to live more pleasantly than does its absence (coll. 13–15).

Philodemos' calculus can shed light on the philosophical modality of *labor* in the *Georgics*. Virgil introduces unrelenting toil as a central feature of the famer's life (1.145–6, quoted above Ch. 3.1) and his characterization of *labor* as troublesome is fully consistent with the Epicurean principle that work is unpleasant and therefore to be avoided.[32] Nonetheless, Virgil shows that due attention to agricultural labour can result in the farmer's enjoyment of the felicity that Philodemos accepts as the goal of property management (*G.* 2.513–31):

> The farmer has parted the earth with his curved plough; here is his year's work (*labor*), hence he sustains his country and small grandsons, hence his herds of cattle and deserving bullocks. Nor is there respite (*requies*), but the year abounds with fruits, or the offspring of the herds, or with the sheaves of Ceres' corn, loads the furrows with produce and overwhelms the storehouses. Winter has come; Sicyon's olive is crushed in the press, the swine return fattened on acorns, the forests give arbutus; autumn serves up varied produce, and high on the sunny rocks the mellow grape clusters mature. Meanwhile his sweet children hang on his kisses; his pure home preserves its modesty; the cows droop milky udders, and on the fertile grass, butting horns, the fat kids struggle with one another. The farmer himself celebrates the holidays stretched out on the grass, with a fire in the middle and his friends wreathe the bowl; and offering you a libation he calls on you, Bacchus, and for the flock's herders he sets contests of the flying javelin on an elm, or they bare their hardy bodies for country wrestling.

Despite the toil and lack of respite that the estate owner endures – cares which are, on the face of it, antithetical to Epicurean pleasure – the landowner enjoys an idyllic life in his possession of the bounty of the seasons that support a flourishing household and festal board for the friends deemed so important in Epicurean philosophy (*KD* 27; *VS* 23, 52; cf. Phil. *De oec.* coll. 15, 18).

Philodemos credits Epicurus' friend Metrodoros, another of the founding fathers of the Garden, with establishing (through 'continuous effort') 'that the occasional disturbances, cares and labours are far more useful in the long run for the best way of life than the opposite choice' (col. 22). Virgil illustrates this principle in his idyllic picture of the desirable outcome that accrues to the landowner from his undesirable labours. This passage celebrating the farmer's life resumes a slightly earlier description (2.458–74, partially quoted Ch. 3.1) of the 'easy living' (2.460) the earth supplies to farmers, their carefree tranquillity (2.467), leisure on broad holdings (2.468), and peaceful sleep (2.470), all characteristic of the ideal Epicurean life. These unqualified goods are there set into strong contrast with the urban cares provoked by political ambition and avaricious luxury (2.461–6), so deleterious to mortal happiness in the Epicurean worldview. Even in these idyllic portraits of the farmer's life, however, Virgil recognizes the labour that subtends the landowner's felicity, with a glancing reference to the youths' experience of work (2.472) and the farmer's year-round toil (2.514).

Some scholars have proposed that Virgil espouses a Stoic line in *G.*,[33] in part because of the poem's emphasis on *labor*. But Virgil's shifting presentation of work in the poem finds a suggestive parallel in Philodemos' sustained recalibration of the costs and benefits of toil and trouble in the administration of property. The felicity the farmer enjoys in the idyllic portraits of the agricultural life in *G.* 2 is also consistent with Philodemos' assessment of the landowner as enjoying 'a pleasant life, a leisurely retreat with one's friends, and a most dignified income' (*De oec.* coll. 23.12–18). It is therefore instructive to consider Virgil's 'praise of the farmer' in the context of the double makarismos of the lives of the philosopher and farmer (2.458–540), which has garnered special attention in the debate about Virgil's presentation of the ethics of farming life,[34] because the poet appears to identify the best life as that of the natural philosopher (2.490–4):

> Blessed (*felix*) is he who could understand the causes of things and trampled beneath his feet all fears and relentless fate and the howl of greedy Acheron. Fortunate (*fortunatus*) too is that man who knows the country gods – Pan and old man Silvanus, and the sister nymphs.

Many commentators have seen in the first beatitude a reference specifically to Lucretius, since Virgil's language is heavily indebted to the Epicurean poet.[35] The philosopher who could account for the origins of the universe sounds very much like the great Latin exponent of Epicurean doctrine of the previous generation, who set out Epicurus' salvific message in Latin verses from which Virgil repeatedly draws in this passage (e.g. *DRN* 3.1071–5, 5.1185). For Lucretius' aim was precisely to trample beneath his feet the fear of death engendered by religious superstition and thus, following Epicurus, to liberate us to enjoy the life of pleasure exemplified by the Epicurean gods (*DRN* 1.78–9, 3.35–40).

The apparent elevation of the Lucretian sage over the Virgilian farmer has occasioned considerable difficulty among scholars who have tried to integrate the passage within the ambit of an Epicurean worldview, not only because they have been reluctant to accept at face value the georgic poet's deference to the poet of natural philosophy, but also because Virgil's commendation of the farmer's knowledge of rustic gods contradicts Lucretius' denunciation of primitive man's credence in the gods and his derision of rustic superstition. Lucretius explains belief in the gods as arising from fear of natural phenomena and illustrates rustic superstition by explicitly citing farmers' belief in Pan and the nymphs (*DRN* 4.586–9, Ch. 2.3).[36] Yet although Virgil's allusion to Lucretius' passage undoubtedly confirms that his farmer is no Epicurean philosopher-poet, it does not necessarily mean that he does not live according to Epicurean principle. For while Lucretius' implacable hostility to religion is engendered by the entirely praiseworthy goal (in the Epicurean worldview) of freeing mankind from the miseries caused by erroneous belief in the gods (*DRN* 1.62–135, 5.1194–240), Epicurus himself was celebrated for his piety (D.L. 10.10) and both he and Philodemos authored treatises on the subject.[37]

Furthermore, the question of what makes for a happy life was a central focus of ancient philosophical disputation from at least the time of Solon (*c.* 638–*c.* 558 BCE), who is reported by Herodotus to have discussed with the Lydian king Croesus how to rank different ways of life according to a theoretical calculus of happiness (Hdt. 1.30.2–33). By explicitly setting his comparison of the lives of the sage and farmer in a ranked order, Virgil enters a long-standing debate about the good life. His verdict invites interpretation as an adaptation of the Epicurean ethical principles articulated by Philodemos in his *De oeconomia*, where he is concerned to assess traditional sources of income (22.6–23.36) according to the hedonistic calculus in order to determine which might be appropriate to the Epicurean. He argues against the conventional view (especially relevant in the contemporary context of Roman Mediterranean hegemony) that the best way of life is military, regarding it instead as the choice of unwise and vainglorious men (col. 22.17–28). By contrast, he is highly laudatory of the landowner's way of life, as long as the master of the estate does not work the land with his own hands (col. 23.7–18, partially quoted above).

Philip Thibodeau has argued that *G.* addresses Italian landowners in just such affluent circumstances,[38] as is implied both in the work's dedication to the rich equestrian Maecenas and in the idyllic picture of the landowner's enjoyment of 'leisure on his broad estates' (*latis otia fundis*, 2.468): *latifundium* was a technical term, current already in this period (cf. Varro, *Rust.* 1.16.4), for the vast estates farmed in Italy by rich absentee landlords. Abundant evidence confirms Virgil's own wealth (Ch. 1),[39] while his close friend and fellow Epicurean Varius also belonged to the senatorial census class.[40] Both biographical and archaeological evidence suggests that the Sabine farm beloved by Virgil's friend and fellow-poet Horace (itself the gift of Maecenas) was also no modest holding but a large and productive estate.[41] Lowell

Bowditch's assessment of the relationship between the latter's wealth and philosophical commitments is applicable, *mutatis mutandis*, to all the members of Virgil's circle of friends and the elite readership to whom he addresses *G.*: 'insofar as Horace's estate ... returns him to himself, such spiritual [or philosophical] commerce depends on very real economic returns'.[42]

At the pinnacle of the hierarchy of lifestyles, Philodemos, like Virgil, ranks the philosopher (23.22–36):

> the first and noblest thing is to receive back thankful gifts with all reverence in return for philosophical discourses shared with men capable of understanding them, as happened to Epicurus, and, [moreover], discourses that are truthful and free of strife and, [in short], serene, since in fact the acquisition of an income through [sophistical] and contentious speeches is [in no way] better than its acquisition through demagogical and slandering ones.

To rank the philosopher at the apex of the hierarchy of ways of life enjoyed a long tradition in classical literature, though Philodemos' exaltation of teaching philosophy as the first and best source of moneymaking is an innovation within this tradition, and must be read in close conjunction with his praise of the landowner, who makes the philosophy teacher's life possible.[43] Virgil can thus be seen to agree with Philodemos' ranking of the relative dignity of the two ways of life in his praise of the sage and farmer, assessing the natural philosopher's life as the happiest, but one which is closely followed by that of the gentleman farmer.

This ranking is entirely consistent with that on display throughout *G.* 2, including the movement from celebrating the fortunate lot of the farmer (2.458–74, partially quoted above) to acknowledging a preference for the lot of the poet of natural philosophy (2.475–86):

> But as for me, first may the Muses, sweet before all things, whose sacred emblems I bear, struck with huge love, receive me, and show me heaven's paths and the stars, the sun's various eclipses, the moon's labours; whence comes a trembling in the earth, by what force the deep

seas swell and, their barriers burst, subside again back upon themselves, why winter suns hasten so to dip themselves in Ocean, or what delay obstructs slow nights. But if the blood round my heart runs cold and prevents me from being able to reach the realms of nature, let me take pleasure in the countryside and the running streams in the valleys; let me love the rivers and the woods, though I live without renown.

The passage encapsulates, in Lucretian language, the themes of natural philosophy set out according to Epicurean principle in the last two books of *De rerum natura* – astronomy, seismology, storms at sea or the tides, and variations in the lengths of day and night.[44] The georgic poet's concern that he may fail in his aspiration to compose a work on natural philosophy is also couched in the language of Epicurean commitment in his self-exhortation to 'take pleasure' (2.485) in the countryside, with its streams and rivers, valleys and woods – the landscape repeatedly eulogized by Lucretius (*DRN* 2.24–36, 5.1391–5) – even though he recognizes that, as a result, he may live 'without renown' (*inglorius*, *G.* 2.486). The adjective evokes Epicurus' injunction to his followers to 'live unknown' and his recommendation to withdraw from society into retirement (*KD* 14 *apud* D.L. 10.143). In the sphragis to *G.* (Ch. 2.2), Virgil represents himself as living in just such 'inglorious leisure' (*ignobilis oti*, 4.564), during his composition of the poem. Like *inglorius* (2.486), its synonym *ignobilis* (4.564) implies the Epicurean principle of living 'unknown' and confirms the biographical tradition that in adulthood Virgil lived 'in retirement' (*secessu*, *VSD* 13).[45]

The poet-*praeceptor*'s praise of the farmer in the double makarismos (2.493–4) rehearses very precisely his praise of the farmer's happy lot at the outset of the passage (2.458–9, quoted above Ch. 3.1). Both beatitudes closely recall Meliboeus' awed recognition of Tityrus' happiness in *B.* 1 (*fortunate senex*, 46, Ch. 2.2). In all three instances, the happiness attributed to the owner of a country holding is characterized as enjoying good fortune (cf. the fortunate farmers of *G.* 2.458–9) rather than the special felicity attributed to the Epicurean sage not only at *G.* 2.490 but also in *B.* 5, where Menalcas entreats the divinized Daphnis, who has ascended to the celestial realms of the Epicurean gods

(Ch. 2.3), to 'be good and felicitous' (*felix, B.* 5.65) to his worshippers. The distinction Virgil repeatedly draws between mortal good fortune and quasi-divine felicity seems to belong to an accepted Epicurean hierarchy of happiness that situates the philosopher at the apex of the scale, but does not impugn the good fortune enjoyed by the farmer, whose happiness Virgil, like Philodemos, ranks second only to that of the sage.[46]

Within this hierarchy of felicity, Virgil illustrates the farmer's good fortune by drawing on the contemporary articulation of Epicurean ethics in Lucretius' *De rerum natura* and Varius' *De morte*, as well as on the master's statements of principle. The fortunate farmer's knowledge of the agricultural gods (*G.* 2.493–4) is balanced by his ignorance of Roman politics, civil war and the avarice and ambition that fuel both (2.495–512):

> Neither elected office nor the purple of kings bends him, and the civil discord leading brothers to betray their faith or the Dacian moving down from the Danube sworn to war, nor Roman politics nor kingdoms doomed to fall; though pitying the poor man he is untroubled, nor does he envy the wealthy man. He harvests the fruits which his boughs and willing fields bear spontaneously, nor has he seen the iron bonds of law, the mad forum, or the office of public records. Others rouse the unknown straits with oars, rush onto the sword in battle, press into the courts and thresholds of kings; this one seeks to visit city and wretched homes with destruction, in order to drink from a jewelled cup and sleep on Tyrian purple; another hoards his wealth and sleeps above his buried gold; this man stands in admiration of the speakers' platform, while the applause of the people and senators, repeated along the benches, has corrupted another; they rejoice, stained with the blood of their brothers, exchange their homes and sweet thresholds for exile, and seek a country lying beneath an alien sun.

The elected office (2.495), unknown to Virgil's farmer, recalls Lucretius' picture of the hell that electoral ambition makes for the would-be politician (*DRN* 3.996–7): 'Sisyphus in life too is before our eyes as the man who seeks elected office, and imbibes a desire for the savage axes, and, always defeated, returns home unhappily'. As Epicurus pithily exhorts his adherents (*VS* 67): 'A free life cannot acquire great wealth, because the task is not easy without slavery to the mob or those in power'. For that reason, Epicurus explains (*VS* 53): 'One should envy no one. For the good are not worthy of envy, and the more good fortune the wicked have, the more they spoil it for themselves'. Just so, Virgil shows the politician and miser suffering because of their misguided ethics. In his depiction of the avarice that animates the ambitious politician, Virgil rehearses Varius' memorable portrait in his 'On Death' (a quintessentially Epicurean topic)[47] of a politician selling the state's land and laws to the highest bidder (frr. 147–8 Hollis): 'This man has sold Latium to the people, and stolen the citizens' farms; he fixed and refixed laws for a price, in order to recline on Tyrian purple and drink from solid gold'. Virgil's praise of the farmer thus shows extensive lexical, ethical and thematic contact with Epicurean philosophy in its engagement with the works of Epicurus and his Italian followers Philodemos, Lucretius and Varius.

Elsewhere too, the poet-*praeceptor* engages with ethical issues current among contemporary Italian exponents of Epicureanism. It has long been recognized that his account of the plague of Noricum at the end of *G.* 3 imitates Lucretius' account of the plague at Athens (*DRN* 6.1138–280), which poses the philosophical issue, much discussed by Epicureans, of how to view death.[48] The focus on animal husbandry in *G.* 3 dictates the progression of Virgil's Noric plague from livestock to wild animals and thence, only at the end, to humankind (3.563–6), the focus of Lucretius' plague narrative. But allusion to 'Lucretius' account of the (human) plague at Athens informs and enriches the Virgilian plague throughout and underlines 'the human applications lurking beneath the surface'.[49] Like Lucretius (and Thucydides before him), Virgil begins with causes and symptoms (*G.* 3.478–85), recapitulating in miniature the movement of Lucretius' description of the plague at Athens. Especially striking, however, is Virgil's abbreviation of his model in such a way as to highlight ethical concerns over scientific issues.

This ethical dimension emerges forcefully at key points in Virgil's presentation of the plague at Noricum. He opens with the shocking scene of a sacrificial bull falling at the altar to the plague, rather than to the ministrant's knife (3.486–93). The vain death of the sacrificial bull recalls Lucretius' repeated expressions of hostility to religious superstition, beginning with his denunciation of the sacrifice of Iphigenia (*DRN* 1.82–6): 'All too often superstition has engendered impious and criminal deeds. At Aulis, for example, chosen leaders of the Danaans, the elect among men, polluted virginal Diana's altar with foul blood'. Virgil's bullock 'falls' prematurely, 'at the moment of death' from the plague (*G.* 3.488), in a verbal reminiscence of the Lucretian Iphigenia led 'trembling' (*DRN* 1.95) to the altar where she falls like a sacrificial beast at her father's blow (*DRN* 1.99), shocking testimony to man's susceptibility to superstition (*DRN* 1.101): 'such heinous evils could superstition prompt'. Virgil's description of 'the woollen fillet's snowy band passed round' the sacrificial victim's brow evokes Lucretius' chilling account of Iphigenia adorned like a heifer for sacrifice (*DRN* 1.87), 'as soon as the fillet went round her maiden locks'. By alluding to Lucretius' programmatic description of Iphigenia's death, Virgil opens his account of the plague at Noricum on a distinctly Epicurean note. With the death of the plough-ox (3.515–24), the poet-*praeceptor* links the implied futility of religious superstition with explicit reflection on the futility of *labor* (3.525–30): 'to what avail are toil and services? Or to have turned the heavy earth with the ploughshare? And yet neither Massic gifts of Bacchus nor the renewal of the feast harmed them. They pasture on leaves and simple grass; their cups are clear springs and rivers streaming in their course, nor does care break up their healthy sleep'. The plough-ox dies like a man – despite his work and services (3.525) and despite the simplicity of his untroubled life, which is quasi-Epicurean in its lack of cares. The term 'services' has a peculiarly Roman valence, being used of the 'favours' exchanged by members of the ruling class to secure political support from one another and from their clients.[50] Its application to the dead plough-ox assimilates the beast to the fortunate farmer of *G.* 2, who similarly eschews the evils of political ambition and luxury in his enjoyment of leisure and a simple life (2.461–74). Virgil contrasts the plough-ox's healthy life, reminiscent of that of the fortunate farmer, with the ambitious and avaricious conduct of men condemned by Lucretius (*DRN* 2.24–36; cf. 5.1392–6) and Varius (frr. 147–8 Hollis, quoted above). As Lucretius caustically observes of the human world, and Virgil here documents in the animal realm, 'fevers quit the body no more quickly' (*DRN* 2.34), whether one indulges in luxury or toils in the farmer's field. The cosmic and civic devastation on display in Virgil's Noric plague narrative is thus systematically underpinned by the Epicurean logic of Lucretius' *De rerum natura* and Varius' *De morte*.

Epicurean ethical sentiment and themes pervade *G*.: the divine saviour, the happy life of the landowner, the futility of religion and the inevitability of death. If Virgil for the most part eschews discussion of the material basis of the universe in the poems, it is not because he rejects Epicurean physics – far from it. Virgil implicitly accepts the Epicurean paradox that 'beneath the superficial variety of things lies a fundamental sameness' in the building blocks of atoms and void.[51] He comments on the Epicurean physical fabric of the farmer's world at the outset of the poem (1.50–61), confirming that 'Nature has imposed these laws and everlasting compacts on particular places, from the first' (1.60–1).[52] Likewise, the opening of *G*. 2 resonates with the Lucretian theme of variety within strict limits (2.9–135).[53] The opening line of this section begins with one of Lucretius' favourite didactic markers, *principio* ('to start with', 2.9), and conflates two lines from Lucretius' anthropology (*DRN* 5.1345, 5.1362) in a ringing motto (*G*. 2.9): 'To start with, Nature has diverse ways of creating [i.e. propagating] trees'. Virgil's argument in this passage is also Lucretian, in its movement from natural methods of tree propagation (2.10–21) to experience (2.22–34).[54] Nonetheless, Virgil's focus in *G*. lies primarily on the technical and, especially, the ethical concerns that inform the life of the landowner rather than on the physical fabric of soil, air, sun and water. Like his Epicurean contemporaries, Virgil engages at greatest length with the ethical dimensions of his subject, such as those that animate Philodemos' treatise *On Property Management* and the long tradition of philosophical inquiry that lies behind it.

3.3 *The Alexandrian Tradition*

Virgil's emphasis on the toil that sustains the farming life has a literary valence in addition to its philosophical underpinnings, and finds inspiration in the Alexandrian literary tradition that valued erudition and stylistic refinement (i.e. care and toil) over copious expression in poetry.[55] Callimachus especially champions the poetics of artistry and erudition, and his attitude is shared by other Hellenistic poets, such as Theocritus and Aratus, and their Roman heirs, the 'Neoteric' poets Catullus, Cinna and Gallus. Thus, for example, Catullus lauds the learning and labour of Cornelius Nepos, the dedicatee of his 'charming little book' of poetry (Catull. *c.* 1.3–7): 'for you, Cornelius, as you were accustomed to think my trifles something, already then, when you alone among Italian authors dared to unfold all of history in three scrolls, learned by god and full of toil'. Even Lucretius values toil in the context of poetic composition, characterizing it as 'sweet' (*DRN* 1.141, 2.730, 3.419) and a 'pleasure' (1.140).[56] Virgil adapts the Callimachean principle of refined artistry in the 'proem in the middle' of his bucolic collection (*B.* 6.3–5, Ch. 2.4), and Richard Thomas has shown that Callimachus remains a key model for Virgil's didactic poem.[57] His influence can be traced not only in the four-book structure of *G.*, but also in the geographical and mythological learning of some of Virgil's most self-conscious lines, such as *G.* 1.138: 'the Pleiades, Hyades, and bright Bear, Lycaon's daughter' (*Pleiadas, Hyadas, claramque Lycaonis Arcton*). The first two words transliterate a Homeric half-line (*Il.* 18.486) and the last two words a Callimachean collocation (*Hymn* 1.41) that exemplifies the Alexandrian poet's erudition in the application of a patronymic to the Greek word for the constellation of the great bear, a constellation that takes its name from the metamorphosis (into a bear) and catasterism (translation to the sky) of Lycaon's daughter Callisto.

Virgil alludes extensively to Callimachus in the proem to *G*. 3 (1–8):

You too we shall hymn, great Pales, and you, celebrated shepherd of the river Amphrysus, and you, woods and rivers of Mt Lycaon. All the rest of the themes, which might have held idle minds with poetry, are already well known: who doesn't know harsh Eurystheus or the altars of accursed Busiris? Who has not told of the boy Hylas and Latona's island Delos, of Hippodamia and [her suitor] Pelops, famous for his ivory shoulder, who was a fierce competitor in horse racing?

The passage combines recondite geographical and mythological learning with sustained allusion to specific Callimachean poetic themes. The Italian pastoral deity Pales appears in the company of Apollo, who received the epithet 'Nomius' ('the herder') 'at that time when he tended the yoke-mares beside Amphrysus, fired by love for the young Admetus' (Callim. *Hymn* 2.47–9). But the invocation of the tutelary gods of animal husbandry familiar from the eclogues (*B*. 5.35) heads a rejection of Callimachean themes: Hercules' murder of the Egyptian king Busiris, who sacrificed strangers at his altars (Callim. *Aet*. 2 fr. 44 Harder); the rape of Hercules' squire Hylas by water-nymphs (Ap. Rhod. 1.1207–357; Theoc. *Id*. 13); and Leto's long search for a place to give birth to her twins, Apollo and Artemis, until Delos offered her sanctuary (Callim. *Hymn* 4). The chariot race between Oenomaus and Pelops, who had abducted his daughter Hippodamia, also appealed to Alexandrian literary taste (cf. Ap. Rhod. 1.752–8), though it does not appear in the extant writings of Callimachus.[58] Paradoxically, Virgil dismisses Callimachus' poetic subjects on Callimachean principle: 'I abhor everything common', the Alexandrian poet says in a famous epigram (27.4 Pf.), echoed here in Virgil's rejection of quintessentially Callimachean themes on the basis of their wide circulation in the poetry of his contemporaries (*G*. 3.6).

The location of Virgil's statement of poetic programme is also indebted to the example of Callimachus, who had famously opened the third book of his four-book *Aetia* with an epinician celebrating the victory of the Egyptian queen Berenice in the horse-race at Olympia.[59]

Praise of the Egyptian royal house was a conventional feature of Alexandrian court literature that Virgil and his contemporaries draw on in their poetry to and about Octavian.[60] The georgic poet signals his debt to Callimachean panegyric in the opening prayer to Octavian, where he suggests that he might wish to rule heaven in the divinized form of a constellation (*G.* 1.32–5): 'or whether you add yourself to the lingering months as a new star, where a place lies open between the Virgin Erigone and the pursuing Claws (already for you the Scorpion himself draws in his arms and has left more than a due share of heaven)'. The formulation 'a new star' is a reminiscence of the same phrase, coined by Catullus (*c.* 66.64) in his translation of Callimachus' epinician poem 'Lock of Berenice' (*Coma Berenices*), which closed the *Aetia* (fr. 110) and commemorated the catasterism of a lock of the queen's hair in an account of the discovery and naming of the new constellation by the Ptolemaic court astronomer Conon.

This disavowal of Callimachean poetic themes at the opening of *G.* 3 heralds Virgil's new embrace of grand epic themes (8–9): 'I must try a path by which I might raise myself from the ground and fly victorious over men's lips'. The humble stance of the erstwhile bucolic singer is here rejected out of hand in the georgic poet's espousal of an unCallimachean ambition to leave behind the earthly realm and essay the more exalted 'path' of lofty epic verse. Virgil underlines his new literary ambition with a reminiscence of the Roman poet Ennius, father of Latin hexameter verse, whose epitaph (spoken in the first person) announced (Enn. *Epigr.* 18 V): 'I fly living over the lips of men'.

Virgil reinscribes his grand epic ambition within the ambit of Hesiodic cosmogony (3.10–12): 'I shall be the first, provided life remains to me, to lead the Muses back to the fatherland from the Aonian height; I shall be the first, Mantua, to bring you back Judaean palms'. The claim to primacy recalls and corrects Lucretius' homage to Ennius, 'the first to bring down from Helicon the crown of perennial foliage' (*DRN* 1.118), for Virgil's adaptation of Hesiod's *Works and Days* more justly entitles him to the title of Roman heir to the Boeotian poet. But while the 'Aonian height' recalls Hesiod's claim, at the opening of the *Theogony*, to have been initiated by the Muses at the foot of Mt Helicon (*Theog.* 1–25), Virgil owes his choice of geographical epithet to Callimachus (fr. 572 Pf.; *Hymn* 4.75), who presented his own initiation into the Hesiodic tradition in a dream set at the 'Aonian' spring of Aganippe (*Aet.* 1 fr. 2b.4 Harder).[61] Virgil thus corrects Lucretius' praise of Ennius as a second Hesiod, while subtly suggesting the Callimachean inspiration of his own Hesiodic poem.

Virgil specifically transplants his Hesiodic-Callimachean poem from Helicon to his own patrimony in Mantua (*G.* 3.13–16): 'and I shall build a temple of marble in a green field beside the water, where my native Mincius wanders in slow bends and weaves its banks with tender reeds. I will have Caesar in the middle and he will hold my temple'. Virgil adopts the pose of a triumphal Roman general, returning from military conquest abroad with spoils rich enough to endow a temple.[62] His temple is clearly a metaphor for a new poetic project, and commentators since antiquity have identified the project with *A.*, because the temple will house statues of the Trojan ancestors (3.34–6) of Octavian and Aeneas, whose genealogy Homer puts into his character's own mouth in the *Iliad* (20.215–40). Virgil's dedication of this temple of song to Octavian, and its decoration with his Trojan ancestors, underwrite the interpretation of *A.* by his biographers as an epic in praise of Augustus (Ch. 1, 5).

The poet anticipates that his ambitious new project will triumph over Envy (3.37–9), another motif associated with Callimachus' poetry (*Epigr.* 21.4, *Hymn* 2.105–12), though he defers the grand undertaking in order to complete the georgic poem promised to his patron (*G.* 3.40–1): 'Meanwhile let me pursue the wood-nymphs' forests and the untouched glades – your mandate, Maecenas, and by no means easy'. Virgil here draws on yet another Callimachean poetic image, in the 'untouched' glades of the *Georgics*, which recall the 'untrodden' poetic paths that Callimachus advocates in the *Aetia* prologue (fr. 1.27–8 Harder). But Virgil closes the proem with the promise of the grander poetry of Homeric epic to come (*G.* 3.46–8): 'Soon nevertheless I shall gird myself to tell of Caesar's blazing battles and bear his name with fame through so many years, as many as separate Caesar from the original birth of [Priam's brother] Tithonus'.

The proem to *G.* 3 announces a new lofty epic ambition, even as the passage retains Virgil's characteristic didactic admixture of Hesiodic subject, Lucretian lexicon and Callimachean poetics.[63] Virgil thereby introduces Homeric themes into *G.*, though an early instance appears already in his account of irrigation in *G.* 1 (104–10):[64]

> Why should I mention how, after sowing the crop, [the farmer] presses on at close quarters in the fields, lays low heaps of bad soil, then admits enough of the following streams of the river, and when the burnt acreage blazes with dying grasses – look! – he draws out water from the brow of a sloping path? The trickle, falling through the smooth rocks, incites a harsh rumble, and tempers the dry fields with jets of water.

The passage adapts a Homeric simile describing Achilles' difficulty in coming to grips with the Trojan river Scamander, with whom he fights in close combat (*Il.* 21.257–62), like a farmer struggling to irrigate his garden. Homer's simile invites us to recall the quotidian activities of the farmstead, momentarily leaving behind the fabled world of epic, in which an extraordinary hero can do battle with a feature of the natural landscape. Virgil accepts the invitation in his adaptation of Homer's georgic simile, but he retains traces of the larger martial epic context in which it occurs, both in the military language that he uses of the farmer's operations ('presses on', 'at close quarters', 'lays low'), and in his farmer's engagement, like Achilles', with the elemental power of water.[65]

By far the most extended treatment of Homeric poetry appears in *G.* 4, where Virgil treats apiculture.[66] He introduces the book's theme with a Callimachean emphasis on the slightness of his subject, the tiny bees, in contrast to the great labour of his literary task (4.1–7):

> Forthwith I shall trace the heavenly gifts of aerial honey: attend to this part too, Maecenas. I shall recount spectacles to be wondered at of slight affairs, great-hearted commanders, the customs of the whole nation in order, their pursuits, people, and wars. There is work (*labor*) in the small subject; but the glory is not small, if propitious gods permit one and Apollo, invoked, hears.

The address to Maecenas (2), the imperative form of the verb 'attend' (2), and the implied obligation encoded in the phrase 'to be wondered at' (3) are all reminiscent of Lucretian didactic style.[67] Yet the didactic tone is juxtaposed, in some tension, to the georgic poet's simultaneous acknowledgement of the small compass of his subject and insistence on the great labour required to treat it, as well as to the martial themes that he will address and the glory that will accrue to him if success attends his work. The project is quintessentially Callimachean in its scope, a learned account in refined style of the tiny bees; but at the same time Virgil evinces an uncharacteristically grand Homeric ambition to celebrate 'great-hearted commanders and their wars'.

Like the georgic poet and the farmer he addresses, Virgil's bees are hard workers (4.156–7): 'mindful of the coming winter they toil at their work in the summer and put up what they have secured in storage'. They sedulously divide up the tasks until 'the work is aglow and the fragrant honey is scented with thyme' (4.169);[68] 'for all there is one respite from their work, and for all one task' (4.184). Virgil likens their work to that of the Cyclopes forging Jupiter's thunderbolts at their smithy beneath Mt Aetna (4.170–5). The contrast between the tiny insects – whom we might see as miniature farmers – and the giant Cyclopes of myth occasions the poet's self-conscious reflection on the (im)propriety of his martial mythological simile: 'if it is permitted to compare small things to great' (4.176). The disparity is especially evident in the literary history – and future – of Virgil's image, for he has drawn the simile from Callimachus' small-scale hexameter *Hymn to Artemis* (3.46–61), but will reuse it unchanged in the narrative of *A.* 8 (449–53) to describe the Cyclopes' manufacture of Aeneas' arms.

A similar concern with scale animates Virgil's treatment of bees swarming, which he describes with full-blown martial imagery (*G.* 4.67–85):[69]

> But if they should go out to battle – for often discord, with a great commotion, has come on between two kings, and immediately you can tell from a distance the courage of the rabble, their hearts beating for war; for the martial peal of harsh bronze reaches them as they delay,

and a summons echoing the intermittent ringing of war trumpets is heard. Then, trembling, they assemble amongst themselves and flash with their wings, they sharpen tiny darts [i.e. their stings] with their beaks and equip their shoulders, and stand around their king, dense-packed at headquarters, and summon the enemy with great cries. And so, when they have obtained a clear spring day and the fields lie open, they burst from the gates and engage; in the high air the sound rings, mixed together they gather themselves into a great orb and fall headlong; no more densely does hail fall from the air nor so many an acorn rain from a shaken holm-oak. They themselves, through the midst of the ranks on their marked wings, display huge courage in small breasts, and struggle on, refusing to yield, until the pressure of the victor has forced one side or the other to turn its back and flee.

The passage anticipates to a startling degree the martial themes of *A.*, where rival commanders muster armies on Italian soil in quasi-civil war (Ch. 4.2). Here in *G.*, however, the stakes are trivial, and a mere handful of dust is enough to put an end to the contest (4.86–7): 'these courageous battles, such great contests, grow quiet when checked by a small toss of dust'. The advice is 'half humorous, as showing the vanity of these tiny ambitions',[70] and half in philosophical earnest, for excessive ambition can destroy a community.

Virgil closes his treatment of apiculture on an ominous note, the failure of the hive – which recalls the Noric plague at the end of the previous book – and its miraculous regeneration through the Egyptian rite of *bugonia*, 'generation from cattle' (4.281–310). Invoking the Muses for the first time in the poem, he asks them to disclose the origin of the rite (4.315–16): 'What god was it, Muses, who brought forth this technique for us? Whence did the strange new knowledge of men take its beginnings?' The introduction of the rite suggests Callimachean, or at least Alexandrian, authority for the material, since Virgil explicitly cites Egypt as the source of the ritual (4.287–92) and emphasizes the technical skill and practical knowledge required. He introduces his subject, by inquiring into the origins of the rite (4.316; cf. 4.285–6, 'I shall expound the whole tale from its first origin, tracing back more deeply'), and addresses the Muses directly, just as Callimachus had done in the first two books of his *Aetia* ('Causes' or 'Origins'), which take the form of a dialogue with the Muses, to whom the poet poses a series of questions.[71] The tale is marked as 'Cyrenaean', like Callimachus himself, who was born in Cyrene. For the mythical cowherd who, 'as the story goes',[72] has lost his bees to plague and famine (4.318) is none other than Aristaeus (*G.* 1.14), the son of the nymph 'Cyrene' (4.321). Both Apollonius (2.500–27) and Callimachus (*Aet.* 3 fr. 75.32–5 Harder) were familiar with the myth of the nymph's rape by Apollo (who thereby fathered Aristaeus) and relocation to Libya, where her eponymous city was later founded (Pind. *Pyth.* 9.39–65).

Despite these hallmarks of Callimachean influence, however, scholars have more frequently seen a Homeric cast to the epyllion and, indeed, the climax of *G.* 4 gives evidence of a new stylistic elevation reminiscent of Homeric epic.[73] The invocation of the Muses 'initiate[s] a Homeric tone, recalling in part the first line of the *Odyssey*, in part the style of *Od.* 9.14, [where] Odysseus begins his own song'.[74] The epyllion opens with Aristaeus' lament at the death of his bees (4.319–20): 'he stood sadly at the sacred source of the remotest stream, lamenting many things, and addressed his mother with these words: "mother, Cyrene mother . . .".' Virgil finds literary inspiration in Achilles' two laments to his sea-nymph mother Thetis in the *Iliad* (1.348–56, 18.79–93), though his Aristaeus also resembles the figure of Gallus in Silenus' song, standing beside the river Permessus (*B.* 6.64) at the moment of his initiation into the Hesiodic tradition of poetry (*B.* 6.69–71, Ch. 2.4).

Aristaeus derives his opening gambit, however, directly from Homer (4.323): 'if only my father is Thymbraean Apollo, as you claim'. Virgil imports an obscure epithet of Apollo from the *Iliad*, which mentions the god's shrine at Thymbra in the Troad (*Il.* 10.430), into his adaptation from the *Odyssey* of the Cyclops Polyphemus' outraged demand that his father Poseidon avenge his blinding by Odysseus (*Od.* 9.528–9): 'hear me, Poseidon . . . If I am truly your son, and you acknowledge yourself my father'. Aristaeus reproaches Cyrene for encouraging him to hope for immortal glory from his consummate skill in farming (4.325–8). Unlike the exemplary farmer of the *Georgics* (and his poet), whom he otherwise resembles in his mastery of agriculture, Aristaeus has devoted himself to *labor* in the expectation of winning glory, like a georgic imitator of Homer's heroes, who stand in the forefront of battle in order to win everlasting fame.[75]

Cyrene too strikes a very Homeric figure, ensconced in her snug apartment deep beneath the waves and surrounded by her sister nymphs spinning and singing (4.333–51). Her posture and situation recall those of Achilles' mother Thetis in *Iliad* 18 (34–147), as her twelve sisters imitate Thetis' Nereid sisters, gathering at her lament (*Il.* 18.38–49). With the significant exception of the singer Clymene (4.345), who appears in both archaic Greek poets (Hom. *Il.* 18.47; Hes. *Theog.* 351, 508), their names coincide with those neither of Homer's catalogue of Nereids nor of Hesiod's twin catalogues of Nereids (*Theog.* 240–64) and Oceanids (*Theog.* 349–61). Rather, their names evoke the pastoral and georgic landscapes of Virgil's poetry (Drymo, 'oak' or 'thicket'; Phyllodoce, a 'leaf-receiver', by contrast to Homer's 'wave-receiver' Cymodoce; both named in 4.336) and his interest in Callimachean poetry (Cydippe from Callimachus' 'Acontius and Cydippe', *Aet.* 3. frr. 67–75; Lycorias a feminized form of Apollo's epithet 'Lycoreus', Callim. *Hymn* 2.19; both named in 4.339). The sisters' spinning recalls the trope that figured poetic composition in wool-working, frequent in classical antiquity,[76] and so Virgil hints in Clymene's self-conscious choice to sing the tale of Vulcan's futile love for his faithless wife Venus and her affair with Mars, a Homeric theme sung by the bard Demodocus in *Odyssey* 8 (266–366). The georgic poet also characterizes Clymene's song as Hesiodic, inasmuch as she recounts the many 'amours of the gods' from the time of Chaos (4.347) in a neat recapitulation of the plot of Hesiod's *Theogony*, which begins with Chaos and ends with the love affairs of the Olympian gods.[77]

The nymph Arethusa takes the lead in drawing Aristaeus' lament to his mother's attention (4.351–6). Arethusa's prominence recalls the eclogue over which she presides like a Muse in the previous collection

(*B.* 10.1) and her lament rehearses Apollo's words there, reminding Gallus that his girlfriend Lycoris has left him to follow a soldier on campaign (Ch. 2.4). The reminiscences of *B.* 10 in these lines have led scholars to speculate that the passage reworks some of the lost poetry of Virgil's friend and fellow-poet Gallus, the dedicatee of the eclogue; and a further reminiscence of Gallus' poetry occurs slightly later, in a brief catalogue of rivers (*G.* 4.360–4). As Aristaeus makes his way to his mother's watery realm he sees, with astonishment, the sources of many different rivers (4.365–7), including 'the resounding Hypanis' (4.370).[78] Before the discovery of the 'Gallus papyrus' in 1978, only one line of Gallus' poetry survived from antiquity, a mannered description of this very river (fr. 144 Hollis), which 'divides two lands with one stream'.[79]

The intensity of allusions to Gallus in this passage is worth considering in connection with Servius' report that Virgil sang 'the praises of Gallus' in the second half of *G.* 4. In his note on *B.* 10.1, Servius reports that 'Gallus was such a good friend of Virgil's that the fourth book of the *Georgics*, from the middle all the way to the end, contained his praise, which he afterwards changed to the myth of Aristaeus on the order of Augustus'. He reiterates this information in his note at the beginning of *G.* 4, where he specifies the occasion of the change as Augustus' renunciation of friendship with Gallus and the poet's subsequent suicide, in 27 or 26 BCE, two or three years after Virgil had finished the poem.[80] Scholarly consensus rejects Servius' report, as it is inconceivable that Virgil could have suppressed any part of a poem already in circulation, given the practicalities of literary 'publication' in antiquity.[81] Many critics think that Servius either confuses the end of Virgil's poem on farming with the end of his bucolic collection, where *B.* 10 does indeed contain explicit praise of Gallus, or presents in garbled version an earlier commentary tradition that recognized Virgil's intense interaction with the style and substance of Gallus' poetry in the Aristaeus episode.[82] The passage is cast as a Callimachean *aetion*, a genre that Gallus is believed, on the evidence of *B.* 6 (Ch. 2.3), to have transplanted to Latin poetry. It takes the form of an epyllion, with Proteus' account of the myth of Orpheus embedded within the poet's tale of Aristaeus' loss of his bees, in a formal structure that was apparently characteristic of Gallan elegy and neoteric poetry (Catull. *c.* 64; Ch. 2.4).[83] The amatory exemplum of Orpheus' obsessive love for Eurydice is also the type of mythological tale that appeared in Gallus' *Amores*, if the myths compiled by his friend Parthenios in his handbook on 'erotic passions' (Ch. 2.4) are anything to go by.

Virgil interweaves reminiscences of Gallus and allusions to Homer throughout the Aristaeus episode. This procedure can be seen even in the catalogue of rivers, where he juxtaposes Gallus' Hypanis with the Italian river Eridanus (the Po), which he describes as 'gilded on both horns of his bull's brow' (*G.* 4.371), in an association as old as Homer (cf. *Il.* 21.237, of the Scamander 'bellowing like a bull'), and as 'flowing through the rich fields to the sea in a purple stream' (*G.* 4.372–3), in an adaptation of a Homeric simile likening Trojan chariots on the battlefield to rivers in spate (*Il.* 16.391). Virgil signals his debt to Homer particularly strongly in Cyrene's offer of 'cups of Maeonian wine' to her son (4.380): the adjective often designates Homer, who was called 'the Maeonian' from his supposed Lydian origin.[84] Her reception of her son (4.376–85) is programmatically Homeric in its reminiscence not only of Thetis' reception of Achilles but also, especially, of Menelaus' hospitality to Telemachus in *Odyssey* 4, where Odysseus' son and his retinue are similarly bathed, anointed with oil, and served food and wine (*Od.* 4.47–58). Her advice to Aristaeus to consult Proteus (*G.* 4.386–414) is also self-consciously Homeric, adapting Menelaus' tale of how, following the advice of the nymph Eidothea, he succeeded in getting the seer to disclose the fates of the Greek chieftains after Troy, including his own future (*Od.* 4.351–570). Like Eidothea's advice to Menelaus, Cyrene's to Aristaeus warns of the stench of the seer's seals, his trick of transforming himself into fire, water and wild beasts, and the concomitant necessity of subduing him in order to gain access to his knowledge. Virgil also owes to Homer his characterization of Proteus as a shepherd, 'who pastures Neptune's huge flocks of evil-smelling seals beneath a marine eddy' (*G.* 4.394–5). But where Homer briefly compares the seer to 'a herdsman among his flocks of sheep' (*Od.* 4.413), Virgil extends the pastoral theme on the authority of Callimachus, who calls Proteus a 'shepherd of seals' (*Suppl. Hell.* fr. 254.6). In accordance with his agricultural subject, Virgil describes Proteus tending his sleeping seals, which 'hav[e] cast themselves up and down the shore; while he himself sat down on a rock in their midst and counted their numbers, just like the guardian of a manger on the mountain, when the evening star leads calves home from pasture to their stalls, and the lambs sharpen wolves' hunger with the sound of their bleating' (4.432–6).

The Homeric scene-setting yields to bucolic and elegy once Aristaeus has subdued Proteus and learns from him that he has lost his bees because he has incurred the vengeful anger of Orpheus and the nymphs for causing Eurydice's death (4.453–9). Proteus' 'Orpheus and Eurydice' (4.453–527) bears a strong likeness to the herdsmen's strains in *B.* and doubtless also to Gallus' own amatory elegy, which Virgil celebrates in *B.* 6 and 10. Particularly striking is the formal line of literary inheritance Virgil establishes in *B.* 6 from Linus and Hesiod through Orpheus to Gallus (6.69–71, Ch. 2.4). Although not mentioned by name, Orpheus lurks beneath the description of Hesiod there bewitching the ash-trees, for 'the power that magicians claimed to charm mountain-ashes from the hillsides was traditionally attributed to Orpheus' music'.[85] In Proteus' tale, too, we find numerous points of contact with the style of poetry Virgil associates with Gallus in *B.* 6 and 10.

Proteus opens his song by detailing the cause of the nymphs' anger at Aristaeus, Eurydice's flight from his lustful pursuit and the snakebite from which she died (*G.* 4.457–63):

> She indeed, the doomed girl, while she fled you headlong through the rills, failed to see beneath her feet the huge water-snake hugging the banks in the tall grass. But a chorus of Dryads, companions of her own age, filled the mountaintops with their cries; Rhodope's citadels wept, along with high Pangaea, the martial land of Rhesus, the Getae, the Hebrus river, and Attic Orithyia.

The pathetic evocation of Eurydice as 'the doomed girl' (4.458) recalls the Virgilian Silenus' emotional invocation of Pasiphaë as an 'unhappy

maiden' in *B.* 6 (46–60, Ch. 2.3), while the snake lurking beside the
riverbank (*G.* 4.458–9) reappears from *B.* 3 (93). The description of
nature mourning Eurydice's death (*G.* 4.460–3) is highly reminiscent of
B. 10, where the Naiads take the lead in mourning the dying Gallus and
the natural world joins in (9–15, Ch. 2.4). Thracian Mt Rhodope too
recurs from *B.* 6, where the mountain is also associated with Orpheus
(30). The Greek musical quality of Proteus' song, especially audible in
lines 461–3, also suggests the mannered style of the Alexandrian poets
and their Roman admirers.[86]

After describing Eurydice's death, Proteus details Orpheus' distress
in equally mannered lines (*G.* 4.464–6): 'He himself, solacing his
grievous love on the hollow tortoise-shell lyre, was hymning you, sweet
wife, you, by himself on the lonely shore – you, when day rose, you
when night fell'. Here too Virgil's theme and technique evoke the elegiac
precedent of Gallus. Languishing in love for his lost wife, Orpheus
endeavours to console himself with song (4.464), just as Virgil represents
Silenus trying to console Pasiphaë in her passion for Minos' bull
(*B.* 6.46); both poets address the subject of their songs directly (*G.* 4.465,
'sweet wife'; *B.* 6.47, 'unhappy maiden'), in the style of the first generation
of Neoteric poets (Ch. 2.4). Orpheus' attitude of lament beside the
lonely seashore recalls Aristaeus in the outer panel of the epyllion and
his literary model Achilles, but also Catullus' Ariadne, abandoned by
Theseus (Catull. *c.* 64.133) – the prototype for many an elegiac lover.
The syntactical symmetry of *G.* 4.466 is especially reminiscent of
neoteric poetry, for example in the balanced construction of a famous
pair of lines from Cinna's epyllion *Zmyrna* (fr. 10 Hollis): 'You the early
Morning Star saw weeping, and you the same saw weeping a little later
as the Evening Star'.

In recounting Orpheus' descent to the underworld to reclaim his lost
bride (*G.* 4.467–84), Virgil reverts to Homeric precedent. The singer's
katabasis recalls that of Odysseus in the *Nekuia* (*Od.* 11), especially
the lines in which Homer describes the shades of the dead surging
forward to crowd around Odysseus' sacrificial offerings (34–43). Virgil
transforms Homer's necromantic scene into a meditation on the power

of Orphic song, which transfixes not only the dead but the house of death itself (*G.* 4.471–84). Virgil will reuse these lines in *A.* 6 (305–12), and Orpheus' triumph over Hades here also recalls the georgic poet's prediction of his (epic) triumph over envy in the proem to *G.* 3 (37–9), for the traditional point of Orpheus' myth was to illustrate the triumph of song over death (Eur. *Alc.* 357–62).

Yet there are indications, even before our poet overturns mythological tradition, that Orpheus' success will be short-lived. For one thing, Virgil describes the shades as 'phantoms of people bereft of the light of life' (*G.* 4.472), adapting a line from Lucretius that describes the material basis of the images we see (*DRN* 4.35–45). Lucretius emphasizes the Epicurean lesson that the dead cannot be brought back to life, and this philosophical message underlies Virgil's revision of Orpheus' tale in *G.* 4, where the bard is unsuccessful for the first time in recorded myth. Virgil overlays this principle of Epicurean physics with the Epicurean ethical precept that enjoins setting a limit to the passion of love (*G.* 4.485–91):

> And now, retracing his steps, he had avoided every mischance, and Eurydice, returned to him, was coming to the upper air, following behind (for Proserpina had imposed this law), when suddenly, madness (*dementia*) seized the unwary lover – pardonable indeed, if the shades knew how to pardon: he stopped still and alas, forgetting, he looked back at his Eurydice already in the light, overcome in his purpose.

Orpheus' failure to set a limit to his passion recalls the similarly phrased failures of Corydon and Pasiphaë in *B.* 2 and 6, where they succumb to amatory *dementia* (2.69, 6.47; Ch. 2.3, 2.4), like the Gallus of *B.* 10. Eurydice's reproach to Orpheus (4.494–5: 'What huge passion, Orpheus, has destroyed me, unhappy, and you?') rehearses the question posed to Gallus by Apollo in the final eclogue (*B.* 10.22): 'Gallus, why are you impassioned?' The same attitude towards the destructive passion of love recurs in *G.* 3, where Virgil broaches the difficulty of managing sexual stimulus in animal husbandry (3.209–11): 'But no work [*industria*] so strengthens their power as to turn them from sexual desire and the stings of hidden love, whether one prefers to deal with cattle or with horses'. Virgil writes within Epicurean parameters, recalling Lucretius' famous description of those afflicted by passion as wasting away 'from a hidden wound' (*DRN* 4.1120). The georgic poet explicitly underlines the applicability to humankind of the disastrous effects of sexual excitement on the animal world, in a Lucretian pastiche at the end of the passage (*G.* 3.242–4): 'Every species of men and beasts on land, every species of sea-creature, flocks and colourful birds, rush into passion and fire: love is the same for all'.[87]

It is therefore not surprising, at least in an Epicurean worldview, that 'all of Orpheus' work goes to waste' (4.491–2) and Eurydice is unrecoverable. Virgil unites Epicurean precept with Homeric precedent in his description of Orpheus' attempt to embrace his dying wife (4.499–502): 'She spoke and immediately fled from his sight, like smoke mixed with thin air, nor saw him again, clutching in vain at the shadows and wishing to say so many things'. Eurydice vanishes like her literary model, Patroclus' ghost in the Homeric Achilles' dream (*Il.* 23.99–101): 'So he spoke, and reached for him with his own arms, but could not grasp him, and his spirit went underground, like vapour, with a thin cry'. But the physics of her dissolution are Lucretian (*DRN* 3.455–8): 'So it is natural to infer that the substance of the spirit too is all dissolved, like smoke into the thin air aloft'.

Like Gallus before him, Orpheus continues to act on his passion rather than setting limits to it. Barred from undertaking a second katabasis (*G.* 4.502–3), he agonizes over how to continue (4.504–5): 'What could he do? Where could he go with his wife twice ravished? With what lament could he move the shades, with what words the divine powers?' His anguished deliberations recall Aristaeus' reproaches to his mother (4.322–5, partially quoted above) and those of mythological figures in neoteric epyllion, such as Ariadne in Catullus' 'Peleus and Thetis' (*c.* 64.177–83). But Orpheus most resembles the Gallus of *B.* 10 as he abandons himself to song in a landscape that reflects his emotions (*G.* 4.507–10): 'They say that for seven whole months in a row, he wept beneath a high crag at Strymon's deserted stream and unrolled these complaints beneath the cold stars, soothing tigers and moving oaks with his song'. The 'Alexandrian' footnote, 'they say', is another neoteric touch, reminiscent of Catullus' epyllion (*c.* 64.76, 124), and Virgil deepens the pathos by reworking a Homeric simile in such a way as to emphasize the elegiac quality of Orpheus' lament (*G.* 4.511–15): 'just so the nightingale, grieving beneath the poplar's shade, laments her fledglings, whom the hard farmer, watching them, plucked from the nest, still immature; but she weeps through the night, and sitting on a branch renews her pitiable song and fills up the place, far and wide, with her sad laments'. Virgil develops a Homeric simile comparing Penelope's concern for her son to that of Itys' mother, who became the nightingale (*Od.* 19.518–23), and conflates it with another in which the tears of Odysseus and Telemachus are compared to birds keening at the loss of their young, taken by farmers (*Od.* 16.216–18). The image also reworks his own earlier vignette of the farmer destroying a bird's nest in the woods to bring new land under cultivation (*G.* 2.207–11). But he draws his lexicon of love, lament and song from the Neoterics' definition of elegy (e.g. Catull. *c.* 65). The elegiac tonality of Orpheus' song, in combination with the bard's posture by the side of a river, especially evokes Gallus' elegiac poetry: the lineaments of *B.* 10's Gallus, adapting himself and his lament for his faithless mistress Lycoris to bucolic, are discernible behind the portrait of Orpheus' single-minded lament for his dead wife in the frigid landscape of Thrace (*G.* 4.516–20), not least because Virgil's Gallus complains of the cruelty of the love god even should he toil in Orpheus' Thrace (*B.* 10.64–6): 'Our efforts (*labores*) cannot change that god, not if we should drink the Hebrus from the midst of its cold waters, and undergo Sithonian snows of wintry sleet'.

Orpheus' intransigence provokes the Ciconian women to tear him limb from limb, and Proteus closes his song with the image of the dead bard's head floating down the Hebrus, still singing (*G.* 4.523–7): 'then too Oeagrian Hebrus, carrying the bard's head, plucked from his snowy shoulders, in the middle of his eddy, rolled it downstream; his voice and cold tongue were calling "Eurydice, ah poor Eurydice" as his spirit fled;

the banks re-echoed "Eurydice" over the whole river'. Gallus is probably
the primary model for the mannered song uttered by Virgil's decapitated
bard with its quintessential neoteric style. The repeated invocation of
Orpheus' dead bride, in conjunction with the neoteric interjection 'ah', is
especially reminiscent of Gallus' despairing address to Lycoris in
B. 10.47–9, which Servius reports Virgil drew verbatim from Gallus'
own poetry (Ch. 2.4). The reference to the river-banks resounding with
the bard's song, with its metapoetic valence of Virgil's 'echo' of Gallus'
poetry, implies our poet's admiration for the wide circulation of his
friend's verse, now due as much to his own efforts as to those of Gallus.

Proteus' song ends with Orpheus', and Virgil represents the seer
immediately 'plung[ing] at a bound into the deep sea' just like his
Homeric model (*Od.* 4.570), leaving Cyrene to explain to her son how
to perform the rite of the *bugonia* and thereby regenerate his bees
(*G.* 4.530–47).[88] Aristaeus performs the rite exactly as bidden, in a final
evocation of Homeric style as Virgil repeats almost every word of
Cyrene's instructions in Aristaeus' actions (4.549–53). The Aristaeus
episode thus sustains to its conclusion the Homeric style and themes
proposed in the proem to *G.* 3, even as Virgil simultaneously integrates
into its fabric the mannered Alexandrian techniques and erotic material
typical of Gallus' elegiac poetry. This carefully calibrated union of poetic
models well illustrates Virgil's intertextual artistry, and offers a salutary
point of reference from which to consider the challenges he faced when
broaching the Homeric literary tradition and its myriad tributaries in
A., where we shall see him unambiguously don the mantle of Homer.

Aeneis

The opening words of *A.* 1 announce Virgil's new project in markedly Homeric terms: *arma uirumque cano*, 'Arms and a man I sing'. The twin themes of warfare and heroism are the focus of Homer's *Iliad* and *Odyssey*, which centre on Achilles' exploits in the Trojan war and Odysseus' travels after Troy's fall respectively. But Virgil has combined and condensed Homer's two twenty-four-book heroic poems into a single twelve-book 'modern' Roman epic that relates the exploits of Augustus' distant Trojan ancestor Aeneas after the sack of his city. The first six books of *A.*, which track Aeneas' travels around the Mediterranean as he searches for the original Trojan 'homeland', constitute the 'Odyssean' half of the epic, while the second six, which detail the Trojans' wars with Italic tribes in order to secure their promised homeland, the 'Iliadic'.[1] Virgil introduces his hero, beset by trouble in his search for a site where he can establish a new city (1.1–7):

> I sing of arms and a man, who, first exiled from the shores of Troy, was fated to come to Italy and the Lavinian strand; he was much buffeted on land and sea by the power of the gods above, because of savage Juno's unforgiving anger, and he suffered much in war too, until he could found a city and settle his gods in Latium: whence came the Latin race, the Alban fathers, and the walls of high Rome.

This hero looks very much like Homer's Odysseus, the nameless 'man' whose travails are summarized in the opening lines of the *Odyssey*

(1.1–5): 'Tell me, Muse, of the man of many ways, who suffered much, when he sacked the holy citadel of Troy; he saw the cities of many men and learned their minds, but experienced at sea much pain in his spirit, struggling for his life and his comrades' homecoming'. Virgil's characterization of his hero is signally 'Odyssean', though his opening period follows that of the *Iliad* more closely in both length and syntactical structure (*Il.* 1.1–7). The temporal sweep of Virgil's opening lines – from the sack of Troy (1184 BCE) to the foundations of Lavinium, Alba Longa and Rome (753 BCE) – also looks to the *Iliad*, which explains Achilles' anger as 'accomplishing the will of Zeus' (*Il.* 1.5, Ch. 4.3), a detail translated in Virgil's characterization of Aeneas' exile to Latium as 'fated'.

Virgil diverges from both Homeric models, however, in his request that the Muse 'recall the causes' that led Juno to 'drive a man outstanding in his dutiful responsibility to undergo so many misfortunes and approach so many travails' (*A.* 1.8–11). Virgil's Latin lexicon imparts an Alexandrian refinement to his large Homeric canvas, for the 'causes' that he asks his Muse to review (1.8) are resonant of Callimachus' *Aetia* ('Causes'), whose first two books featured the Greek poet in conversation with individual Muses.[2] The hero's travails (*labores*, 1.10) imply not only Aeneas' epic feats but also Virgil's painstaking Alexandrian artistry.[3] In probing the motivation for Juno's anger (1.8–9: 'for what affront to her godhead, or grieving what?'), Virgil also hints at the crucial role that the whole of the literary tradition will play in his epic, and he offers an allusively phrased partial answer a few lines later (1.25–8): 'the causes of her anger and savage grief had not yet slipped her mind; the judgement of Paris remained deeply embedded in her memory, the insult to her scorned beauty, the hated race and ravished Ganymede's honours'. Homer treats neither the Judgement of Paris (though cf. *Il.* 24.28–30) nor Ganymede's ascension to Olympus as Jove's cupbearer, but both myths appear in the 'epic cycle' supplementing the Homeric history of the Trojan war and the Greek heroes' disastrous homecomings.[4]

4.1 *The Homeric Tradition*

Virgil's paramount model is Homer, whose *Iliad* and *Odyssey* supply the 'code' models for his essay in heroic epic (Ch. 3.1). Georg Knauer, in a monumental study of Virgil's Homeric sources, has documented both the broad ambition and detailed artistry of the Latin poet's revision of this material,[5] and Alessandro Barchiesi has identified the fourfold significance of Virgil's sustained imitation of Homeric epic as combination, continuation, repetition and inversion.[6] The opening movement of *A.* 1 well illustrates Virgil's approach. After the proem, he maintains the focus on Juno and her hostility to Troy and the Trojans, which he contrasts with her traditional love for Greek Samos and, even more, for Carthage, a city in Libya that she intends should rule the world; but she has heard that the Fates plan otherwise, that a race descended from Trojan blood will destroy Carthage. Fearing this future and brooding on the past, she has kept the Trojan survivors wandering the Mediterranean for years, when she catches sight of them on the high seas and decides to drive them off course in a storm. The Virgilian Juno derives both her larger plot (*A.* 1.34–3.718 = *Od.* 5.263–12.453) and her detailed tactics from the Homeric epics. She imitates Poseidon in raising a storm against her enemy at sea, while the shipwreck of Aeneas' fleet at Carthage is modelled on the storm that wrecks Odysseus' raft and casts him ashore on Scheria. Her manipulation of Aeolus, the king of the winds, whose help she secures with the promise of a wife (*A.* 1.50–80), is based on Hera's manipulation of Sleep in *Iliad* 14, whose help she secures with the promise of a wife (*Il.* 14.225–79).

In the midst of the storm, Aeneas re-enacts the role of the shipwrecked Odysseus in *Odyssey* 5, but recalls his own experience of Iliadic warfare (*A.* 1.92–101):

> Immediately Aeneas' limbs were loosened with chill fear; he groaned and raising both hands to the stars repeated such words aloud: 'O three and four times blessed were those who met their deaths before their fathers' faces beneath Troy's high walls! O Diomedes, bravest of the race of Greeks! Could I not have fallen in Iliadic fields and poured out

my life by your right hand, where savage Hector lies dead by Patroclus' arrow, where huge Sarpedon lies, where the Simois snatched so many men's shields and helmets, and rolled their brave bodies beneath his waves!'

In naming Aeneas here for the first time in his epic, Virgil depicts his hero in strikingly Odyssean guise, for in just such a storm at sea Odysseus' knees give way from fear and the Greek hero reflects on his troubles in a speech partially 'repeated' here by Aeneas (*Od.* 5.306–9): 'Three and four times blessed were the Greeks who died then in broad Troy, bringing favour to the sons of Atreus. So I wish I'd died and followed my fate on the day when the most Trojans cast their bronze-tipped spears at me over the body of Peleus' dead son'. But Virgil overwrites Odysseus' exploits at Troy with Aeneas' recollection of his own narrow escape from Diomedes (*Il.* 5), and the deaths of the Trojan prince Hector (*Il.* 22) and his Lydian ally Sarpedon (*Il.* 16). He marks his contamination of an Odyssean speech with Iliadic material in his application of the epithet 'Iliadic' (*Iliacis, A.* 1.97) to the plain before Troy.

Nor does Virgil restrict his adaptation of archaic Greek poetry to the *Iliad* and *Odyssey*. He also draws on the 'Homeric' hymns, which supply the inspiration for Aeneas' encounter with his mother Venus as he explores the Libyan countryside after the storm (*A.* 1.314–15): 'his mother went to meet him in the middle of the forest, with a maiden's face and bearing'. On first meeting her son, Venus rehearses her epiphany to his father Anchises in the hymn to *Aphrodite*, and her departure also follows the hymn's precedent (*A.* 1.402–4 ~ *Aphr.* 172–5).[7] The allusions impart an erotic undertone to Virgil's scene, especially in the revelation of Venus' identity (*A.* 1.402–4): 'turning away she glowed from her rosy neck, and her ambrosial hair wafted a divine odour from her head'. Her beauty and perfume recall the preparations she makes to seduce Anchises in the *Aphrodite* (61–3): 'There the Graces bathed her and anointed her with ambrosial oil such as always covers divine beings, ambrosial oil which she had by her in full fragrance'. Aeneas responds to her subtle eroticism with a flattering speech that likens her beauty to that of a goddess (*A.* 1.327–9), on the model of the shipwrecked Odysseus, who begins a complimentary speech to the nubile Phaeacian princess Nausicaa (*Od.* 6.149–85) with the question, 'are you goddess or mortal?' (6.149), and compares her to Artemis (6.151–2), the goddess whom Venus resembles when she appears to Aeneas here (*A.* 1.315–20), 'wearing the arms of a Spartan maiden, or like Thracian Harpalyce who wearies horses and outstrips the swift river Hebrus in her flight. For, in the manner of a huntress, she had hung from her shoulders a handy bow'.

Aeneas diverges sharply from the hymnic model, however, after his mother reveals herself to him (1.406–8): 'when he recognized his mother, he pursued her with such words as she disappeared: "why do you so often – you're cruel too – delude your son with false images?"' Virgil here conflates his hero's recognition of his 'Homeric' lineage with the charge of Venus' cruelty from *B.* 8 (*crudelis tu quoque, A.* 1.407 = *B.* 8.50). The charge that Venus characteristically 'deludes with false images' draws on Epicurean ethics (Ch. 2.3, 4.3) and anticipates the goddess' instigation of the ill-fated love affair between Aeneas and Dido, Queen of Carthage (*A.* 1.657–60): 'But the Cytherean goddess devised new stratagems, new plans in her breast – that Cupid, transformed in face and mien, should attend instead of sweet Ascanius, inflaming the impassioned queen with gifts and instilling the fire of love in her bones'. Venus plots to delude Dido with false images, when she instructs Cupid to 'deceive [Ascanius'] face with a trick, just for one night, and a boy yourself assume the boy's well-known face' (1.683–4).

Though modelled on Odysseus' dalliances with Calypso (*Od.* 5), Nausicaa (*Od.* 6–8) and Circe (*Od.* 10–12), all of whom (along with many others) are condensed in the figure of Dido,[8] Aeneas' amatory sojourn in Carthage (*A.* 1–4) is marked as 'elegiac' by the erotic turn that Virgil's lexicon takes at this point in the narrative.[9] It is fitting that the love goddess should intervene to direct Virgil's epic narrative into amatory channels, for she and her son Cupid/Amor preside over the genre of Latin love elegy. Worrying that Dido's 'blandishments' (*A.* 1.670–1), the elegiac lover's seductive words, will entrap Aeneas in

Carthage, Venus mounts an elegiac counter-offensive. In her instructions
to Cupid (1.664–88), she deploys a series of amatory tropes (1.673–5):
'I plan to beset (*capere*) the queen with tricks first and surround her
with flames, to prevent her from changing at the prompting of some
god; let her be gripped with a great love for Aeneas on my side'. Venus'
metaphor of love as a military siege derives from martial epic, but fire
and treachery are also elegiac *topoi*.[10] Propertius opens his first elegiac
collection (*c.* 29 BCE) with siege imagery (1.1.1): 'Cynthia with her eyes
first captured (*cepit*) me, unhappy'. Venus' fears are as much for her
grandson Ascanius, 'my greatest care' (*A.* 1.678), as for her son Aeneas,
and she articulates her 'love' for Ascanius in the language of Gallan love
elegy (Ch. 2.4). It is Dido, however, who is the focus of Venus' cruel
elegiac plot, as she instructs Cupid (1.687–8): 'when she embraces you
and gives sweet kisses, you can breathe hidden fire into her and deceive
her with poison'.

   The seeds of love sown by Cupid at the banquet in the first book come
to fruition in the fourth, where Dido takes on the profile of an elegiac
lover (4.1–2): 'But the queen, long since wounded by grievous care, feeds
the wound with her lifeblood and is wasted by an invisible fire'. Aeneas'
image appears constantly before her eyes, leaving her sleepless (4.4–5):
'fixed in her heart his face and words stick fast, nor does love allow her
limbs peaceful repose'. Her grievous passion first makes her wretchedly
unhappy, like an elegiac lover (cf. Prop. 1.1.1, quoted above), and then
drives her mad (*A.* 4.68–9): 'unhappy Dido burns and wanders through
the whole city in her madness' (cf. 4.300–1, quoted below). Her love-
madness specifically recalls Virgil's depiction of the elegist Gallus, mad
with passion for Lycoris, in *B.* 10 (Ch. 2.4).[11] Dido thinks she 'recognizes
the traces of the old flame' (*A.* 4.23) that she felt for her first husband
Sychaeus, unaware that she has been deluded by false images. In a
moment of self-conscious narratorial reflection on his plot, the epic poet
expresses qualified sympathy for her predicament (4.412): 'Cruel Amor,
to what ends do you not drive mortal hearts!' The question recalls Pan's
assessment of the love-god's cruelty in *B.* 10 (28–9): 'Amor has no
concern for such things: cruel Amor is not satisfied with tears'.

Virgil's scepticism about elegiac eroticism (Ch. 2.3, 3.3) emerges not only in the Lucretian lexicon that colours his treatment of Dido's passion (Ch. 4.3) but also in the tragic hues with which he introduces her story in *A*. 1. Venus' unusual self-fashioning as a Spartan maiden recalls her amatory hunting of Anchises in the Homeric hymn, but her footwear is drawn from tragedy (1.336–7): 'It's the custom of Tyrian maidens to carry a quiver, and bind their ankles high with the purple buskin' (*cothurno*).[12] The high-heeled boots she wears in her encounter with Aeneas were a conventional attribute of the tragic actor, and Virgil has set the scene for tragedy in his description of the Libyan harbour, where Aeneas' shipwrecked fleet finds shelter after the storm, for the Trojans make landfall in a natural setting that features the characteristic stage-front (*scaenae frons*) of the ancient theatre (1.164–6), against which the tragic drama conventionally played. Venus' account of Dido's bloody family history unfolds like a tragic prologue (1.338–41): 'You see the Punic kingdom, Tyrians and Agenor's city; but the territory is Libyan, a nation unmanageable in war. Dido holds sway, having left the city of Tyre, fleeing her brother'. Like her Greek counterpart Aphrodite in Euripides' *Hippolytus*, Venus sets out a backstory that orients the audience to the ensuing action (1.341–2): 'It's a long story of wrong, long and twisting; but I shall follow the main points of the matter'.

In Tyre Dido survives an internecine family feud, a conventional theme of classical tragedy (1.346–50): 'her brother Pygmalion, more abandoned to crime than all others, held the kingdom of Tyre. Between the two men mad passion intervened and before the altars her brother, blinded by love of gold, impiously overwhelmed [her husband] Sychaeus all unaware, secretly stabbing him'. Intrafamilial conflict and the opposing claims of human ambition and divine law lie at the heart of ancient tragedy, and Dido finds herself at the centre of the drama. Pygmalion successfully conceals his crime until her husband's ghost visits Dido in a dream, uncovers his wounds, and discloses the dark family secret. The intervention of a ghost is another tragic convention derived from Homeric epic, and the apparition duly instructs Dido to flee with the buried treasure that had originally inspired his murder.

Pygmalion looks like a historical tyrant (*tyranni*, 1.361), as his enemies join Dido's cause and she equips a navy (1.363–4): 'the wealth of greedy Pygmalion was carried overseas; and the leader of the expedition was a woman'.

Virgil identifies love as the cause of Dido's tragic ruin. The queen admits a nascent interest in the shipwrecked hero to her sister Anna (4.15–19): 'If my intention weren't fixed and immovable not to ally myself to anyone in the conjugal bond, after my first love deceived and cheated me by Sychaeus' death; if I weren't tired of the marriage bed and torch, I could perhaps have succumbed to this one – fault' (*huic uni forsan potui succumbere/ culpae*).[13] Like the confidante, who conventionally encourages the tragic hero to embark on a misguided course of action, Anna urges her sister not to resist her burgeoning love but to detain Aeneas in Carthage (4.54–5). When another storm arises, on the occasion of a royal hunt, Aeneas and Dido find shelter alone in a cave and there celebrate a 'marriage' (4.169–72): 'That day first was the cause of death, first the cause of evils. For moved by neither appearance nor reputation, Dido no longer thinks of a secret love; she calls it marriage and veils her fault with this name'. Roman poets conventionally represented the elegiac love affair as clandestine, so Dido's decision to publicize her love implies her transition from elegiac lover to tragic hero.

The 'fault' to which Dido succumbs evokes the Aristotelian analysis of the tragic hero's 'flaw',[14] an 'error' vividly instantiated in the queen's propensity to wander Carthage in a frenzy of passion (4.68–9, quoted above). When she discovers that Aeneas is secretly preparing to abandon her, her frenzy assumes an explicitly tragic profile (4.300–1): 'out of her mind, she rages and raves (*bacchatur*), aflame, through the whole city, like a Bacchant, excited by the commotion of the sacred objects, when the biennial rites incite her with the cry of "Bacchus" and Mt Cithaeron echoes by night with the noise'. Bacchus was the tutelary god of Athenian tragedy and Virgil's simile underlines not only Dido's surrender to maenadic passion but also her assimilation to the god's proprietary genre. Her numerous speeches (nine in *A*. 4) further contribute to her tragic characterization. She dreams that Aeneas tracks her as she wanders alone, 'just as mad Pentheus sees the ranks of the Eumenides, and thinks a twin sun and double Thebes show themselves, or like Agamemnon's son Orestes, pursued by the Furies, when he flees his mother, armed with torches and black snakes, and the avenging goddesses sit at the threshold' (4.469–73). The comparison to Pentheus and Orestes at their most desperate moments on the Athenian stage, in Euripides' *Bacchae* and Aeschylus' *Orestes*, confirms Dido's impending doom, while the death she chooses, by the sword, though uncharacteristic of women in Greek tragedy, is that of the tragic hero.[15]

The depiction of Dido as an elegiac lover and tragic protagonist stands in striking contrast to Virgil's sustained characterization of Aeneas as quintessential epic hero. At the banquet in Carthage in *A*. 2–3, Aeneas narrates the sack of Troy and the Trojan survivors' subsequent travels around the Mediterranean in a bravura recapitulation of Odysseus' storytelling at the Phaeacian court in *Odyssey* 9–12. The account of the sack of Troy in *A*. 2 is commonly interpreted as an Iliadic intrusion into the Odyssean first half of Virgil's epic, though the battle did not feature in the *Iliad*, but was the subject of the cyclic epic *Ilioupersis*. Aeneas focuses on three moments of heightened pathos in the narrative of Troy's fall: the Greeks' deception of the Trojans with the wooden horse (2.1–249), the night battle for Troy (2.250–558), and his own decision to flee the sacked city (2.559–729). His opening words emphasize the city's tragic fate, and hint at the long tradition of tragedies, both Greek and Roman, that treated the fall of Troy (2.3–6): 'you bid me renew unspeakable pain, queen – how the Greeks overthrew Troy's riches and sorrowful realm, a most pitiable sight that I saw myself and in which I played a great part'.[16]

The foundational account of the Trojan horse was that of Homer, who put it into the mouth of the Phaeacian bard Demodocus in *Odyssey* 8. In beginning his own narrative with the tale, therefore, Aeneas self-consciously adopts the posture of an epic poet. The Trojan priest Laocoon, who interprets the horse as a trick of the Greeks (Ch. 4.3), and the perfidious Greek Sinon, who encourages the unsuspecting Trojans to believe that the horse is a peace offering to the gods, appear first in the *Ilioupersis*, though we have better evidence of their roles in the fragments of eponymous Sophoclean tragedies of the fifth century BCE. Aeneas' account bears other hallmarks of tragedy: reversal of fortune, as when Laocoon is attacked and killed while performing blood sacrifice or the Trojans who take in Sinon out of pity and are in turn betrayed by him to the Greeks; religious misinterpretation and superstition, as when the Trojans ignore Laocoon's advice 'to fear Greeks even when they bear gifts' (2.49); and the mysterious workings of the gods and fate. Aeneas emphasizes the Trojans' naïveté in bringing the horse into the city, the tragic gulf between their actions and the consequences (2.241), and Virgil heightens the dramatic irony by giving Aeneas here a reminiscence of a line uttered by Hector's widow Andromache in Ennius' lost tragedy of the same name (fr. 87 Jocelyn), which intensifies the tragic pathos of the Trojans' embrace of the Greek emblem of their destruction.

The central action of *A.* 2 is the night battle for the city. Aeneas wakes from a dream, in which the ghost of Hector entrusts him with the city's gods and instructs him to flee.[17] The dream vision of Hector, still bearing the wounds of his fatal combat with Achilles, has an epic genealogy, recalling not only the appearance of Patroclus' ghost to Achilles to ask for burial in *Iliad* 23, but also the report by Ennius, at the outset of his epic *Annales*, of the appearance of Homer's ghost to him. Virgil thus characterizes his hero as both a leading warrior and a signal poet. Aeneas responds to the dream vision with Iliadic battle-frenzy (*A.* 2.337–8): 'Into the flames and weapons I was carried, where the savage Fury and roar of battle called me'. In his battle lust, Aeneas exemplifies the attitude of the Homeric warrior, who fought for personal glory rather than from a larger sense of civic and familial obligation, and his battle lust is explicitly framed as at odds with the new responsibility to his community demanded by Hector's ghost. Only when he sees Priam killed by Achilles' son Pyrrhus, and recognizes in the king's death the climax and emblem of Troy's destruction, does Aeneas realize that his martial ethos has imperilled his family.

The last section of *A*. 2 focuses on Aeneas' decision to flee Troy, and a series of incidents that imperil his plans. As he hastens home from Priam's palace, he sees Helen in the temple of Vesta and in a blaze of anger determines to kill her.[18] Venus intervenes to hold him back, however, on the model of Athena restraining Achilles from killing Agamemnon in *Iliad* 1, and she reveals to him the divine forces at work in Troy's destruction. Like Hector, she urges Aeneas to abandon Troy, sending him home to save his family. His father Anchises, however, categorically refuses to leave and Aeneas, distracted from his purpose, is 'again carried into the fray, desiring death in his great misery' (2.655; cf. 2.337, quoted above). Although Aeneas' wife Creusa begs him to stay and protect his family, Aeneas prepares to return to battle, calling his men to bring weapons (2.668). At this crisis, Ascanius' hair bursts into flames and Anchises, interpreting the prodigy as propitious, asks for and receives a confirmatory sign (2.693–4): 'a star fallen through the shadows, trailing a torch with much light, streaked down the sky'. The falling star evokes the comet that was believed to commemorate Julius Caesar's apotheosis (Ch. 2.2) and links the *sidus Iulium* to Ascanius, through the image of his blazing hair (Ch. 4.2). Anchises therefore agrees to depart and Aeneas arranges his small household for flight, setting his father on his shoulders and taking his son by the hand, but leaving Creusa to bring up the rear (2.711): 'let my wife follow my footsteps from afar'.

In the confusion of their flight, however, Creusa is lost, and Aeneas returns to Troy only to find her ghost, who reveals to him his heroic destiny in Italy (2.783–4): 'there you will find fortunate circumstances, a kingdom and a royal consort: no need to lament beloved Creusa'. Modern scholars have been troubled by Aeneas' disposition of his family convoy in a gendered hierarchy of value, quite literally elevating male kin over female and blood relation over marital, with the resulting loss of Creusa.[19] Virgil rejects the Latin tradition of her departure from Troy with Aeneas, preserved by the early epic poet Naevius, because his hero can hardly indulge in epic dalliance with Dido in Carthage or contract a dynastic marriage in Latium with his wife along on the voyage. Instead, he conflates a later variant of the myth, in which she was rescued by Aphrodite and/or Cybele, with his own treatment of Orpheus and Eurydice in the fourth *Georgic* (Ch. 3.3). His contamination of the two myths is facilitated by the precedent of Creusa's original name in Roman myth, Eurydica (i.e. Eurydice), and the similarity of Aeneas' night passage through the labyrinthine twists and turns of the sacked city of Troy to Orpheus' return from the underworld.[20] The episode ends with the overlay of two different Homeric scenes along with Virgil's own Orpheus and Eurydice, on Aeneas' threefold attempt to embrace his wife's ghost (2.790–4): 'When she finished speaking, she left me weeping and wishing to say much, and she receded into thin air. Three times there I tried to throw my arms round her neck; three times her image, clasped in vain, escaped my hands, like light winds and most similar to a fleet dream'. Virgil underlines the magnitude of Aeneas' love and loss in his evocation of Achilles' effort to embrace Patroclus' ghost (*Il.* 23), Odysseus' attempt to embrace his mother's shade (*Od.* 11), and Orpheus' final loss of Eurydice (*G.* 4.499–502, Ch. 3.3).

Virgil's emphasis on his hero's desire to stay and fight, rather than run or hide, has been attributed to the need to exculpate Aeneas for abandoning Troy rather than dying in the city's defence. Over the course of the book, Virgil redefines the nature of epic heroism, moving away from the Homeric conception of a singular pre-eminent warrior's martial prowess or an extraordinary individual's intrepid resourcefulness to the Roman communitarian ethic of overlapping responsibility to gods, society and family captured in the Latin word *pietas*, 'dutiful respect'. Only at the end of *A.* 2 is Aeneas ready to assume the leadership of the Trojan survivors, 'a huge number of new comrades, mothers and men, youth gathered for exile, a wretched crowd' (2.796–8), who constitute the Trojan 'remnant' under Aeneas' leadership.

A. 3 offers Virgil an opportunity to explore another mode of classical epic in the foundation legend or colonization narrative of 'ktistic' epic (from Greek *ktisis*, 'foundation').[21] The Trojans' goal is the 'Westland', a locale clarified in the course of the book by a series of oracles and portents, conventional in colonization narratives. As Juno in her role of

Aeneas' divine antagonist persecutes the Trojans, so Apollo guides them both in his universal role of oracular god and divine patron of city-foundation, and in his specific role of tutelary divinity of the Trojans and, especially, Aeneas.[22] The Trojans sail westward from the Aegean sea, where the first third of the book is set, via Greece, and eventually reach Sicily and the Italian peninsula, before Juno blows them off course to Libya.[23]

The first stop is in 'martial' Thrace, a land with a well-deserved reputation for savagery, impiety and warfare. Taking the auspices upon landing, Aeneas makes a horrifying discovery (3.26–9): 'I saw an amazing prodigy that makes me shudder to speak of it. For from the tree I first plucked from the ground, snatching it by its roots, there flowed drops of black blood and they stained the ground with gore'. Aeneas' violation[24] of the corpse of Priam's youngest son Polydorus, sent to his brother-in-law Polymestor in Thrace along with a vast quantity of Trojan gold only to be murdered on the final overthrow of Troy, confirms the city's lasting destruction and the end of Priam's line. Trojan foundations in the area were known in Aenus, on the Hebrus, and Aeneia in Chalcidice, but Virgil innovates in bringing Aeneas to the site of Polydorus' murder, which was best known from Euripides' tragedy *Hecuba*. His innovations in the Trojan tradition repeatedly contaminate epic with tragedy, but he strictly isolates his hero from the ruin of the tragic protagonist: in his encounters with tragic figures, Aeneas consistently maintains an epic profile as the leader of the Trojan survivors.

Leaving the impious land behind, the Trojans make landfall at Delos, the birthplace of Apollo and an important site of the god's worship in antiquity. To Delos, Virgil transfers the Pythian tripod and the bay, both attributes of Apollo's oracle at Delphi, which Greek colonists traditionally consulted for guidance about colonization. Welcomed by Apollo's priest, Aeneas prays for guidance and is instructed to 'seek their ancient mother' (3.94), interpreted by Anchises to mean Crete. As in Thrace, however, where the lasting destruction of Priam's line is confirmed by the discovery of Polydorus' corpse, so on Crete the final annihilation of

Troy is corroborated by the plague that strikes the colonists. In the midst of the devastation, Aeneas receives a dream vision of the divine Penates, who reveal the true meaning of the oracle (3.161–8), and the Trojans' Italian origin from Dardanus, which Virgil derives from the genealogy of the Homeric Aeneas, who claims Dardanian descent (*Il.* 20.215–40). The Trojans are thus 'native' Italians, returning to their true homeland, like the Homeric Odysseus and his crew before them.

The Trojan ships next put in on one of the Strophades, 'islands of turning', which they reach after a disorienting passage from Crete. There they see hills and smoke at a distance but find herds of cattle and flocks of goats apparently untended. With this detail, Virgil signals his Homeric intertext as the arrival of Odysseus and his crew on the island where the Sun god pastures his cattle: in *Odyssey* 11, Teiresias warns Odysseus not to eat the cattle, for anyone who does so will lose his homecoming, but in *Odyssey* 12, ignoring his prohibition, Odysseus' crew slaughter and eat the cattle, thereby forfeiting their return to Ithaca. In *A.* 3, the Trojans slaughter the animals and prepare a feast after sacrificing to Jupiter and the other gods, only to find themselves attacked by the Harpies ('Snatchers'), monstrous creatures depicted by Homer and Hesiod as personified winds, but portrayed in classical literature and art as birds with the faces of women (*A.* 3.214–18).[25] As women in avian form, the Virgilian Harpies are also evocative of Odysseus' encounter with the Sirens, winged women who entice men to their deaths, though Virgil's primary model is Apollonios of Rhodes, who portrays the Harpies as stinking, ravenous bird-like creatures, befouling and stealing the food of the Thracian king Phineus for betraying divine secrets (*Arg.* 2.178–235).[26]

The abortive sacrifice on the Strophades is successfully renewed when the Trojans land at Actium, and they sail thence to Buthrotum, where Aeneas discovers a miniature Troy ruled by Hector's brother Helenus, now married to Hector's widow Andromache, as prophesied in Euripides' *Andromache*. Walking up from the harbour, Aeneas comes upon Andromache 'weeping and filling the whole place with lament' (3.312–13), the very incarnation of tragic mourning.[27] Andromache appears in several important scenes in the *Iliad*, but she also enjoyed a fertile afterlife in classical tragedy, on which Virgil draws in her characterization.[28] In his depiction of Helenus, by contrast, he focuses on the prophet's Homeric lineage to offer further revelations about the Trojan mission intertwined with Roman ritual prescriptions. Throughout the episode, Virgil strongly contrasts the pair's retrograde focus on the Trojan past – confirmed by Andromache's lament and Helenus' onomastic renewal of the Troad in the landscape of Buthrotum – with the forward narrative impetus of Aeneas and the proto-Roman mission.[29]

The final episodes of *A.* 3 occur off southern Italy, in Sicily, where the Trojans encounter Achaemenides, a member of Odysseus' crew abandoned in his haste to flee the Cyclops' island.[30] Virgil here approaches Homer's subject matter most closely in time and space, as Aeneas meets the only survivor, besides Odysseus himself, of the Greek hero's return from Troy. The episode offers Aeneas the opportunity to reconsider the Trojans' hospitable reception of Sinon in *A.* 2, which resulted in the fall of their city, and Virgil the opportunity to reassess the heroism of Homer's Odysseus. Aeneas' reception of Achaemenides with the same compassion as that with which Priam had received Sinon documents the continuity of the Roman virtue of *pietas* with the Trojan past. But Virgil represents Aeneas as exemplifying a heroism of larger moral purpose than his Greek model Odysseus, whose Homeric resourcefulness is undermined in Achaemenides' report of the encounter with the Cyclops, the most famous of Odysseus' exploits.[31] For 'Achaemenides' narrative *omits* all of Ulysses' brilliant stratagems, involves fewer days, fewer men lost, a less dominant role for Ulysses overall, and culminates in his abandonment of one of his crew'.[32] Virgil thereby documents not only the greater moral stature of his own hero, but also the larger ambition of his own epic project. Yet the book ends on a note of profound pathos with the death of Aeneas' father Anchises, who has played a central role on the voyage from Troy.[33]

In *A.* 4 Dido responds to Aeneas' narrative with passionate love and a plan to keep him in Carthage rather than material aid and the resources to help him realize his mission. The genuineness of her hospitable reception of the Trojans has already been called into question not only by Venus' deceptive stratagems and Cupid's impersonation of Ascanius, but also by Jove's instructions that Mercury instil in her 'a mild spirit and kindly purpose' (1.303–4). After Aeneas declares his intention to leave for Italy, Dido's passionate love turns to furious hatred (Ch. 4.2) and Mercury advises him to sail before she can harm the Trojans (4.569–70): 'Come on, curtail your delays! A varying and always changeful thing is the female'.[34] Aeneas immediately rouses his comrades for departure, and they watch with trepidation from the open sea as Carthage burns at the outset of *A.* 5, until a storm blows them back to Sicily, a year to the day after they had buried Anchises and been driven off course to Carthage.[35] Aeneas' return to Sicily has been interpreted as a retrograde journey in both space and time, as the hero, though motivated by *pietas*, mourns his father (but not Dido) and further delays his mission.[36]

   A. 5 is devoted to the Trojans' celebrations of the anniversary of Anchises' death and appropriately marks a new beginning for the first of the epic's four central books. To commemorate his father's death Aeneas announces a ritual sacrifice and feast, to be followed by athletic contests. These games comprise the focal episode of the book and showcase Virgil's intertextual artistry.[37] Their primary model lies in the funeral games Achilles holds for the dead Patroclus in *Iliad* 23, and so they constitute another 'Iliadic' intrusion into the 'Odyssean' first half of *A.* But the *Odyssey* too features athletic contests at the Phaeacian court in *Odyssey* 8, in a structurally analogous position before the epic hero's katabasis. Apollonios of Rhodes combines both sets of Homeric games in his own athletic contests of *Argonautica* 4, which furnish Virgil with a model for the simultaneous imitation of both Homeric poems.[38] In all four epics the games facilitate the reintegration of the hero into his community. By honouring Anchises with funeral games, Aeneas reintegrates himself into Trojan society after his erotic digression in Carthage and re-establishes his leadership of the Trojan remnant.

Virgil distils Homer's eight Iliadic games into half their number, and organizes them more artistically, alternating longer and shorter episodes that foreshadow events in the second half of the epic: ship-race, foot-race, boxing, archery and the non-competitive 'Troy game' of equestrian manoeuvres, in which Aeneas' son Ascanius distinguishes himself. The athletic contests can be read as a microcosm of the plot of the *Aeneid*, with the Trojans' travels by sea in *A.* 1–6 yielding to their travails on land in *A.* 7–12, and the land-based games increasingly resembling the martial skills they will deploy in the war with the Italians.[39] Comic failures in the games anticipate tragic events in the larger narrative: in the ship-race, one of the captains throws his hapless helmsman overboard, foreshadowing the death of Aeneas' helmsman Palinurus at the end of the book; in the foot-race, Nisus loses his lead when he slips in sacrificial gore but helps his friend Euryalus to win, prefiguring not only the friends' mutual devotion but also the failure of their mission in the night raid of *A.* 9; in the boxing match, Entellus kills his prize, a sacrificial steer, with a blow, rather than 'sacrificing' his human opponent, as Aeneas will do in the funeral rites for Pallas in *A.* 11; and in the swift-moving archery contest, the final contestant shoots into the air an arrow that catches fire and vanishes like a shooting star, in another prefiguration of the *sidus Iulium*. At the end of Anchises' funeral games, the Troy game turns into a real martial exercise when Ascanius leads the youths against the Trojan women, who have set fire to the ships.[40] On the advice of the elderly Nautes, Aeneas establishes a city in Sicily for those Trojans too old, too weak or too female to continue on the voyage to Italy (5.715–17): 'aged old men and mothers tired out from the sea, whatever in your company is weak and fears danger – choose them, and let them have this territory'. He thereby underlines the disjunction between a Trojan retrograde fixation on the past and his own new tenacity of Roman purpose.

A. 5 ends with the death of another person close to Aeneas, his helmsman Palinurus. As with Creusa at the conclusion of *A.* 2, Anchises at the close of *A.* 3 and Dido at the end of *A.* 4, so Palinurus is in some sense sacrificed to Aeneas' heroic mission. The element of sacrifice is particularly clear in his death, which results from a bargain Venus strikes with Neptune to keep Aeneas safe on the passage from Sicily to Italy. Neptune agrees, but on one condition (5.814–15): 'There will be only one lost, whom you will seek from the depths; one life will be given for many'. A similar transaction occurs in *A.* 6, in connection with a different life and a different journey, when Aeneas reaches Cumae and, in accordance with the instructions imparted by his father in a dream vision at the end of *A.* 5, requests the Sibyl's guidance to the underworld in order to learn his destiny. She explains that he must first expiate another death (6.149–52): 'moreover the body of your friend lies dead (alas, you don't know), and pollutes the whole fleet with his death while you seek advice and hang on our threshold. Bring him back to his resting place before and bury him in a tomb'. Misenus' death in advance of Aeneas' descent to the underworld rehearses that of Odysseus' crewmember, Elpenor, before the Homeric hero's journey to the underworld, where he meets his shade (*Od.* 11). The Roman hero discharges his duty of burial with exemplary piety, felling trees for Misenus' funeral pyre, erected on a site that will bear his name (Misenum). The act of cremation is closely associated with the Trojan–Roman communal enterprise, with the community taking possession of the land by naming it.

Upon his arrival in Cumae, Aeneas seeks a prophecy from the Sibyl but stops briefly to admire the reliefs crafted by Daedalus on the doors of the Temple of Apollo. The doors commemorate the gratitude of the archetypal Greek artist and inventor for his escape from Crete, where he had been imprisoned by the Cretan king Minos, either because he helped the king's wife Pasiphaë consummate her desire for a bull (*B.* 6, Ch. 2.3) or because he helped Ariadne save Theseus from the Minotaur (Catull. *c.* 64). Daedalus' art commemorates the terrible crimes and dark passions of the Cretan royal house, but cannot represent the death of his beloved son Icarus, who flew too close to the sun and so melted the wax that held the feathers on the frame of his wings and drowned in the Icarian Sea. The artistry of the doors stands in a *mise-en-abyme* relation to the artistry of *A.*: Virgil's themes of erotic passion and paternal love summarize the plot of the epic thus far and establish a tone of solemn mystery for Aeneas' encounter with the Sibyl and subsequent journey to Hades.[41]

Before the descent to the underworld, however, Aeneas witnesses the Sibyl's oracular frenzy and hears her riddling prophecy (6.86–97):

> Wars, terrible wars, I descry, and the Tiber frothing with much blood. You will lack neither of the Trojan rivers Simois and Xanthus, nor Greek camps; another Achilles has already been born to Latium, also the son of a goddess; nor will Juno, dogging Teucer's descendants, be anywhere absent, while all the time, a suppliant in desperate circumstances, what peoples among the Italians, what cities won't you beseech! The origin (*causa*) of such great ills is again a foreign bride for the Trojans, again an alien bridal.

Her prophecy condenses the plot of the 'Iliadic' second half of the *Aeneid*, implying a recurrence of Iliadic warfare on Italian soil and foretelling the appearance of another Achilles and Helen in Italy. The Sibyl closes on a happier note, however, with her prediction that the Trojans will find help from an unexpected source, 'a Greek city' (6.97).

Aeneas' katabasis, with the Sibyl as his guide, is the central episode of *A.* 6. Virgil is indebted for the subject to Homer, whose hero Odysseus descends to the realm of the shades in the 'Nekuia' ('book of the dead', *Od.* 11), in order to consult the prophet Teiresias about his fate. Virgil's hero, by contrast, enjoys a full tour of the underworld, culminating in his meeting with his father in Elysium and review of his Roman descendants (Ch. 4.2) in an extravagant Orphic-Pythagorean vision (Ch. 4.3). As Aeneas journeys through Hades' realm with the Sibyl he encounters different groups of people: the unburied, exemplified by Palinurus; mythological heroines who killed themselves for love, exemplified by Dido; the heroes of Greek mythology, exemplified by Priam's son Deiphobus, Helen's second Trojan husband; and the famous sinners of Tartarus. Virgil models his catalogue of mythological heroines on Homer's catalogue of women in *Odyssey* 11, but he refines his Homeric source by particularizing its members as women who died for love and locating them in the 'Mourning Fields'. The focus on unhappy love reflects the taste of the Hellenistic Greek and Neoteric Latin poets for psychological and emotional extremes of passion. In this company, Aeneas meets Dido, who cursed him and the Roman race on her deathbed after he abandoned her in the fourth book (Ch. 4.2). At the very centre of the sixth book, the poet thus brings the former lovers together for a final encounter, which simultaneously recalls and reverses their last meeting in *A*. 4.

A. 6 constitutes a pivotal turning point in the *Aeneid*, as Aeneas revisits important events and people from his past and recalibrates his mission to focus on the future. Troy, Carthage and his Odyssean wanderings are now finished, and an Italian prospect opens before him in the 'Iliadic' war narrative announced at the outset of the next book (7.37–45):

> Now come, Erato, I shall lay out the kings, the circumstances, the state of affairs that existed in ancient Latium, when a foreign army first beached its fleet on Ausonian shores, and I shall recall the beginnings of the first battle. You, goddess, you, advise your poet. I shall tell of terrible wars, I shall tell of battle lines and kings driven to their deaths by courage, a Tuscan band and the whole of the Westland driven to take up arms. A greater sequence of events opens before me, I embark on a greater work.

In antiquity the *Iliad* was viewed as the 'greater' of Homer's two epics, and Virgil signals his epic's entry into the 'greater' subject of Iliadic warfare not only in the repetition of the adjective, but also in his reference to the 'terrible wars' prophesied by the Sibyl (6.86, quoted above). The postponement of the 'proem in the middle' from the head of the book is due to the narrative model of the *Odyssey*,[42] in which Odysseus' katabasis is followed by the burial of Elpenor at Circe's palace and the departure of Odysseus and his crew, who catch a following wind that drives them to the Sirens before falling. Aeneas tracks Odysseus' movements on his return from the underworld, beginning in *A*. 7 with the burial of another member of the Trojan remnant, his old nurse Caieta, whose death is based on that of Elpenor and thereby 'doubles' that of Misenus in *A*. 6.

The rich intertextual artistry with which Virgil develops his 'Iliadic' opening can also be seen in his unexpected invocation of the muse of love, Erato ('Beloved', *A.* 7.37), on the model of Apollonios of Rhodes, who invokes her at a parallel juncture in his *Argonautica* (3.1–5), as he turns from the outward voyage of the Argonauts to their arrival in Colchis, where Medea will fall in love with Jason. Erato is the muse who presides over erotic themes in classical literature and so Virgil appropriately invokes her at the start of his Iliadic books, which will turn on the issue of Aeneas' marriage to the Latin king's daughter Lavinia. Like Nausicaa, she is the only daughter of an ageing king, and erotic undercurrents accompany her introduction into the narrative (7.53–7): 'now ready for a man, she was marriageable, of fully developed years; many sought her from great Latium and the whole of Ausonia; Turnus seeks her, the handsomest of all and powerful in his ancestral descent, whom the royal consort, with an amazing love, hastened to be joined in marriage, her son-in-law'. The Latin elegiac lexicon returns here,[43] and hints at the central role that passion will play in the Iliadic *A.* 7–12.

The three major sections of *A.* 7 bring the Trojans and the Italians to the outbreak of war. With the arrival of the Trojans in Latium, Virgil reviews the portents indicating divine opposition to the marriage of Lavinia and Turnus, to explain Latinus' welcome of the Trojan embassy and invitation of a dynastic marriage between their leader and his daughter. At this promising juncture, however, Juno catches sight of the Trojans in Latium and devises a plot to undo the marriage compact, threatening a dowry of blood in warfare between the two peoples. Summoning the Fury Allecto from the underworld, Juno unleashes chthonic power to raise hellish passions on earth and instigate war:[44] Allecto maddens first Latinus' wife Amata ('Beloved'), then Turnus, and lastly Ascanius' hunting hounds, until the Italians demand war. The final section of the book opens with Juno symbolically opening the gates of war (Ch. 4.2) and ends with the muster of the Italian ranks.

While *Iliad* 2 supplies the overarching structure of the book, with the false dream sent to Agamemnon corresponding to Allecto's incitement of the sleeping Turnus to war, and the catalogue of ships to the catalogue of Italians, Virgil enriches this Homeric framework with tragic motifs and elegiac conventions. A tragic Fury besieges Amata's threshold, enflaming erotic passion to Bacchic madness and thereby engendering a war between two peoples destined to be one nation (Ch. 4.2). As the generic progression from elegy to tragedy suggests, *A.* 7 recapitulates the action of *A.* 1 in 'greater' compass. Where Juno deploys the winds against the Trojans in *A.* 1, she raises the forces of the underworld against them in *A.* 7; the history of Carthage in *A.* 1 is superseded by the history of Latium in *A.* 7; both Dido and Latinus seek to ally their peoples with Aeneas' Trojans; and both Dido and Turnus suffer wounds, respectively erotic and martial, that embroil their people in war with the proto-Roman Trojans.

Book 8 turns away from Turnus and the Italians to follow Aeneas up the Tiber to Pallanteum, an Arcadian settlement on the future site of Rome. Aeneas seeks allies against the Italians and looks first, just as the Sibyl had predicted, to Greek settlers from Arcadia, King Evander and his son Pallas. From them he hears about Hercules' killing of the monster Cacus and foundation of the 'greatest' altar, and he tours the site of early Rome before receiving a divinely manufactured set of arms. *A.* 8 stands in the same structural relationship to *A.* 2 as *A.* 7 stands to *A.* 1: with the fall of Troy in *A.* 2, Virgil depicts the Trojan past; with the tour of early Pallanteum in *A.* 8, he explores the site of the Roman future. The events of *A.* 8 enact in microcosm the temporal progression from past to future: the story of Cacus' theft of Hercules' cattle and death at the hero's hands constitutes the aetiology for the foundation of the *ara maxima* in the past; Evander's tour of Pallanteum showcases the 'present' state of Italian culture; and the shield of Aeneas heralds the future of the Roman people.

Homer provides a description in *Iliad* 18 of Achilles' shield, made at the request of the hero's mother Thetis by the divine craftsman Hephaistos, before Achilles re-enters the war. Virgil follows his model with an ecphrasis describing Aeneas' shield, made at the request of his mother Venus by her husband Vulcan. Containing scenes of mostly peaceful life, the shield of Achilles shows what the Greek hero consciously forgoes by returning to war (since he knows that he will die at Troy). By contrast, the shield of Aeneas records important moments in the history of the Roman people and thereby documents the continuity between the hero's dutiful acceptance of his mission to establish the Trojans in Italy and his descendants' achievements. The scenes on the shield of Aeneas eschew Greek mythology to relate stories from Roman history that fall into three broad categories: early Roman legends, the Battle of Actium, and the triple triumph of Augustus (Ch. 4.2). The shield thus brings the narrative of the *Aeneid* into close contact with events of the poet's own day as the narrator reflects on the significance of the refoundation of Rome by Aeneas' descendant Augustus.

As *A.* 8 belongs to Aeneas, so *A.* 9 belongs to Turnus, who takes centre stage in the absence of Aeneas: the primary Homeric model is *Iliad* 8–12, where Hector leads the Trojans against the Greek ships in the absence of their greatest champion, Achilles. *A.* 9 opens with Turnus inciting the Italians to fire the Trojan ships, though his stratagem is frustrated by the fleet's metamorphosis into 'goddesses of the great sea' (9.101–2). The Italians take heart from the portent, which Turnus interprets as isolating the Trojans in their camp. In the course of the book, Turnus emerges as the foremost warrior on the field until, in personal combat with the Trojan Pandarus at the climax of his *aristeia*, he claims the mantle of Achilles (9.741–2): 'begin, if you have any courage, and engage in battle; you will tell Priam you found Achilles even here'. In fashioning himself another Achilles, Turnus boldly reworks the Greek hero's words to Hector in their climactic duel (*Il.* 22.268–9).

But *A.* 9 also explores the heroism of the 'next generation' of Trojan warriors: Nisus and Euryalus undertake a night embassy to the absent Aeneas; Ascanius is victorious against an Italian foe in his first trial of strength; and the brothers Pandarus and Bitias, flushed with Trojan martial success, open the gate they guard to the Italians, allowing Turnus entry.[45] Ascanius' success in the central episode contrasts with the tragic deaths of the four other youths. Nisus and Euryalus inaugurate a series of youths killed in the Italian war before they reach adulthood. Their heroism is motivated by the twin themes of love of glory and love for one another,[46] neither of which is sufficient for them to realize their mission, as their night embassy (modelled on the embassy to the absent Achilles in *Il.* 9) turns into a night raid on the Rutulian camp (modelled on the *Doloneia* in *Il.* 10) that leaves them burdened with spoils and hindered in their flight when an Italian scouting party discovers them. Of particular thematic significance for the last four books of the epic is the friends' excessive zeal for spoils, which they mistake for glory but which cost them their mission and their lives. In *A.* 10, Turnus exhibits a similarly excessive lust for plunder when he strips Pallas' corpse of his sword belt, while in *A.* 11 Camilla pursues a richly equipped Trojan warrior. All three scenes underline the warriors' youth and inexperience, with Euryalus and Camilla killed immediately, betrayed to the enemy by the spoils they pursue so incautiously. It takes longer for the motif to catch up with Turnus, as he enjoys signal success in battle in *A.* 9, though he squanders his opportunity to open the Trojan camp to the Italians. *A.* 9 emphasizes the futility of fighting for individual glory, the Homeric warrior's goal, in the newly dynastic context of the Trojans' proto-Roman mission. Nisus and Euryalus, Pandarus and Bitias all come to grief as a result of their individualistic martial ethos, while Turnus accomplishes nothing for the Italians by his singular heroics in the Trojan camp.

At a Council of the Gods in *A.* 10, Jupiter decrees that the gods must refrain from assisting their favourites on the battlefield, and so the opposing forces of the Trojans and Italians fight their first full-scale battle in massed ranks, with general scenes of killing alternating with focused duels. Aeneas, on his return from Pallanteum at the beginning of *A.* 10, rallies the Trojans' spirits with his Etruscan and Arcadian recruits, and his young ally Pallas emerges as the leader of the latter. Pallas' *aristeia* brings him briefly into contact with his Italian counterpart Lausus, the son of Turnus' exiled Etruscan ally Mezentius, but the two youths are not fated to be matched against one another. Instead Pallas, with unlucky gallantry, confronts the more experienced warrior Turnus, whose *aristeia* culminates in the young Arcadian's death. In the second half of the book, Aeneas, enraged at the death of his ally, embarks on a killing spree, seeking to kill Turnus, whom Juno has lured from the battlefield with a phantom. Baulked of his prey, Aeneas instead kills first Mezentius' son Lausus and then Mezentius himself at the climax of his *aristeia*.

The different reactions of Turnus and Aeneas to the deaths of young warriors show Virgil both adhering to and diverging from his Homeric model.[47] Turnus seeks the combat with Pallas, challenging and attacking him, while Aeneas is attacked by Lausus and even tries to decline the duel; Turnus expresses a desire for Pallas' father Evander to witness his son's death, while Aeneas reacts with fatherly pity for Lausus and reflects on paternal love at his death; Turnus follows the Homeric script of vaunting over his dead enemy and stripping his corpse before returning Pallas' body to his father, while Aeneas eulogizes Lausus and sends his body back to his father unspoiled. When Turnus strips the prostrate Pallas of his baldric, he follows the model of Hector stripping Patroclus in *Iliad* 17. There, Zeus censures Hector's rash action, which dooms him to death at Achilles' hands in *Iliad* 22. Similarly, in *A.* 10, the epic narrator censures Turnus' inability 'to observe the limit' (10.502), and anticipates his regret for despoiling Pallas, an action which dooms him to death at Aeneas' hands in *A.* 12. Aeneas, by contrast, seeks to kill not the inexperienced Lausus but a more evenly matched foe, Lausus' father Mezentius.

A. 11 opens with a series of funerals for the war dead of the preceding book. Aeneas dedicates a monument to the gods in *pietas* for his defeat of Mezentius, an oak-trunk 'trophy' clad in the fallen warrior's arms. But it is Pallas' funeral that is most pressing, and an Achillean Aeneas dispatches his dead Patroclus back to Evander in Pallanteum, accompanied by an honour guard and rich offerings. Evander's reception of his son's body intertwines his own tragedy with demands for vengeance that inspire Aeneas' actions in the epic's final books. On the Italian side, Turnus' enemy Drances accepts the Trojan terms for truce to bury their dead, extolling Aeneas' prowess in war and justice, and hinting that many Italians still hope for alliance with the Trojans. Drances also plays a leading role in the second movement of the book, the Italian debate, which opens with the report of an embassy (dispatched in *A.* 8) to Aeneas' old enemy Diomedes, now resettled in Italy and unwilling to fight the Trojans again. King Latinus seizes the opportunity to renew his proposal for an alliance with the Trojans, by settling them on Etruscan land and inviting them to build a city there, and Drances supports Latinus, urging him to seal the alliance with the dynastic marriage of his daughter to Aeneas. Out of hatred for Turnus, Drances reviles him for endangering Italian lives and goads him to face Aeneas in single combat. In his abuse of Turnus, Drances acts the part of Thersites abusing Agamemnon in *Iliad* 2, but his specific argument (supporting Lavinia's marriage to Aeneas) recalls Antenor's proposal in *Iliad* 7 that Paris return Helen to Menelaus, and characterizes Turnus as a Trojan bride-thief. Turnus' passionate defence of the war, and of his Achillean heroism, are cut short by the Trojans' renewal of battle, and the debate ends with Turnus' rushing out to meet his ally Camilla, whose *aristeia* and death constitute the final episode of the book.[48]

Camilla has long been recognized as modelled on the Amazon Penthesileia, who, in the epic cycle's *Aethiopis*, joins the Trojan cause after Hector's burial. Introduced in the final position of the catalogue of Italians in *A.*7, Camilla leads the Volscian contingent of Turnus' army. Virgil represents her as the very essence of primitive Italy in her hardy upbringing. Dedicated by her exiled father to the goddess Diana, Camilla bears a name which marks her as the deity's 'attendant' (Varr. *Ling* 7.34). A huntress who shuns marriage and the traditional pursuits of women, she leads a band of Italian Amazons on the battlefield, but at the height of her *aristeia*, she falls to the Trojan warrior Arruns while 'she incautiously pursues' the Trojan priest Chloreus, 'ablaze with a feminine love of booty and spoils' (11.781–2). Her death confirms the gendered structure of epic warfare, explicitly thematized in the poem's second word, *uirum* (*OLD* s.v. 1): 'an adult male person (in expressed or implied contrast with a woman)'. The friction between Jupiter and Juno on the divine level symbolizes the gendered struggle between good and evil, order and chaos, that pervades the *Aeneid* and reappears in the opposition between Aeneas and Dido on the mythological level and Augustus and Cleopatra on the historical level (Ch. 4.2).[49] Camilla dies, however, every inch the Iliadic warrior (11.828–31): 'then, chilled, she was released little by little from her body and, abandoning her weapons, laid down her neck slowly and her head was seized by death; with a groan her life fled, protesting, to the shades'. The last line echoes the deaths of both Patroclus and Hector in the *Iliad* (16.856–7 = 22.362–3): 'and his soul, flying from the limbs, went to Hades lamenting his fate, leaving behind manhood and youth'.

A. 12 opens in the expectation of the climactic duel between the Trojan and Italian heroes, but delay after delay intervenes. At the beginning of the book, Turnus is compared to a Punic lion recruiting his strength for battle after suffering a chest wound (12.4–9). Homer frequently uses lion similes of his warriors, and Virgil takes his primary model from *Iliad* 20, where Achilles is compared to a lion wounded by hunters as he faces Aeneas on the battlefield. He unites this simile with an earlier Homeric simile applied to Patroclus, closing on the hero Kebriones 'with the pounce of a lion who has been struck in his chest while ravaging the pastures, and his own might destroys him' (*Il.* 16.752–3), in a combat that leads directly into his fatal engagement with Hector. Virgil's conflation of the two Homeric similes characterizes Turnus as simultaneously an Italian Achilles (about to face the Trojan warrior Aeneas) and his doomed friend Patroclus. But both the Punic setting and the chest wound ominously recall Dido, for Turnus' wound is apparently erotic, provoked by the possibility of losing Lavinia (12.70): 'love troubles him and he fixes his eyes on the maiden' Lavinia.[50]

Disdaining deferral of his duel with Aeneas, Turnus declares 'there's no delay' in him (12.11), and agrees to face Aeneas in single combat for the right to marry Lavinia. 'He burns for arms' (12.71), but the compact is broken and a general mêlée breaks out. Turnus wreaks havoc on the sidelines while Aeneas marshals his troops to assault Latinus' city, and this assault causes Amata to kill herself, in the belief that Turnus is already dead. Her chosen method of hanging is characteristic of the shameful death commonly chosen by women in Greek tragedy.[51] The tragic resonance of her death, and its motivation by love, closely recall Dido's demise in *A*. 4: like Dido, Amata is a queen (12.54; cf. 4.1), unlucky (12.598; cf. 1.749, 4.450, 596), bent on death (12.602; cf. 4.308, 415, 519, 604) and driven by sad passion (12.601; cf. 4.91, 101, 433, 501, 697). In Amata's death, as in Dido's, Virgil foreshadows the fall of the queen's city (12.593–4).

When a messenger reports the city's danger to Turnus, he returns to fight with Aeneas before their assembled armies in the poem's final scene. As the two heroes meet, Virgil characterizes them in two contrasting similes, the first describing Turnus plunging down a mountain like a landslide (12.684–90) and the second comparing Aeneas to the upward thrust of a mountain (12.701–3). Virgil thereby anticipates Aeneas' victory in the contest: 'The plunging rock (Turnus) which leaves a downward path of destruction is contrasted with the majestic power of the enduring mountains (Aeneas) ... darkness with light, falling with rising, defeat with victory, "barbarian" with "Roman," wild violence with cosmic order.'[52] As they launch their attacks, Virgil compares them to bulls fighting over a heifer, adapting a description from *G*. 3, which draws on a brief bull simile from Apollonius of Rhodes; in *A*. 12, Virgil has restored georgic reality to its literary origins in epic simile.[53]

The combat ends where Virgil's Homeric architecture necessarily demands, with the vanquished warrior begging the victor for his life. Wounded in the thigh, Turnus acknowledges Aeneas' victory (12.930–2). His suppliant posture, however, belies his words, as he immediately pleads for his life (12.932–6): 'if any love for a wretched parent can touch you, I beg you (and such was your father Anchises), take pity on Daunus' old age and return me, or if you prefer my corpse, to my people'. In the *Iliad*, there are no instances of successful supplication on the battlefield: at the height of his *aristeia* in *Iliad* 21, Achilles memorably declines to spare the life of the Trojan prince Lycaon, while in the aftermath of striking Hector's deathblow in *Iliad* 22 he savagely denies him even the burial for which he begs. The Homeric intertext that makes Aeneas an Achilles 'redivivus' requires him to kill Turnus. But Turnus' appeal to Aeneas' love for his father Anchises activates another Homeric intertext that complicates the morality of his inevitable death at Aeneas' hands – Priam's supplication of Achilles for the ransom of Hector's body in *Iliad* 24, which succeeds precisely through the Trojan king's appeal to the Greek warrior's love of his father (*Il.* 24.486–7, 503–4). Turnus' appeal to Aeneas' memory of Anchises has also reminded many readers of Aeneas' last conversation with his father in the underworld, where Anchises instructed his son (6.852–3) 'to impose habit on peace, spare the conquered and battle down the proud'. But Aeneas, provoked by the sight of Pallas' baldric on Turnus' prostrate form, acts on the model of Achilles. The epic ends with the flight of Turnus' soul, 'groaning', to the shades (*A.* 12.952), in a line that repeats the death of Camilla and its echo of those of Patroclus and Hector in the *Iliad*.

4.2 *History and Politics*

Homer's epics were the central documents of Greek culture and education (*paideia*), and enjoyed pride of place in the instruction of the history and values of Hellenism throughout the ancient world. Homer was even regarded as the source of all literary genres, including prose forms. Virgil's ambitious synthesis of the Homeric epics lays claim to the same cultural aspirations for the Latin-speaking world. In this he follows the model of Ennius, the first hexameter Latin epicist at Rome, whose *Annales* (completed in 18 books by the time of his death in 169 BCE) constituted an important engagement with the Homeric tradition.[54] In his epic treatment of Roman legend and history from the city's foundation by Aeneas down to the wars of his own day, Ennius united Roman tradition with Greek universal history in a synthesis that put Rome, formerly peripheral to the currents of Greek history and culture, at the centre of Mediterranean history, philosophy and literature.[55] Early in the *Aeneid*, Virgil seems to reflect on Ennius' project in Aeneas' response to Venus' account of Dido's history (1.372–4): 'O goddess, if, by going back to the very beginning, I press on and you have time to hear the chronicle (*annales*) of our troubles, the evening star will sooner close the sky and lay the day to sleep'. In Virgil's tendentious framing, Ennius' epic manner is obliquely invoked as formless historical chronicle rather than artistically shaped epic, and Venus emphatically rejects Aeneas' invitation, cutting him off mid-stream to send him on to Carthage (1.385–6). Their exchange provides crucial insight into Virgil's aims and methods in the inclusion of historical material in his epic.

The narrative of the *Aeneid* reveals a sustained interest not only in the details of Trojan myth and its resonances in Greek literature but also in Roman history, which is evoked in portents and prophecies, intertextual allusions and descriptions of artworks. Unlike a chronicle, Virgil's epic begins *in medias res*, with Aeneas on the high seas between Troy and Latium and at the mercy of the elements in the storm that carries his ships off course to Carthage. In the first simile of the poem soon after, Virgil compares Neptune quelling the waves to a Roman politician calming a frenzied mob (1.148–52): 'and just as when often trouble has come up in a large group, and the common crowd rages in their temper; now torches and rocks fly, madness supports their arms; then, if perhaps they've caught sight of a man important for his good deeds, they fall silent and stand with their ears ready'. Virgil casts this politician in idealizing Roman mould, as a man who can diffuse civil unrest (1.153): 'he directs their minds with his words and soothes their breasts'. Two such men appear in the immediate aftermath of the storm. The first is Aeneas, who cheers his shipwrecked comrades with a speech specifically designed to 'soothe their grieving breasts' (1.197). The second is his distant descendant Augustus, whom Jupiter evokes in his own soothing speech to Venus after the storm, promising that Aeneas' progeny will one day preside over a golden age of peace (1.291–5): 'then harsh generations will lay war aside and grow mild . . . the dread gates of war will be shut with tight bars of iron; impious Madness seated inside on his savage weapons, bound with a hundred bronze knots behind his back, will rage wildly with bloody mouth'. The detail of the closed gates of war reinforces the identification of Aeneas' descendant as Augustus, for Livy reports that only three men had shut them (1.19): Numa (*c.* 710 BCE), T. Manlius (241 BCE) and Augustus (29 BCE).

In his prophecy, Jupiter confirms that 'the fate of [Venus'] descendants remains unchanged' (1.257–8), and that his daughter 'will see the city and promised walls of Lavinium, and carry great-souled Aeneas aloft to the stars of heaven' (1.258–60). Jupiter fashions himself an annalist in his promise to 'unroll the secret records of fate' (1.262), but although he proceeds in chronological order from Aeneas to Augustus, he offers a highly curated account of the Roman future.[56] First, he explains, Aeneas will rule for three years after the war in Italy, before rule passes to his son Ascanius, whose byname 'Ilus' (derived from Ilium, another name for Troy) the god changes to 'Iulus', thereby aligning the Trojans with the 'Iulius' (Julius) family of Alba Longa, which Ascanius will found. There Hector's compatriots will rule for three hundred years 'until the royal priestess Ilia, pregnant by Mars, will bear twin offspring' (1.273–4). Jupiter thus arrives at the foundation story of Romulus, who traditionally establishes Rome in 753 BCE. At the centre of his speech, the god promises that the Romans will enjoy 'power without end' (1.279), and he assures Venus that Juno too will be reconciled with these future 'masters of the universe' (1.282). Under her descendants' rule, dominion will pass from Asia, through Greece, to Rome, and she will see the worldwide fame of the Trojan 'Julius Caesar, his name derived from great Iulus' (1.286–8). Thus, in his own carefully scripted *annales*, Jupiter focuses on the key personalities and temporalities of Roman history from the perspective of the Julian family: Aeneas, Ascanius, Romulus, Julius Caesar, Augustus.[57]

Jupiter's prophecy is amplified at the climax of Aeneas' katabasis in *A.* 6, when Anchises reveals to his son a select group of souls awaiting birth (Ch. 4.3) who will glorify Rome, and instructs him in their exploits in the annalistic 'Parade of Heroes'.[58] He begins with the Alban kings and Romulus, whose Julian descendants, especially Augustus, he eulogizes at the centre of his speech (6.792–4): 'This is the man, this is he whom you so often hear is promised to you, Augustus Caesar, son of a god, who will again establish a golden age for Latium in the fields once ruled by Saturn'. Anchises cannot believe that Aeneas could disavow his mission after seeing such an inspirational sight (6.806–7): 'are we still hesitating to develop our manly worth by deeds, or does fear prevent us from settling in Ausonian land?' After this first climax, he reverts to chronological order and enumerates the kings of Rome who followed Romulus and the early leaders of the republic, before focusing out of order on two future leaders whose civil war will wreak universal havoc. Anchises identifies them as the father-in-law (6.830) and son-in-law (6.831), Caesar and Pompey, united by the marriage of the former's daughter Julia to the latter in 59 BCE, and he addresses them directly in his anguish at the prospect of their civil war (6.832–5): 'don't, children, don't let such great wars be natural to your hearts, nor turn strong forces against your fatherland's vitals; you first forbear, you who derive your lineage from Olympus; cast your weapons down, child of my blood!'

After this second emotional climax, Anchises enumerates a final series of republican heroes, even quoting Ennius' *Annales* (e.g. *A.* 6.846 = *Ann.* 363 Sk). This is the context of Anchises' famous statement of the Roman civilizing mission of peace (6.851–3, Ch. 4.1). But he cannot resist drawing his son's attention to one more hero, M. Claudius Marcellus, who in 222 BCE killed the commander of the Insubrian Gauls in personal combat and so won the *spolia opima*, spoils stripped from an enemy general (Livy 4.20).[59] Only once, at this very juncture, does Aeneas interrupt his father to inquire about an individual soul, who walks in the shadow of the triumphant Marcellus. Anchises identifies him sorrowfully as another Marcellus, the son of Augustus' sister Octavia and husband of his daughter Julia, who died at the age of 19 in 23 BCE. Virgil's portrait of this 'exceptional youth' (6.861) recalls the young heroes whose untimely deaths he commemorates in the Italian war (Ch. 4.1). In his depiction of Marcellus, Virgil most closely approaches the momentous events of his own day, as Anchises closes on a note of familial piety (6.882–6): 'alas, pitiable boy, if you breach your harsh destiny, you will be Marcellus. Let me scatter lilies, deep red flowers, with full hands; let me at least present my heir's soul with these gifts, and discharge an empty rite'. The scene concludes with Anchises instructing his son, now 'fired by love for the glory to come', in the details of the wars he will face in Italy (6.889). Anchises offers fuller insight into Roman history than Jupiter, broadening it well beyond the family of Julius Caesar and complicating the tenor of the nation's history to include both imperial expansion and internecine civil war. Although framed as genealogical protreptic in chronicle form, Anchises' speech repeatedly strays from strict chronology to present Roman history as a series of emotional tableaux that bear the moral weight of exemplarity for both his internal and external audiences.

Aeneas' shield constitutes Virgil's final historical set-piece in the epic (8.625–731), and here the poet eschews annalistic presentation altogether in conscious emulation of Homer (Ch. 4.1).[60] Vulcan is 'well versed in prophecy' (8.627), and we are invited to compare his manufacture of the shield to the prophecies of Jupiter and Anchises, in the presentation of 'Italian history and the Romans' triumphs' (8.626). At the centre of the shield, Vulcan (like Jupiter and Anchises before him) glorifies Augustus, whom he depicts leading the Italians to victory at the Battle of Actium over Antony and Cleopatra. Like the episodes of early Roman history depicted on the shield, the battle is drawn as a confrontation between the forces of good and evil: with Augustus Caesar stand the senators and Roman people, household and state gods, while 'his father's star' (*patrium sidus*, 8.681) shines above his head; with Antony and his Egyptian wife come barbarian wealth, oriental polyglot troops[61] and the bestial gods of Egypt. The contrast between good and evil portrayed on the shield recalls that in the account of Hercules' confrontation with Cacus (Greek *kakos*, 'bad, evil') reported by Evander (Greek *eu-anêr*, 'good man') earlier in the book: Jupiter and his son Hercules, Evander, Pallas and the Arcadians represent the cosmic order, which supports Venus, Aeneas and the Trojans; they are pitted against the forces of cosmic disorder, led by Juno and the chthonic gods (Aeolus, Allecto), Cacus and history's losers (Dido, Cleopatra, Turnus, Mezentius,

Camilla). The parallels between Hercules, Aeneas and Augustus are reinforced by the synchronicity of Aeneas' arrival in Pallanteum on the very day commemorating Hercules' arrival in Latium, defeat of Cacus and establishment of the *ara maxima*, which provided the aetion for the annual celebration on 12 August of his festival, and Augustus' arrival at Rome on 12 August 29 BCE and celebration of his triple triumph the next day. Considerable irony and unresolved tension remain, however, in Vulcan's paradoxical position as father of the monster Cacus, cuckolded husband of Venus and artisan of her son's shield.

The most notorious scandal of Virgil's historical imagination appears in his anachronistic introduction in *A.* 1 of Carthage, which was traditionally founded in 814/13 BCE, 370 years after the fall of Troy (1184 BCE) and 364 years after Aeneas' arrival on Dido's shores (1178 BCE).[62] Venus tells her son he 'will see huge walls and the rising citadel of new Carthage' (1.365–6), in a formulation that underlines the etymology of the name Carthago, which Servius reports meant 'new city' in Punic. Aeneas 'admires the massive towers, once Punic huts; he admires the gates, the noise and the paved streets' (1.421–2). His admiration is especially excited by the Carthaginians' zeal in their work (1.423–6), which offers a model for Aeneas' own ktistic ambitions. Their buildings and construction techniques are distinctively Greco-Roman (1.427–9): 'here some dig out a port, here others place the deep foundations of a theatre, and quarry huge columns from the rocks, suitable decoration for the future stage'. Even the decoration of the great temple to Juno is incongruously Greco-Roman in its focus on the Trojan war (1.456–7): 'he sees Iliadic (*Iliacas*) battles in order and wars now bruited abroad throughout the whole world'.

Aeneas' disastrous sojourn in Dido's city provides the aetiology for the century of 'Punic' wars fought between Rome and Carthage (264–241, 218–201, 149–146 BCE). When Aeneas abandons Dido, she invokes Juno, Hecate and the 'Dread Goddesses' to avenge her death and demands that her Tyrians (4.622–4) 'incite your descendants and the whole future lineage with hatred, and send this tribute to our ashes. Let there be no love nor compacts between our peoples'. She calls for 'some avenger' to 'rise from her bones and harry the Dardanian colonists with fire and sword, now, hereafter, at whatever time the opportunity will present itself' (4.625–7). The unnamed avenger is Hannibal, the brilliant Carthaginian general of the Second Punic War: Dido's curse underwrites the century of wars between the two Mediterranean powers (4.628–9).

From another perspective, however, Virgil's treatment of Aeneas' dalliance with Dido and the building projects he oversees in Carthage evoke the more recent history of Roman dynasts in Egypt. After the wedding in the cave, a rumour circulates that the pair 'keep the long winter warm together in luxury, forgetting their kingdoms and enthralled by shameless passion' (4.193–4). This prompts the Libyan king Iarbas, whose advances Dido had earlier rejected, to complain to Jupiter that 'an infamous Paris with his eunuch retinue, having tied a Lydian turban on his chin and pomaded hair, has taken possession of [Iarbas' own] booty'. Dido's treasure is reminiscent of Egypt's wealth in Virgil's day, while the pair's immoral indulgence in lust and luxury evokes Caesar's stay in Egypt after the Alexandrian war (48–47 BCE), when he confirmed Cleopatra on the throne and they became lovers. Even more striking is the implication that Aeneas and Dido have abandoned themselves to the extravagance and self-indulgence for which Antony and Cleopatra were notorious (Plut. *Ant.*). Worse still, when Jupiter dispatches Mercury to recall Aeneas to his mission, his messenger finds Aeneas building the wrong city (*A.* 4.259–61): Aeneas here assumes the profile of Antony, who after Philippi assigned to himself the administration of Egypt and the eastern provinces of the empire. Further immoral hedonism is visible in Aeneas' attire (4.261–4): 'His sword was starred with yellow jasper, and hanging from his shoulders glowed a cloak of Tyrian purple, gifts that wealthy Dido had made him'. Cicero in the *Philippics* denounces Caesar for wearing a purple toga and Antony for wearing a luxurious Greek cloak, while Florus reports Antony's immoral opulence in Egypt, where he wore a sceptre, scimitar and a purple cloak encrusted with precious stones. Aeneas' dependence on Dido and enjoyment of her wealth earn

Mercury's contempt, vividly seen in the god's application to him of the epithet *uxorius* (4.266), 'belonging to a wife', which recalls Octavian's propaganda that Antony was 'enslaved to a woman' (Dio Cass. 50.26.5). The god's epiphany recalls Aeneas to his mission, but there is no reprieve for Dido, who in death looks very like Cleopatra on the shield of Aeneas (8.707–10): 'the fire-god had depicted [the Egyptian queen] amidst the slaughter, pale with approaching death'. Virgil portrays the Carthaginian queen at the moment of her death in similar terms (4.642–5): 'but Dido, trembling and wild in her awful purpose, rolling bloodshot eyes, with her quivering cheeks stained with spots of blood, and pale with approaching death, burst into the innermost court of her palace'.

The historical and political resonances of Dido's Carthage in the first half of the *Aeneid* are balanced in the second half by those of the Italian war, which rehearses both the historical conquest of the Italian peninsula by Rome, culminating in the enfranchisement of the Italians after the 'allied war' of 91–87 BCE, and the century of Roman civil wars from the Gracchi to the Battle of Actium (133–32 BCE), ending in Augustus' promise of peace throughout the empire (*pax Augusta*).[63] In his prophecy, Jupiter reassures Venus of Trojan conquest in Italy (1.263–5: 'Aeneas will wage a huge war in Italy, crush savage peoples, impose institutions on the men and build walls, until a third summer has seen him rule in Latium') and he later recalls Venus' assurance that her son 'would be the kind of man to rule Italy, a land great with opportunities for power and savage in war' (4.229–30).

More prominent in Virgil's narrative are suggestions of civil war in the Italian war. There are indications that the Latins are already divided amongst themselves. Latinus displays in his palace statues of ancestral kings 'who suffered martial wounds, fighting for their fatherland' (7.181), along with 'many weapons on his doorposts' (7.182), where 'captive chariots and curved axes hang, helmets and huge door-bolts, arrows, shields, and prows seized from ships' (7.184–6). They have long practised the custom of opening the gates of war to initiate battle (7.607, 611–14). But the war between Trojans and Italians is also proleptically cast as civil war. Juno frames the war between the two peoples as a conflict between marital relations (7.317–19): 'let son-in-law and father-in-law come together at this price for their own peoples: you will be dowered, maiden, in Trojan and Rutulian blood, and the war goddess Bellona awaits you as your maid of honour'. The phrase 'son-in-law and father-in-law' evokes the relationship of Pompey and Caesar in an image of the civil wars that ended the republic, while the verb Juno uses for their bloody union normally indicates meeting in war (*OLD* s.v. *coeo* 1) rather than forming an alliance (ibid. 10). She invites Allecto's aid precisely because the Fury 'can bring like-minded brothers to war under arms and overwhelm houses with hatred' (7.335–6), and Allecto claims signal success in the enterprise (7.545): 'look, your civil dissension (*discordia*) has been sealed in savage war'. The term *discordia* is key to Virgil's design of the Italian war, in relation to both its literary history (alluding to Ennius' characterization of the Second Punic War, *Ann.* 225 Sk.) and its political valence in contemporary rhetoric, where it connotes civil war.[64] The war Aeneas fights in Latium has elements of civil war because it is fought between two peoples destined to form one nation (*A.* 12.503–4). In order for the two warring peoples to unite, Jupiter must conciliate Juno in her guise as the Carthaginian goddess Tanit to the Trojan settlement in Italy. She concedes that the two peoples will be united but asks that the Trojan name die (12.821–4). Jupiter's confirmation of her conditions ends, on the divine plane, the anger that drives the epic plot (12.834–6).[65]

4.3 *Philosophy and Religion*

The *Aeneid* bears the imprint throughout its narrative of Virgil's lifelong study of philosophy. As in literary background and historical record, so in philosophical doctrine, the epic can be interpreted as an ambitious synthesis of traditions. The important relationship between religion and philosophy is urgently sounded at the outset, when the epic poet asks his Muse (1.11): 'does such great anger belong to heavenly minds?' The Epicurean answer is a resounding no (Lucr. *DRN* 1.44–9 = 2.646–51):

'the whole nature of the gods in and of itself ... is neither won by good deeds nor touched by anger'. Nor were the Epicureans alone in this view, as Cicero comments (*Off.* 3.102): 'this indeed is common to all the philosophers ... that god never gets angry and never does harm'. Homeric theology, in which anthropomorphic gods are driven by human emotions to act on partisan ambitions, was a scandal for all the ancient philosophical schools, and they expended as much energy in debating the ethics of Homer's characters as in discussing his politics and poetics.[66] Virgil too poses questions of philosophical and religious import throughout his epic, and tests answers proposed by the critical and cosmological traditions.[67]

Critics have often identified Jupiter with the providential god of the Stoics, especially in view of the Roman destiny he prophesies to Venus.[68] Virgil associates him from the outset with the 'end' (*finis*) or 'telos' of the epic action (1.223–4), and at the conclusion of the poem, the god asks Juno (12.793) 'what now will be the end, wife?' Virgil inherits the association of Jupiter with the goal of epic action from Homer, who asserts in the proem to the *Iliad* that the will of Zeus was 'fulfilled' (*eteleieto*) by Achilles' anger (*Il.* 1.5, Ch. 4.1). By the late republic, both Greek *telos* and Latin *finis* had become technical terms for the ethical 'goal' of philosophical doctrine: in 45 BCE, for example, Cicero composed a treatise 'On the ends of goods and evils' (*De finibus bonorum et malorum*) dealing with the question of the highest good and greatest evil. But Jupiter's Stoic credentials are difficult to maintain in the *Aeneid*: he is prey to partisan anxieties for the proto-Roman mission and repeatedly intervenes in the action to ensure the very destiny that he ostensibly underwrites, sending Mercury down in *A.* 1 to secure Dido's goodwill and again in *A.* 4 to remind Aeneas of his mission (Ch. 4.1). At the end of the epic, he dispatches a Fury-like *Dira* to prevent Juturna from further aiding her brother Turnus on the battlefield. Two *Dirae* make their home in the upper air, where they 'attend the throne of Jove, on the threshold of the savage king, and sharpen the fear of suffering mortals' (12.849–50). The noun *Dira* was etymologized in antiquity as meaning 'anger of god' (*ira deum*), an etymology that illuminates the Fury's purpose in this scene and returns us to the very question with which the epic opens. Virgil thus radically undermines the traditional theology of Homer even as he reanimates it.

Aeneas too has been interpreted in Stoic terms, as an exemplar of the Stoic wise man or his precursor, 'the man who makes progress in wisdom and virtue' (*prokoptôn*).[69] The Stoic sage disciplines his emotions, especially before the onslaughts of fate, though the *prokoptôn* may relapse in the struggle. Aeneas has been seen as the latter in *A.* 2, where his battle-lust repeatedly overwhelms his judgement; but when he suppresses his own grief in order to console his comrades in *A.* 1, he has been read as acting in accordance with Stoic principle (1.208–9, Ch. 4.1). He rehearses the same trajectory while marooned in Carthage, succumbing to lust and luxury before making the dutiful decision to leave Dido as a result of Mercury's epiphany, after which he remains impervious to her pleas (4.393–6). Stoic doctrine taught the importance of following gods' commands, but another setback, on Sicily, when the Trojan women fire the ships, requires the intervention of the elder Nautes to show Aeneas the Stoic path (5.709–10): 'wherever fate draws us in its ebb and flow, let us follow; whatever will happen, every fortune must be overcome by enduring it'. Seneca echoes this formulation in his famous statement of Stoic virtue (*Epist.* 107.11): 'fate leads the willing man, drags the unwilling'. Aeneas has the opportunity to demonstrate his moral progress early in *A.* 6, when he assures the Sibyl, 'no new or unexpected aspect of trouble can occur for me; I have anticipated and traversed all things beforehand in my mind' (6.103–5). Seneca quotes these lines as a statement of Stoic principle (*Epist.* 76.33), and Cicero specifies the verb 'anticipate' as a technical term of Stoic thought (*De off.* 1.80–1). Aeneas' Stoic profile, however, waxes and wanes in the course of the epic. His killing of Turnus at the end of the book is especially difficult to align with Stoic ethics, for he acts in the grip of a Junonian rage (12.945–7): 'after he drank in the sight of the memorial of savage grief, the spoils of Pallas, he blazed with fury, terrible in his anger'. Aeneas' rage is Iliadic in its Achillean intensity as he kills his 'Hector' (Ch. 4.1), but the thematic complex of memory, savagery, fury and burning rage that drives Aeneas to kill his suppliant enemy is consistently associated in the epic with Juno, whose 'mindful anger' drives the plot (Ch. 4.1).[70] All the passions, and especially anger, were viewed as problematic by the Stoics, and in his treatise 'On Anger', Seneca argues for its complete eradication (*De Ira* 1.5–8, 3.42).[71] Contemporary critics have therefore preferred to interpret Aeneas' rage according to Aristotle's or Philodemos' analyses of anger.[72]

If Aeneas cuts a quasi-Stoic figure in the epic, Dido assumes an Epicurean profile that begins positively but ends as a negative exemplum of the sect's principles. Her first words to the shipwrecked Trojans echo Lucretian cadences, as she grants them 'freedom to speak' (1.520) and allays their cares and fears (1.562). Her words counsel the Trojans in the goal of Epicurean psychology (Lucr. *DNR* 2.18–19), 'that the mind enjoy pleasant sensation, removed from care and fear'. If the regal interior of Dido's palace would never have won the approval of Lucretius, who denounces gold and silver ornamentation, coffered ceilings and the music of the cithara (*DRN* 2.24–8), her luxurious banquet, with its hospitality of wine, food and song, is an exemplary instance of the leisure activities of good kings according to Philodemos in his treatise 'On the Good King According to Homer', which explicitly addresses the question of royal parties.[73] Good order is maintained throughout the banquet in *A*. 1, the toasts succeeding the banquet in due succession, followed by Iopas' philosophical song (1.740–6),[74] and the varied conversation (1.748) approved by Philodemos (*Epigr.* 27 Sider).

This positive picture of Dido's Epicureanism swiftly recedes in *A*. 4. Virgil sounds a number of hints throughout the closing movement of the first book that foreshadow Dido's subsequently disastrous royal career. The unhappy queen fixates on Aeneas' young son and the gifts that the Trojan hero has brought her with a thoroughly un-Epicurean emotional engagement. Virgil's lexicon recalls Lucretius' diatribe against love: a grave illness inflames Dido as she gazes at Iulus (1.713), just as Lucretius describes the lover's breast 'blazing with dread desire' (*DRN* 4.1090) and explains lovers' inability to sate their desire by looking (*DRN* 4.1102) at their beloveds. Especially relevant is Lucretius' chilling account of the insidious progress of love-sickness (*DRN* 4.1068–9): 'for the wound lives and grows old by nourishing it and the passion increases every day and the trouble grows worse'. His lines supply the imagistic complex for Dido's passion in *A*. 4, where Virgil confirms Lucretius' Epicurean worldview by showing how Dido's rule is fatally undermined by love (1–5, quoted above, Ch. 4.1) and superstition (56–67), two of the chief causes of human misery according to Epicurean philosophy.[75]

Critics have been divided about how to reconcile the Epicurean portrait of Dido with the generally more favourable presentation of the sect's principles in Virgil's earlier poetry.[76] Like Aeneas' killing of Turnus at the end of the epic, the Dido episode has frequently been seen as a proving ground for competing ethical approaches to the epic.[77] Some scholars have argued that Dido and her Epicurean worldview are proved 'comprehensively wrong' in the epic,[78] while others have noted the Epicurean disdain with which Virgil consistently treats obsessive love (Ch. 2.3, 3.2). Pamela Gordon has also drawn attention to Dido's positive reception amongst imperial Roman philosophers, their favourable interpretation of her penultimate speech (*A*. 4.653: 'I have lived and accomplished the course that fortune granted') and suicide (Sen. *Vit. Beat.* 19; *Ben.* 5.17.5; *Epist.* 12.9).[79]

The philosophical centrepiece of the epic is to be found in *A*. 6, where Anchises instructs his son in an Orphic–Pythagorean–Platonic account of the purification and transmigration of souls in the bodies of his descendants. Aeneas and the Sibyl reach an 'Orphic' Elysium, where the first individual shade to emerge from the crowd of singers and musicians is Orpheus (6.645–6). Scholars have long seen Virgil working with the model of Orpheus' katabasis because Aeneas cites his precedent already in his conversation with the Sibyl (6.119–20). At the threshold of their descent, the Sibyl instructs 'the uninitiated to depart' (6.258), as in the ritual opening lines of our earliest Orphic theogony (frr. 1a, b, *PEG* 2.1, p.2 Bernabé; ibid. fr. 3): 'the doors are closed, the impure are excluded, and the theogony is addressed to initiates alone'.[80] The portentous lines marking Aeneas' entry into the underworld also carry an Orphic charge (6.264–7): 'gods, to whom belongs power over souls, silent shades, Chaos and Phlegethon, silent places of night, let it be right for me to reveal the mysteries, to disclose with your consent matters hidden deep in the darkness under the earth'.

As both musician and religious teacher, Orpheus belongs naturally to the company of the blessed shades in Elysium, who conventionally engage in music and dancing. But his presence also signals the importance of the mystery cult of Orphism to the scene that follows, and the surrounding lines sound a conventional Orphic emphasis on purity and purification, in references to the healing god Apollo's paean and laurel, along with 'chaste priests' (6.657–61).[81] In this company, Virgil includes Orpheus' traditional associate Musaeus, a poet and musician especially prominent in Orphic and Eleusinian literature and ritual, whose name marks him out as the founding priest of the cult of the Muses. He guides the Sibyl and Aeneas to Anchises, whom they find reviewing the souls of his descendants 'penned in' and awaiting rebirth in Elysium – a first, brief allusion to the Pythagorean doctrine of metempsychosis, or transmigration of souls. Virgil represents these souls as 'flitting' around the underworld river Lethe, 'just as when in the meadows bees in still summer settle on various flowers and swarm around white lilies, and the whole plain buzzes with their hum' (6.707–8). The simile is Homeric (*Il.* 2.87–90) and Apollonian (*Arg.* 1.879–82), but the imagery also draws on the classical association of bees with poets and poetry, as well as on Plato's representation of 'winged' souls 'travelling through the air' (*Phaedr.* 246c) and the Orphic conception of bees as oracular (*Orph.* fr. 749 Bernabé). These are the souls, Anchises explains, that will be reincarnated after they undergo purification by drinking from Lethe.

When Aeneas asks why 'the wretches feel such dread desire for the light' (6.721), Anchises expounds a detailed cosmology and anthropology that mingles elements of Stoic, Orphic and Platonic doctrine in Lucretius' Epicurean lexicon. The cosmology is Stoic (6.724–7): 'First breath within nourishes sky and lands and liquid plains, the shining globe of the moon and Titan stars; and mind, infused through the limbs, moves the whole mass and mingles in the great body of the universe'.

'Breath' and 'mind' are synonyms for the Stoic 'world soul', present in all living beings, whose seeds exhibit the 'fiery character' (6.730) of Stoic doctrine, at least to the extent that earthen flesh and mortal limbs allow, 'closed within darkness and the blind prison' of the body (6.734). In his emphasis on the body clogging and dulling our celestial seeds, Anchises turns away from Stoicism to Plato, who attributes impurity and defilement to the soul from contact with the 'guilty' body (6.731), and thence to Orphism, which prescribes penalties of wind, water and fire after death for misdeeds in life.

Anchises concludes his eschatology with the Orphic–Pythagorean cycle of reincarnation–metempsychosis (6.745–7), 'the long interval, with the cycle of time completed, [that] has removed the engrafted stain and leaves pure the ethereal sense and breath of elemental fire'. Anchises even prescribes the length of time required to purify the souls before they can return to bodily form (6.748–9): 'all of these souls, when the cycle has revolved through a thousand years, god summons in a great rank to the river Lethe'. In the myth of Er, Plato stipulates the interval as a thousand years and specifies that the souls drink from the 'forgetful river' before they return to earth (*Rep.* 10.615b, 621a). His picture of the immortality of the soul was rendered into Latin by Cicero, who himself claimed allegiance to Plato's philosophical school, in the *Somnium Scipionis* ('Scipio's Dream'), an important source for Virgil's union of eschatology and commemoration of great statesmen.[82] This model is confirmed by the return of Platonic imagery, after the intervening Parade of Heroes (Ch. 4.2), in Virgil's depiction of Anchises, Aeneas and the Sibyl 'wander[ing] around the whole region in the broad fields of air and survey[ing] everything' (6.886–7). Scholars have interpreted 'the broad fields of air' as a reference to the souls' ascent to the moon, where they enjoy 'astral immortality', 'a complicated nexus of beliefs, attested from the fifth century BCE ... belonging to the Platonic tradition'.[83]

The intricate philosophical genealogy of Virgil's underworld may help to explain the peculiar passage of Aeneas and the Sibyl from the underworld (*A.* 6.893–8):[84] 'there are twin gates of dreams, of which one is said to be horn, from which is granted an easy exit for true shades; the other gleams with shining ivory, but the shades of the dead send false dreams to heaven. With these words, then, Anchises there accompanies his son together with the Sibyl, and sends them from the ivory gate'. In the *Odyssey* (19.560–9), Penelope describes 'two gates through which insubstantial dreams pass', one of polished horn, through which pass dreams that 'accomplish the truth', and the other of sawn ivory, through which pass dreams that 'cheat with empty hopes'. The Homeric model implies that Aeneas' katabasis is an insubstantial dream vision of the afterlife and the souls he sees there, including the parade of heroes, though the antiquity of the epic tradition lends mystery and gravity to the Virgilian hero's dream-journey. In the *Somnium Scipionis*, Cicero grapples with a similar disjunction between the Platonic source of Scipio's dream vision in the myth of Er, which awards immortality to the soul of the man who has cultivated virtue (rather than power or glory) in life, and his own fervently held view, as a leading Roman statesman, that national saviours, culture-heroes, rulers and statesmen are most deserving of immortality of the soul. By clothing Aeneas' Homeric katabasis in the fabric of Cicero's Platonic eschatology, Virgil imbues epic tradition with philosophical significance. Aeneas, however, apparently remembers nothing of what he sees in the underworld (despite Anchises' protreptic purpose), just as he fails to understand the images of 'the fame and fate of his descendants' engraved by Vulcan on his shield (8.731).[85] Servius comments that Virgil intended his gates of sleep to signify 'all that he said should be understood as false', but Virgil's late antique and Christian readership preferred to interpret Aeneas' katabasis through the lens of Cicero's Platonic *Somnium Scipionis* and to see in it not only the history of Roman power but also the philosophical revelation of religious truth.

Reception

Virgil's first poetry collection made him famous and his works have never since gone out of fashion.[1] His friend and contemporary Horace (Ch. 1) celebrates him as a favourite of the rural muses for his 'tender and elegant [bucolic] verse' (*Sat.* 1.10.44–5). Individual eclogues were performed on stage as mimes or pantomimes, and the poet himself recited the *Georgics*, with the assistance of his friend and patron Maecenas, to the future emperor Augustus in the first performance of his didactic poem (Ch. 1). Yet, according to Donatus (*VSD* 43–6), Virgil never lacked critics. His *Bucolics* were mocked by a certain Numitorius, in a two-poem work that circulated under the title 'Antibucolica' (*VSD* 43), and when Virgil, at a public recitation of his *Georgics* (*VSD* 43), began the line 'naked plough, sow naked . . .' (Ch. 3.1) someone in the audience quipped 'you'll catch a fever from the cold', impugning the poet's verse as 'frigid', a term of disapprobation in ancient literary criticism.[2] Nonetheless, both works entered the school curriculum in the poet's own lifetime, when the grammarian Q. Caecilius Epirota, after the death of their mutual friend Gallus (*c.* 26 BCE), established a select school and inaugurated the practice of reading Virgil 'and the other new poets' (Suet. *Gram.* 16).

Virgil's deathbed expression of a desire to burn his unfinished *Aeneid* (*VSD* 39–41) was also widely known.[3] Ovid in his exile poetry claims to have fed his unfinished *Metamorphoses* to the flames (*Tr.* 1.7, 4.10.61–2), while the elder Pliny (*HN* 7.114) and Gellius (*NA* 17.10.7) both attribute Virgil's deathbed disavowal of the *Aeneid* to his modesty (cf. *VSD* 11). The posthumously published poem was immediately recognized as a classic of Latin poetry, and Virgil as the Roman Homer. Even before his death, Propertius had hailed the poem as 'greater than the *Iliad*' (Ch. 1), and the elegies of his fourth and final book are in constant dialogue with Virgil's epic, to which he probably had pre-publication access through his relationship with Maecenas (his patron, as well as Virgil's and Horace's). Tibullus too, in his elegy 2.5 (composed in the 20s BCE, but published after his death in 19), offers sustained reflection on Virgil's epic achievement in his own treatment of the myth of Aeneas. Horace and Ovid also repeatedly allude to Virgil's epic, Horace at least as early as 23 BCE when he published his three-book collection of *Odes*, in which he addresses a poem to Virgil embarking on a sea-journey (1.3), probably a metaphor for his composition of Homeric epic.[4] Ovid begins a career of Virgilian allusion in the opening line of the first poem of his earliest collection of poetry (*Am.* 1.1.1: 'arms in heavy measure [*arma graui numero*] and violent wars I was preparing to publish'), which recasts the *incipit* of the *Aeneid* (1.1, quoted Ch. 4). Over a century later, Quintilian quotes Domitius Afer's assessment of Virgil's accomplishment as second only to that of Homer in all of classical literature, 'and closer to first place than to third' (*Inst. Or.* 10.1.86).

Not even the *Aeneid*, however, was immune from criticism (*VSD* 44): to Carvilius Pictor, Donatus attributes an 'Aeneomastix' ('scourge of Aeneas/*Aeneid*'); to Herennius, a collection of Virgil's literary 'faults'; and to Perellius Fausta, a collection of his 'thefts'. Q. Octavius Avitus too, he reports, produced an eight-volume work in Greek, entitled *Likenesses*, that documented Virgil's literary 'thefts' and quoted their sources (*VSD* 45). In response to these and other critics, Asconius Pedianus (*c.* 9 BCE– *c.* 76 CE) authored a work 'Against the Detractors of Virgil', in which he collected some of the charges dealing with history and the borrowings from Homer, and it is to him that we owe Virgil's riposte to the charge of Homeric plagiarism (*VSD* 46): 'Why do those critics not try the same thefts too? But they would understand that it's easier to steal Hercules' club than a line of Homer'.

Virgil's critics, however, were vastly outnumbered by his admirers. His first two poetry collections entered the school canon while he was still alive, and the *Aeneid* was already being imitated by contemporary poets while he was still composing it. Quotations of his poetry in graffiti at Pompeii confirm the widespread circulation of his verse among all social registers in the first century after his death.[5] His epic themes were also taken up in both the public and private visual and plastic arts soon after his death. The Augustan 'altar of peace' (dedicated 9 BCE) features Aeneas on a panel corresponding to that of Romulus, and its imagery has been connected to the fourth eclogue and the *Aeneid*.[6] The Augustan forum (dedicated 2 BCE) included facing hemicycles with matching statue groups of Aeneas leaving Troy with Anchises and Ascanius and Romulus carrying the *spolia opima* respectively, and contained complementary statuary programmes in the facing porticoes where members of the Julian family and Alban kings stood on the north and the 'greatest men' of the Roman republic on the south, in an arrangement indebted to the parade of heroes in *A*. 6. Among the frescoes recovered from Pompeii (preserved by the eruption of Vesuvius in 79 CE) are paintings of the death of Laocoon, Aeneas rescuing his father and son from the sack of Troy (even parodied, in figures bearing monkey's heads and tails), Dido and Aeneas, and the wounded Aeneas being healed.[7] Virgil's literary career even became a defining model for later poets, as he rose in a poetic *cursus honorum* from humble bucolic through more elevated didactic to the summit of martial epic.[8]

The reign of Nero (54–68 CE), last of the Julio-Claudian emperors, was an especially rich period of literary experimentation that witnessed prolific composition across all of the verse forms that Virgil essayed and extensive allusion to his poetry throughout the entire range of literary texts, both prose and verse. The *Bucolica* inspired a particular vogue for pastoral poetry in this period, with seven in the Virgilian manner ascribed to the shadowy figure of Calpurnius Siculus. As in Virgil's collection (Ch. 2.2), there is praise for a young saviour-prince (Nero) who will renew the golden age at Rome, reference to a comet (that of 54 CE, 1.77–83), a singer Corydon (*B*. 1, 4, 7), and his patron Meliboeus (*B*. 1, 4). From early in the reign of Nero also come two 'Einsiedeln' eclogues, so named from their discovery in a tenth-century manuscript at

Einsiedeln in Switzerland, which praise Nero (in the first) and announce the restoration of a golden age (in the second). The same manuscript that preserves Calpurnius' bucolics includes another four by a late third-century CE author Nemesianus, who enriches his Virgilian themes with an admixture of Calpurnian elements.[9] Of particular interest in all three authors is the prominence of ruler panegyric and the influence of the 'Messianic' fourth eclogue, the latter already renowned well before Christianity became the official religion of the Roman empire.[10]

Virgil's *Georgics* initiated an even earlier, and longer sustained, vogue than his *Bucolics*, for they inspired three didactic poems during the Augustan age alone: Ovid's elegiac 'Art of love' (*Ars amatoria*, *c.* 2–1 BCE) and 'Cures for love' (*Remedia amoris*, *c.* 2 CE); his friend Grattius' hexameter didactic poem 'On hunting' (*Cynegetica*, mentioned by Ovid in *Pont.* 4.16.34); and the late Augustan/early Tiberian Manilius' 'On Astronomy' (*Astronomica*), a hexameter work in the didactic mode with a strong Stoic disposition. Three later classical Latin didactic poems bear the stamp of continuing Virgilian influence, two datable to the Neronian period. The single-book *Aetna*, on volcanic phenomena, was actually attributed to Virgil in antiquity (though Donatus reports scepticism about the attribution, *VSD* 19), and must have been composed before 62 CE when a powerful earthquake struck in the region of Vesuvius (dismissed by the author as 'now cooled for many years', 431–2), precursor to its eruption of 79. Another Neronian author of Virgilian didactic is Columella, who derived his title and the (mostly) prose form of his twelve-book *De re rustica* (60–5 CE) from the Latin republican prose tradition of agricultural treatises (esp. Varro, Ch. 3.1), but who composed his tenth book 'On the cultivation of gardens' (*De cultu hortorum*) in hexameters, in homage to Virgil, who passes over the subject of gardens in *G.* 4. A final specimen of Virgilian didactic comes from Nemesianus (the author of four bucolic poems mentioned above), whose *Cynegetica* takes its title and theme from Grattius but far outstrips its model in Virgilian style.[11]

It was the *Aeneid*, however, that dominated both the Roman educational curriculum and imperial Latin literature. Virgil's masterpiece initiated the efflorescence of historical and mythological epic by the greatest poets of imperial Rome. Ovid's *Metamorphoses* (8 CE), his only hexameter poem, has long been recognized as inspired by Virgil's union of the mythological tradition with universal history; Ovid even retells Aeneas' travels and wars after the fall of Troy in *Met.* 13–14. Ovid's twelve-book calendar poem *Fasti* (unfinished in six books at his death in 17 CE) also addresses questions of Roman history and religion indebted to Virgil. The Neronian period in particular ushers in widespread renewal of grand epic in the Virgilian manner: Petronius (*c.* 27–65 CE) included a 'civil war' epic sketch of 295 lines in his *Satyrica*,[12] while Seneca's nephew Lucan (39–65 CE) wrote a full-blown, though unfinished (in ten books), historical epic *Bellum Ciuile* on the civil war between Caesar and Pompey. Both works were presumably put into circulation after 65, when their authors were forced to commit suicide by Nero. In the Flavian period (69–96 CE), epic remained a popular verse form in the hands of C. Valerius Flaccus (died *c.* 90 CE), who wrote an unfinished (in eight books) *Argonautica*; P. Papinius Statius (*c.* 45–*c.* 96 CE), who wrote a twelve-book *Thebaid* and an unfinished (in one and a half books) *Achilleid*; and Ti. Catius Asconius Silius Italicus (*c.* 28–*c.* 103 CE), who wrote a historical epic *Punica*, on the theme of the Second Punic War, in seventeen books.[13]

Nor was the study of Virgil restricted to poets and students in the classical period: the elder Seneca (*c.* 50 BCE–40 CE) cites him more frequently than any other Latin poet in his two collections of early imperial Roman declamation, *Controuersiae* and *Suasoriae*, while his son, the philosopher of the same name (*c.* 4 BCE–66 CE), reveals his familiarity with Virgilian poetry on every page of his works, which span the genres of philosophical epistle and dialogue, tragedy and epigram. Like his father, the younger Seneca quotes Virgil more often than any other Latin poet in his prose works, while his tragedy *Thyestes* overlays its mythological subject with a contemporary historical urgency that owes a great deal to the model of the *Aeneid*. Even the family freedman L. Annaeus Cornutus (*fl.* 60 CE), a Stoic grammarian, wrote commentaries (now lost) on Virgil's poetry, which Gellius censured for their criticism of the poet's lexical choices and literary decorum. It is in the Neronian period too that the tradition of scholarly exegesis on Virgil's works gains momentum: especially important was the grammarian M. Valerius Probus (*c.* 25–105 CE),[14] whose annotations on Virgil supplied material that Hadrian's imperial secretary C. Suetonius Tranquillus (*c.* 69–126 CE) included in his biography of the poet in his *Lives* 'Of Illustrious Men' (Ch. 1). Quintilian (M. Fabius Quintilianus, *c.* 35–*c.* 100 CE), the first holder of the chair of Roman rhetoric endowed by the Flavian emperor Vespasian, also quotes extensively from Virgil's poetry in his 'Education of the Orator' (*Institutio oratoria*), on the theory and practice of rhetoric, to illustrate exemplary rhetorical technique. The greatest prose stylist of imperial Rome, the historian Cornelius Tacitus (*c.* 56–*c.* 120 CE), has also been shown to shape his accounts of the reigns of the Julio-Claudian and Flavian emperors by reference to Virgil.[15]

In the late fourth century CE, the emperor Theodosius declared Christianity the state religion, but we can see Virgil's reception reflected in Christian texts even before this edict, because their authors had early attributed messianic import to Virgil's poetic prophecies (Ch. 2.2). The Christian apologist Lactantius (*c.* 240–*c.* 320 CE) interpreted the Sibyl of *B.* 4 (Ch. 2.2) as announcing the advent of Christ in her prophecy of the birth of a child to renew the golden age (*Divinae Institutiones* 7.24), and the emperor Constantine treats the Christian interpretation of the eclogue in a speech of 323 CE. The child of *B.*4 was interpreted as Christ; the 'maiden' (*uirgo*) as the Virgin Mary; and the extinction of the serpent (*B.* 4.24) as the destruction of the snake in *Genesis* 3:15. Christian exegetes also draw on Anchises' Orphic–Platonic eschatology of *A.* 6 (Ch. 4.3), to show Virgil looking forward in these passages not to a new golden age under the earthly rule of Augustus but to a new religious order under the spiritual rule of Christ.

Early Christian writers, especially the North Africans, defend the Carthaginian queen Dido's chastity against Virgil's 'calumnies', for the Augustan poet was well known to have distorted the chronological record in order to bring Aeneas to Dido's Carthage (Ch. 4.2). The church father Augustine of Hippo (354–430 CE) famously recalls his own spiritually unhealthy interest in Dido in the first book of his *Confessions* (398). He compares Aeneas' literal wanderings (*errores*) in the *Aeneid* to his own faults, to which he was so blind that he wept for Dido instead of his own spiritual destitution (1.13). In comparing Dido's pursuit of death to his own pursuit of the things most remote from God, he contrasts the misplaced pain of erotic passion with the real pain of his soul caused by reading the damaging literature of the secular school curriculum. *Confessions* 3 is Augustine's 'Carthage book', and like Virgil's 'Carthage book' (*A*. 4), it begins with erotic love. Augustine models his departure from Carthage for Rome in *Confessions* 5 on Aeneas' abandonment of Dido at the end of *A*. 4. His mother Monnica becomes, like Dido, an abandoned lover, a victim in her excessive love for her son, which impedes his spiritual progress. But the context of Augustine's departure anticipates the decisive conversion to Christianity: Aeneas abandons Dido to her death on the pyre, while Augustine leaves Monnica to pray at a tomb. Both 'heroes' abandon their women deceitfully, guided by divine authority. The sequence constitutes both a sustained literary allusion to Aeneas' fated destiny on the part of the 'enlightened' Augustine and a deliberate literary re-enactment of the Virgilian hero's divine mission on the part of the sinful Augustine turning to Christ. Here as elsewhere, Augustine's allusions reflect not just literary modelling but a life shaped by imitation of the epic.[16]

In the *Confessions*, Augustine also bears witness to the important role in late antiquity of divination by 'lots' (*sortes*), a technique derived from classical Latin prophecy which involved opening at random an important book such as the Bible or Virgil's *Aeneid*. Augustine's conversion to Christianity is secured by biblical *sortes* (*Conf.* 8.12); hearing a child repeating the words 'take it and read, take it and read', he picks up the Bible and reads a passage in Paul's letter to the Romans (13:13–14: 'put on the Lord Jesus Christ'), which he interprets as divine guidance for his conversion. In the same period, the late fourth-century CE *Historia Augusta*, a history of the Roman emperors from Hadrian on, depicts Roman emperors consulting the 'Virgilian lots' (*sortes*

Vergilianae) for divine guidance. Their earliest recorded use is that of Hadrian, who consults the lots about the imperial succession. Chancing upon the passage immediately following the lines on Augustus in the 'Parade of Heroes' (Ch. 4.2), about Numa Pompilius, the second Roman king, Hadrian interprets the passage to portend his succession to the imperial purple following Trajan. Several emperors are represented as receiving or citing the lines about the premature death of Augustus' nephew Marcellus in Anchises' speech in *A.* 6, while another popular passage for such citation is the prophecy of Jupiter in *A.* 1.[17]

Late antiquity also saw the first flowering of Christian Latin epic, which runs through the whole of the middle ages and into the European renaissance, and constitutes another important chapter in the history of Virgil's reception. These epics range from the Virgilian centos, 'patchwork' texts that weave together unconnected lines and half-lines from all of Virgil's poems, through the biblical epics that propound biblical history and revelation in Latin hexameters, to the medieval Latin epics on European historical and Christian philosophical themes. Over fifteen Virgilian centos survive from late antiquity, including four that turn Virgil's pagan Latin verse to Christian use. The two most famous Virgilian centos are the pagan *Cento Nuptialis*, 'Wedding cento', by Ausonius (*c.* 310–95), and the longer Christian *Cento Vergilianus de laudibus Christi*, 'Virgilian cento on Christ's praises', by Faltonia Betitia Proba (*c.* 310–60). Ausonius takes as the subject of his short cento the wedding of Gratian, the son of the emperor Valentinian I, and concludes with a notorious thirty-line tour-de-force of sexual description on the defloration of his bride. By contrast, Proba's cento, which has been thought to be the first Christian example of the genre, retells stories from early Genesis and the life of Christ from the Gospels in over 600 Virgilian hexameters.[18]

The Spanish aristocrat and priest Juvencus (*fl.* first third of the fourth century CE) inaugurated the genre of biblical epic, though only his *Evangeliorum libri quattuor*, 'Four Books of the Gospels', of *c.* 329 survives. Juvencus praises the 'sweetness' of Virgilian poetry in his preface, and draws on all three of Virgil's poems throughout his epic, in order, it has been thought, to appeal to the educated readership of his day, which found the style of the Christian Bible unsophisticated.[19] Juvencus' focus on the Christian 'New Testament' was followed by Sedulius (second quarter of the fifth century CE), who wrote an 'Easter Song' (*Carmen paschale*) also based on the Gospels; and Arator (mid-sixth century CE), who wrote a two-book *Historia apostolica* or *De actibus apostolorum*, 'on the Acts of the Apostles'. Three epics on the 'Old Testament' are also extant: *Hepteuchos*, on the first 'Seven Books' of the Hebrew Bible (early fifth century CE, authorship unknown); *Alethia*, 'Truth', on the opening chapters of Genesis (first quarter of the fifth century CE), by Claudius Marius Victorius; and *De spiritalis historiae gestis*, 'Spiritual history', on *Genesis* 1–3, 6–8, and *Exodus* 1–15 (c. 490 CE) by Avitus. All these poems directly recall and creatively imitate Virgil's *Aeneid*, viewing it alongside the Hebrew Bible as 'sacred scriptures that point towards Christian completion'.[20] In these biblical epics, the influence runs both ways: as they rehearse scripture in Virgilian tones, so Virgil's *Aeneid* acquires a Christian cast.

The middle ages continued to witness the composition of Virgilian epic and its exegetical handmaid, commentary. In the mid-sixth century, the North African Fulgentius authored an allegorical commentary in dialogue form on the *Aeneid*, *Expositio continentiae Virgilianae secundum philosophos moralis* ('Exposition of the content of Virgil according to moral philosophers'). The shade of Virgil instructs Fulgentius in Aeneas' education in virtue, with particular attention to *A.* 1 and 6. Following in the tradition of the late antique commentators Servius and Macrobius, who portray Virgil as a sage and his works as the repository of all knowledge, Fulgentius interprets Aeneas' career both allegorically, depicting the Roman hero as an everyman bettering himself in the course of his life, and anagogically, treating the hero's epic journey as the soul's quest for ethical perfection. To the medieval French scholar and poet Bernardus Silvestris (*fl.* 1130–50) has been ascribed a commentary on *A.* 1–6 in the same allegorizing vein as that of Fulgentius: Bernardus allegorizes Aeneas as 'spirit', Anchises as 'heavenly Father' and Venus as 'natural justice'; he interprets Aeneas' travels in

A. 1–5 as representing his maturation in the stages of life; and he reads the katabasis of *A.* 6 as an allegorical search for wisdom. Both works are Neoplatonic in their intellectual allegiances, and respond especially intensely to Virgil's Platonic eschatology at the end of *A.* 6 (Ch. 4.3).

Virgil continued to be studied in school throughout the middle ages; indeed, instruction in Virgil was instruction in Latin. He remained the foremost authority on Latin grammar, rhetoric and philosophy, an exponent of ancient wisdom and exemplar of moral virtue as the poet of Aeneas' *pietas* (both 'piety' and 'pity') and, most importantly, a prophet of Christ because of the fame of *B.* 4. All extant medieval Latin epics take Virgil for their 'code' model (Ch. 3.1, 4.1), and the four greatest, written in northern France in the last quarter of the twelfth century, interact with Virgil's poetry, as well as with one another, in the classical tradition of intertextuality, through sophisticated displays of literary imitation and rivalry: Joseph of Exeter's *Ylias*, Walter of Châtillon's *Alexandreis*, Alan of Lille's *Anticlaudianus* and John of Hauville's *Architrenius*.[21] Also twelfth-century is the *Roman d'Eneas*, an anonymous old French poem (*c.* 1155–60) in the form of a chivalric saga, which transposes Virgil's epic of Roman imperialism into a meditation on courtly love and the competitive ethos of chivalric spectacle. Aeneas' liaison with Dido receives extended treatment in the *Roman*, as does his newly passionate love affair with the Italian princess Lavinia, called Lavine.

The Italian poet Dante Alighieri (c.1265–1321) was heir to the developed medieval traditions of philosophical allegory and Latin epic in his *Commedia* (completed 1320), which reflects throughout on Virgil's poetic authority. The ancient poet enters the *Commedia* early in the *Inferno* (1.62–3) as a character 'who seemed faint through long silence', testimony to the temporal and religious gulf that lies between the Christian poet and his pagan 'master and author' (*Inf.* 1.85). Virgil appears to Dante in the underworld and guides him through *Inferno* and *Purgatorio*, as Anchises had appeared to Aeneas and the Sibyl in Elysium at the end of *A.* 6 to instruct his son in philosophical and historical wisdom. Virgil the character suggests the importance of

Virgil's master-text, the *Aeneid*, to the pilgrim Dante on his voyage of spiritual salvation, and to the poet Dante in his characterization of Limbo in *Inf.* 4, modelled on the Elysium of *A.* 6. Virgil illuminates the path of Dante-pilgrim in *Inferno* and *Purgatorio*, but as a pagan he is denied Christian salvation and so yields to Beatrice in *Paradiso*; Statius acts as an intermediary between the pagan wisdom Virgil represents and the salvific message of Christianity that Beatrice will reveal to Dante-pilgrim. Dante models the final disappearance of Virgil from his poem in *Purgatorio* 30 on the moment of profound loss at the end of *A.* 6, where Anchises' lament for the young Marcellus sounds the cost of Roman imperialism (Ch. 4.2). The Christian poet unites the Latin Vulgate line 'blessed are you who come' (*Purg.* 30.19) with Anchises' tribute to the prematurely dead youth in the angels' song 'give lilies with full hands' (30.21).[22] Dante thereby transmutes Virgilian tragedy into Christian salvific bliss, as Dante-pilgrim is greeted by Beatrice, dead even younger than Marcellus but redeemed by Christian hope, faith and love.

In the next generation, the Tuscan-born Petrarch (1304–74) wrote extensively in Latin as well as in Italian, and Virgil is one of his three paramount classical models, along with Cicero and Seneca. His Latin epic *Africa* (unfinished), in nine books of Virgilian hexameters, is closely modelled on the *Aeneid* and describes Rome's rise to Mediterranean hegemony in the Second Punic War. A century after Petrarch lived, another Italian humanist, Maffeo Vegio, composed a *Supplement* to the *Aeneid*, often called its thirteenth book, at the precocious age of 21 (1428).[23] His supplement begins with Turnus' death and ends with Aeneas' death and deification, three years later. Both his style and subject are consummately Virgilian, and he is resolutely classicizing in the exposition of his narrative, bringing his *Supplement* to a close with the hero's apotheosis, in fulfilment of the hints Jupiter gives in his conversations with Venus and Juno in *A.* 1 (Ch. 4.2) and 12 (Ch. 4.3). Vegio's *Supplement* enjoyed such popularity that it was printed together with the *Aeneid* in early modern editions, and was even translated as the final book of Virgil's epic.[24]

Many English versions of Virgil's *Aeneid* have been essayed since Geoffrey Chaucer inaugurated the practice with his epitome of Aeneas' arrival in North Africa and meeting with Dido at Carthage, in *The House of Fame* and *The Legend of Good Women*.[25] But few later English translators of Virgil have shared Chaucer's well-documented interest in women in classical myth and literature. Most seem rather to have been drawn to translation of the *Aeneid* because of its political and military commitments, for many enjoyed public careers, principally as politicians, bureaucrats and diplomats, and many also saw military service.[26] Chaucer himself may have served in the military in 1359–60 with Edward III's army in France during the Hundred Years' War, before later undertaking diplomatic missions (1367–78) and sitting as a justice of the peace and member of Parliament (from 1385), while William Caxton, author of the earliest complete English version of the *Aeneid* (albeit a prose paraphrase rather than a poetic rendering, and from a French translation of the *Aeneid*, *Le Liure des Eneydes*, rather than the original) worked as a wool merchant, diplomat, translator, author and printer.

The earliest complete translation of the *Aeneid* into English is that of Thomas Phaer (the first seven books, published 1558), whose work was completed by Thomas Twyne after his death in 1560; their jointly authored complete version was published in 1573, and republished in 1584 with the inclusion of a translation of Vegio's *Supplement*. Thomas Phaer (*c.* 1510–60) trained as a lawyer and doctor, and authored medical and legal treatises in addition to his translation of the first seven books of the *Aeneid*, which he dedicated to Queen Mary Tudor a few months before she died in November 1558. The royal dedication implies the translator's Catholicism along with a monarchist politics congenial both to the *Aeneid* and to an earlier 'age, when Virgil's Rome could be used to evoke the universal authority of the Church'.[27]

The career of John Milton (1608–74) in some ways exhibits the most points of convergence with Virgil's poetic career and epic achievement of all the English poets, but his puritan faith and republican politics made the pagan religious and monarchist imperial plot of the *Aeneid* anathema to him, even in his twelve-book epic *Paradise Lost*.[28] More attuned to Virgil's monarchist subject was John Dryden (1631–1700), author of a celebrated translation of the *Aeneid* that appeared in 1697 (second edition 1698). A royalist Catholic, whose loyalty to the exiled King James II occasioned his loss of the Poet Laureateship in 1688, Dryden was a professional author and court poet who held a succession of political offices (first under Cromwell's Secretary of State, 1654–8; Poet Laureate 1668–88; Royal Historiographer 1670–88) until James II was deposed and the protestant William of Orange acceded to the throne as King William III along with his wife Mary, James II's daughter.[29]

T.W. Harrison has well discussed the disintegration of the seventeenth-century royalist reception of the *Aeneid*, given its most powerful form by Dryden, in the eighteenth century 'insistence on the criteria of the sublime and the pathetic' along with 'the concentration on intense but small pieces', as English poetry moved 'towards a lyric norm'.[30] Harrison connects this shift in taste to the nineteenth-century innovation of translating Virgil into prose.[31] Only in the second half of the nineteenth century, with a new interest in the middle ages and medieval balladry, does sustained verse narrative enjoy popular appeal again. In this context, William Morris (1834–96) – textile designer, artist, writer and libertarian socialist – provides a telling contrast with both Phaer and Dryden in his socialist political commitments, which emerged from humble beginnings in 1876, the very year in which his *Aeneids of Vergil* were published.

To pass from William Morris in the nineteenth century to C. Day-Lewis (1904–72) in the twentieth, is to offer the sharpest break we have yet seen in the reception of Virgil, though this disjunction inaugurates a series of critical ruptures spanning the twentieth and twenty-first centuries. C. Day-Lewis – English schoolmaster, poet, novelist, Professor of Poetry at Oxford (1951–6), Poet Laureate (1968–72) – came to the *Aeneid* after successfully translating the *Georgics* into English verse, and it was his experience with the *Georgics* (published 1940) that seems to have led him, out of *pietas*,[32] next to the *Aeneid* (1952) and finally to the

Eclogues (1963). In the late 1930s, his first wife's brother, who was teaching at Winchester, asked him to translate a short piece of the fourth *Georgic* that had been set as an examination passage. Day-Lewis, newly removed to a cottage on the border between Devon and Dorset, was running the local Home Guard and took as an epigraph for his translation of the *Georgics* a passage from the Latin poem itself, which in his translation runs (*G.* 1.505–11):

> ... there's so much war in the world,
> Evil has so many faces, the plough so little
> Honour, the labourers are taken, the fields untended,
> And the curving sickle is beaten into the sword that yields not.
> There the East is in arms, here Germany marches:
> Neighbour cities, breaking their treaties, attack each other:
> The wicked War-god runs amok through all the world.

The contemporary resonance of Virgil's account of a world at war, with the East under arms and Germany on the march, may have stimulated Day-Lewis to turn to the *Aeneid* after completing the *Georgics*.

T.S. Eliot famously called the *Aeneid* 'the classic of all Europe' in his 1944 presidential address to the Virgil Society, 'What is a Classic', later published in *On Poetry and Poets* (London 1957). In the address, Eliot identifies 'maturity' as the hallmark of 'the universal classic, like Virgil', and he defines the requisite maturity as belonging not only to the poet's mind, but also to his civilization, its manners, language and literature. Like Day-Lewis, Eliot responds to Virgil's refinement of language and, writing at an epochal moment towards the end of the Second World War, he is especially conscious of the role of history in both Virgilian poetry and European culture. He lauds Virgil's 'comprehensiveness' and 'universality', though today we might view those characteristics of his poetry as the result, rather than the source, of its reception history.

Day-Lewis and Eliot stand at the high-water mark of Virgil's reception in twentieth-century Anglo-American criticism and literature, but the tide turns rapidly. Already by the end of the 1950s, W.H. Auden (1907–73) could frame an attack on political poetry as an attack on Virgil's *Aeneid*, in a poem perhaps from 1959 entitled 'Secondary Epic' (vv. 1–5): 'No, Virgil, no:/ Not even the first of the Romans can learn/ His Roman history in the future tense./ Not even to serve your political turn;/ Hindsight as foresight makes no sense.' Although his own early poetry, and three plays co-authored with Christopher Isherwood in the late 1930s, had brought him fame as an author of left-wing political views, Auden projects his subsequent disavowal of political themes onto the Latin poet (vv. 47–9): 'No, Virgil, no:/ Behind your verse so masterfully made/ We hear the weeping of a Muse betrayed'. The betrayed Muse is not only Virgil's. Auden's own continuing attraction to political poetry (and to Virgil's *Aeneid*) can still be felt in his composition of another 'prophecy' for inclusion in Anchises' parade of heroes (vv. 35–46):

> . . . *Now Mainz appears and starry New Year's Eve*
> *As two-horned Rhine throws off the Latin yoke*
> *To bear the Vandal on his frozen back;*
> *Lo! Danube, now congenial to the Goth,*
> *News not unwelcome to Teutonic shades*
> *And all lamenting beyond Acheron*
> *Demolished Carthage or a plundered Greece:*
> *And now Juturna leaves the river-bed*
> *Of her embittered grievance—loud her song,*
> *Immoderate her joy—for word has come*
> *Of treachery at the Salarian Gate.*
> *Alaric has avenged Turnus. . . .*

Auden's 'Virgilian' prophecy contains no triumphalist imperial message, but rather heralds the revenge of history's 'losers' in the sack of Rome by the Visigoth leader Alaric in 410 CE. The Anglo-American poet especially savours the historical irony of the name of the last western emperor, 'Romulus Augustulus', who was deposed by the German Flavius Odoacer, a vassal of the eastern emperor Zeno in 476 (vv. 50–5, 57, 61–2): 'Your Anchises isn't convincing at all:/ It's asking too much of us to be told/ A shade so long-sighted, a father who knows/ That Romulus will build a wall,/ Augustus found an Age of Gold . . ./ Would mention them both but not disclose .../The names predestined for the Catholic boy/ Whom Arian Odovacer will depose'. In his witty meditation on the oracular form in which Virgil presents Roman history in the *Aeneid*, Auden reveals his own continuing commitments to European literature and history in his craft, even as he focuses on the anti-climactic finale of Virgil's 'empire without end'.

A similarly subtle reading of the *Aeneid* and its narrative architecture informs the 1950 poem 'Falling Asleep over the *Aeneid*' by the American poet Robert Lowell.[33] Although his title suggests the classics' loss of cultural capital after the Second World War, the poem offers a masterful assessment of the crucial role of Pallas in Virgil's narrative. At the head of his poem Lowell includes a brief 'key': 'An old man in Concord forgets to go to morning service. He falls asleep, while reading Vergil, and dreams that he is Aeneas at the funeral of Pallas, an Italian prince'. The importance of Pallas to Virgil's 'Iliad' cannot be overstated, and it is instructive to trace the intricacy of Virgil's intratextual relations through Lowell's verses, whose Aeneas presides over Pallas' funeral holding 'the sword that Dido used' (v. 15) and admiring the dead youth's beauty (vv. 26–30): 'Face of snow,/ You are the flower that country girls have caught,/ A wild bee-pillaged honey-suckle brought/ To the returning bridegroom—the design/ Has not yet left it, and the petals shine'. The floral imagery recalls the flower simile applied to Pallas on the bier in *A.* 11, as also that applied to Euryalus in death in *A.* 9, while the bridegroom analogy evokes Pallas' baldric and its image of the Danaids' murdered bridegrooms in *A.* 10. Dido returns to the dream-Aeneas' thoughts, as she does in Virgil's description of the funerary cortège in *A.* 11, as the weaver of the robe in which Pallas is wrapped for delivery to his father (vv. 35–9): 'But I take his pall,/ Stiff with its gold and purple, and recall/ How Dido hugged it to her, while she toiled,/ Laughing—her golden threads, a serpent coiled/ In cypress. Now I lay it like a sheet'. The latent threat Dido poses to the hero and his proto-Roman allies is echoed in the dreamer's assessment of the gods' role in the war (vv. 50–2): 'Our cost/ Is nothing to the lovers, whoring Mars/ and Venus, father's lover'. Lowell focuses the epic's narrative sweep, and the Roman history it surveys, on the dead youth Pallas, whom he represents, like Virgil in his eulogy of Nisus and Euryalus (*A.* 9.446–9), as an image of specifically literary memorial (vv. 61–70):

> ... At the end of time,
> He sets his spear, as my descendants climb
> The knees of Father Time, his beard of scalps,
> His scythe, the arc of steel that crowns the Alps.
> The elephants of Carthage hold those snows,
> Turms of Numidian horse unsling their bows,
> The flaming turkey-feathered arrows swarm
> Beyond the Alps. 'Pallas', I raise my arm
> And shout, 'Brother, eternal health. Farewell
> Forever' ...

A final development in Virgil's reception at the dawn of the twenty-first century may be mentioned by way of conclusion. The suffragette movement of the late nineteenth and early twentieth centuries gave rise in the twentieth and twenty-first to politically empowered feminist authors and critics, who have used their access to the Latin and Greek classics to draw attention to the institutional 'androcentrism' of the classics, including Virgil's *Aeneid*, with its focus on a singular 'man' and its celebration of the great 'men' of Roman history (Ch. 4.2).[34] The first two complete female-authored versions of the *Aeneid* in any language appeared in the twenty-first century.[35] Yale University Press, which published Sarah Ruden's translation of the poem in 2008, publicized the fact that she was the first woman to offer a full translation of the epic, probably as a sales strategy to secure readers for the new version. Her line-by-line translation is very plain, aiming to suggest the length of the Latin verses while paring away the Latinate expressions of translators such as Dryden, in order to offer instead, like Day-Lewis, a contemporary idiom based on an English lexicon that makes sparing use of Latin derivations.

While in no way a translation of the *Aeneid*, the American novelist Ursula Le Guin's *Lavinia* both draws on, and reflects upon, the Italian second half of Virgil's epic, as it also gives voice to its mostly silent women, including Lavinia, who speaks not one word in the epic. Le Guin herself explains her motivation as 'a translator's yearning to identify with the text' (Le Guin 2008, 273): 'This is what urged me to take some scenes, some hints, some foreshadowings from the epic and make them into a novel—a translation into a different *form*—partial, marginal, but, in intent at least, faithful'. Her project, like Ruden's, 'is an act of gratitude to the poet, a love offering' (2008, 273). But in her 'Afterword' Le Guin also credits a feminist foremother with aiding her research, Bertha Tilly, whose *Vergil's Latium* (Oxford: Blackwell, 1947) records her travels in Lazio during the 1930s. Le Guin's narrative belongs to Lavinia, as Virgil's belongs to his hero. Le Guin's is a gynocentric story, written by a woman about a woman. She changes the perspective of the events of the Italian war to show us women's responses to courtship, war, farming and domestic labour, and she is particularly interested in the Bronze Age context of Virgil's poem, sharing the Roman poet's interest in the religious details of early Latium. The novel is a fitting tribute to the continuing interest that Virgil's poetry inspires far away in both time and place from the historical, political and religious contexts in which it was composed.

Notes

Chapter 1

1 The ancient lives are conveniently collected and translated in Ziolkowski and Putnam 2008, 179–403. On Suetonius' *Vita Vergili*, see Kaster 2014; on Donatus' redaction of Suetonius, see Naumann 1981; Daintree 1990; and Ziolkowski and Putnam 2008, 180–1. Donatus' *Vita Vergili*, the fullest of the extant ancient lives, is also included in the second volume of the Loeb edition of Suetonius' *Lives*; on its circulation in the middle ages, see Stok in Powell and Hardie 2017, 133–52. On the late antique grammarian Servius, whose commentary on all three of Virgil's poems is the only such ancient work now extant, see Kaster 1988, 169–97; Murgia 2003; Ziolkowski and Putnam 2008, 180.

2 Testimonia and reception collected in *EV* 5: 429–33. See also Ziolkowski and Putnam 2008, 179–468; Powell and Hardie 2017.

3 Lefkowitz 2012[1981]; Fairweather 1974, 1981, 1984; cf. Horsfall 1995 and Starr 1995.

4 Blum 1991.

5 On the horizon of expectations brought to the ancient *Lives* by their authors and readers, see Hardie and Peirano Garrison in Powell and Hardie 2017, ix–xiii and 1–28 respectively.

6 Cf. Smolenaars and Powell in Powell and Hardie 2017, 153–72 and 173–97 respectively.

7 Sen. *Clem.* 9. On Augustus, see Eck 2007.

8 Graziosi 2009, esp. 156–7 with n.54.

9 Gordon 1934.

10 See Lefkowitz 2012[1981] and Fairweather 1974, 261–5.

11 On Siro, see Kroll 1927, and Gigante 1990.

12 In addition to *De fin.* 2.119, cf. Cic. *Pis.* 68–72, 74; *Or. post red. in sen.* 14–15. See Sider 1997, 227–34.

13 Cavallo 1983, 41 and 54–5; Gigante and Capasso 1989.

14 On Epicurus' life and philosophy, see Rist 1972; Inwood and Gerson 1997; Warren 2009.

15 On Varius, see Cova 1989; Courtney 1993, 271–5; Hollis 1996 and 2007, 253–81.

16 On Cinna, see Wiseman 1974, 44–58; Courtney 1993, 212–27; and Hollis 2007, 11–48.

17 On the impact of Horace's portrait of Virgil on the latter's biographical tradition, see Peirano 2012, 97 n.86, with further bibliography.

18 On Maecenas, see Paturzo 1999; Le Doze 2014; Chillet 2016. On his poetry, see Courtney 1993, 276–81; Hollis 2007, 314–25.

19 On Quintilius Varus, see *RE* 24, 899, s.v. Quintilius 5; Körte 1890, 172.

20 Sider 1997, 21.

21 Sider 1997, 21.

22 On Virgil's relations with Philodemos, see Freer 2014 and 2019; Xinyue and Freer 2019.

23 Don. *VSD* 19. On Octavian's distribution of land to his veterans, see Keppie 1983.

24 Horace: Suet. *Vita Hor.* 1.1–2; Propertius: Prop. 1.21–2, 4.1; Tibullus: Tib. 1.1.19–22 and 41–2.

25 On Pollio, see André 1949; Zecchini 1982; Néraudau 1983; Courtney 1993, 254–6; Hollis 2007, 215–18; Cairns 2008. On Varus, see Nisbet and Hubbard 1970, 227–8; Cairns 2008, 49–50. On Gallus, see Ross 1975; Courtney 1993, 259–70; Hollis 2007, 219–52.

26 Cf. Aug. *Ep.* Fr. xxxv Malc.; V. *G.* 4.564–5; *P.Herc. Paris.* 2.

27 Plut. *Lathe biôsas* 1128–9. On the doctrine, and the misunderstandings it has engendered, see Roskam 2007.

28 Peirano 2012.

29 On performances of individual eclogues, see Highet 1974; Panayotakis 2008; Höschele 2013; cf. Hunter 1996, 7–10, on the importance of mime to Theocritus' *Idylls*.

30 Cf. Quint. 10.3.8, citing Varius; Gellius 17.10.23, citing Virgil's 'friends and intimates'.

31 The historicity of both anecdotes has been called into question: Horsfall 1995, 15–16, reviews the evidence. Smolenaars in Powell and Hardie 2017 documents the chronological plausibility of the second anecdote.

32 Donatus also reports Maecenas' freedman Melissus' unflattering assessment of Virgil's rhetorical skills (*VSD* 16): 'in speech he was very slow and nearly similar to an untaught rustic'. Scholars have wondered how to reconcile the report of Virgil's effective recital of verse with this dismissive report of his pleading skills, but the elder Seneca (*Contr.* 3 *praef.* 8) is an early witness to the difference between the two skills.

33 On the date of the correspondence, see Deufert 2013.

34 White 1993 offers a balanced discussion of the history of the question.

35 On the recitation or performance of Virgil in ancient reception, see Ziolkowski and Putnam 2008, 162–78.

36 Horsfall 1995, 9.

37 Cf. the popular report of Epicureans not only living and eating together, but also sharing their women, discussed by Gordon 2012, 75–104.

38 The sex lives of the rich and famous were traditionally subject to speculation in ancient biography: Fairweather 1974, 263–4. For ancient biographical interpretation of the homoerotic narratives of *B.* and *A.*, cf., e.g. Mart. *Epigr.* 8.56.12, Juv. 7.69.

39 On the tendency in ancient biographies to defend the morals of the deceased, see Peirano 2012, 96–7.

40 On Calvus, see Gruen 1967; Courtney 1993, 201–11; Hollis 2007, 49–86.

41 On Gallus in Pollio's letters to Cicero, see Gelzer 1982; Cairns 2008, 62–3.

Chapter 2

1 Horsfall 1981, 108–9; Clausen 1994, xx n23; Perutelli 1995, 27–8. On the MS tradition of Virgil, including the *Bucolics*, see Zetzel 1973; Courtney 1981; Reynolds 1983, 433–6.

2 On the bucolic programme articulated in *B.* 1, and the special significance of line 45, see Wright 1983.

3 On Theocritus' bucolic poetry book, and the place of *Idyll* 1 in it, see Gow 1950, 1.lxvi–lxix; Gutzwiller 1996, 123–8; Hunter 1999, 5–12. For Callimachus' collected edition, see Gutzwiller 1998, 183–8.

4 On Virgil's Theocritus, see Vaughn 1981.

5 On Theocritus' urban mimes, see Buxton 1995.

6　On the impact of Virgil's ten-poem collection on his contemporaries, see
　　Leach 1978.

7　On Virgil's onomastic conventions, see Hubaux 1927; Perutelli 1995, 42–4;
　　Hubbard 1998, 45–139; Jones 2011, 89–106. On Roman names in Virgilian
　　bucolic, see Jones 2011, 107–12.

8　Gutzwiller 1996, 133–7; Hunter 1996, 92.

9　Sicilian settings in the *Bucolics*: 4.1–3, 6.1, 10.1–4; cf. 1.54, 2.21, 10.51. See
　　further Thill 1979, 46–9; Jones 2011, 47–8.

10　For clearness, or shrillness, as the hallmark of the syrinx and thence of
　　pastoral poetics, see Hunter 1999, 69; cf. *B*. 9.36 for Virgil's bucolic ideal
　　of the 'clear-voiced swan'.

11　The title of Hollander 1981, who considers pastoral echo at 1981, 12–15;
　　cf. Rosenmeyer 1969, 148–50, 185–6.

12　For Virgil's debt to Theocritus, see Posch 1969, 15–27; Lipka 2001, 28–65.

13　Perutelli 1995, 49–50; Hubbard 1998.

14　On amoebean verse, see Karakasis 2011. On imitation and emulation as
　　the constitutive features of pastoral, already in the Greek pastoral tradition,
　　see Hubbard 1998, 19–44; in Virgil, Hubbard 1998, 45–139.

15　Coleman 1977, 109–29; Clausen 1994, 86–118; Lipka 2001, 37–44. On *B*. 3,
　　see Segal 1967; Putnam 1970, 119–35; Henderson 1998 (= Volk 2008a,
　　125–54); Hubbard 1998, 68–74 (= Volk 2008a, 101–8).

16　Cf. Hubbard 1998, 68–75.

17　Hubbard 1998, 68–9. Donatus (*VSD* 9) and Servius (on *B*. 2.1) identify
　　Corydon as Virgil's alter ego in the collection; see Breed 2006, 30.

18　Cf. Jones 2011, 157 n.3.

19　On the programmatic function of the beech in Virgilian bucolic, see
　　Hubbard 1998, 49 n.11 and 88; Lipka 2001, 209 index s.v. *fagus*; Saunders
　　2008, 10–21; Jones 2011, 29–32.

20　Hubbard 1998, 72.

21　On comedy in the eclogue, see Currie 1976; cf. Coleman 1977, 109;
　　Clausen 1994, 92–3.

22　The term is that of Rosenmeyer 1969, 179–205.

23　Hunter 1996, 23–4, commenting on Theocritus' literary erudition and
　　allusive play in *Id*. 7.

24　The closest Theocritus seems to come to naming a patron is in *Idyll* 7.93,
　　where Simichidas (often interpreted as a mask for Theocritus) claims that
　　his songs' reputation has 'perhaps reached the throne of Zeus', i.e. the court

of Ptolemy Philadelphos in Alexandria: see Hunter 1996, 22 and 1999, 179, on *Id.* 7.93. *Idylls* 16 and 17 have been interpreted as requests for patronage from Hiero of Syracuse and Ptolemy Philadelphus, respectively: see Hunter 1996.

25 The title of Rosenmeyer 1969.

26 On the politics of Virgilian representation, see Connolly 2001; on Virgil's bucolic fiction, see Kania 2016.

27 Coleman 1977, 89–91 notes how little Theocritean material there is in the eclogue; cf. Lipka 2001, 31–2, 59.

28 Appian, *B Liv* 5.12–13; Dio *Cass.* 48.6–12: see Keppie 1983; Eck 2007, 18–19.

29 Powell 2008, 190–2. On Sextus Pompey, see Hadas 1966; Powell and Welch 2002.

30 Partisan support: Powell 2008, 190–2; inappropriate to herdsmen: Coleman 1977, 71–91.

31 Cf., e.g. Cic. *Phil.* 2.113, 5.21, 6.19, 13.1; *ad Brut.* 1.16.9. See Syme 1939, 154–5; Wirszubski 1950; Weinstock 1971, 133–48; Fears 1981, 869–75, 892–7. On *libertas* and the practice of politics in the late Roman republic, see Arena 2013.

32 Weinstock 1971, 143, citing *RG* 1.1, *BMC R Emp.* 1.112.

33 The title of Alpers 1979.

34 Weinstock 1971, 370–84.

35 Weinstock 1971, 191–7.

36 On the optimism with which the comet was greeted, see Pandey 2013.

37 On the extensive allusions to Catull. *c.* 64 in *B.* 4, see Lipka 2001, 82–3, 86; Coleman 1977 and Clausen 1994 ad loc.

38 The identification is first extant in Augustine: see Benko 1980.

39 Cairns 2008 supports this interpretation.

40 Livia, already the mother of a son (Tiberius, later Augustus' successor, the emperor), bore a second son on 14 January 38, three months after her marriage (or betrothal – the sources are confused) to Octavian: see Fantham 2006, 21–3, discussing *B.* 4.

41 On the Theocritean echoes, see Posch 1969; Coleman 1977, 158–65; Clausen 1994, 152–3; Lipka 2001, 44–6.

42 For the Ambarvalia, cf. Cato, *Agr.* 141; Tib. 1.1.24–4, 2.1.1–26; and see further Coleman 1977, 169, on *B.* 5.75; Clausen 1994, 110, on *B.* 3.76–7; Scullard 1981, 17–18, 26, 124–5.

43 Alpers 1979, 107–11, 143; *contra* Kronenberg 2016, who interprets Daphnis as an allegory for Lucretius.

44 Quintilian (*Inst. Or.* 8.6.46) accepts the identification of Menalcas with Virgil here, and Donatus and Servius assume it, on the basis of the setting near Mantua, the Virgilian character of the verses quoted by the herdsmen in the poem and attributed to Menalcas, and the similarity of *B.* 9 to Theocritus' autobiographical *Idyll* 7.

45 Horsfall 1995, 12–13; cf. Starr 1995. Winterbottom 1976 discusses the little that can be gleaned from *B.* 1 and 9 independent of biographical speculation.

46 Weinstock 1971, 371.

47 Rosenmeyer 1969, 65–97.

48 For Lucretian echoes in the *Bucolics*, see Lipka 2001, 65–87; Davis 2012; Kronenberg 2016.

49 On Epicurean resonances in *B.* 1, see Davis 2012, 17–39; Lipka 2001, 66–70.

50 Jones 2011, 19–22; Kronenberg 2016, 26–7.

51 On the Athenian Garden, see Clay 2009.

52 It must be noted, however, that Virgil's bucolic collection shows an uneasy awareness of the fragility of philosophical tranquillity in the troubled period after the assassination of Caesar.

53 Bing 2016.

54 Davis 2012, 28. On the monthly banquets, instituted in Epicurus' will (D.L. 10.16–22), see Clay 2009, 22–5; cf. Philodem. *Epigr.* 27 Sider.

55 Clausen 1994, 48–9.

56 See, e.g. Coleman 1977, 20 and 80; Clausen 1994, ad loc. Mayer 1983 and Cairns 2008 are rare dissenters.

57 Maltby 1991, 320 s.v. *iuuenis*; cf. O'Hara 1996 on *G.* 1.500.

58 Clay 2009, 11.

59 Cf. *KD* 6, 7, 14, 39, 40; *VS* 58, 81. Epicurus' prohibition of a political career has engendered much discussion among both ancients and moderns. The state of the question has been set on a wholly new footing by Roskam 2007, 29–66, treating qualifications of the principle at 2007, 49–66.

60 Momigliano 1941; Castner 1988; Griffin 1989; Benferhat 2005; Roskam 2007; Sedley 2009; Fish 2011; Gilbert 2015.

61 Gilbert 2015: Chapters 4 and 5.

62 Griffin 1989; Gilbert 2015.

63 On Epicurean currents in *B.* 5, see Mizera 1982; Davis 2012, 79–97; Kronenberg 2016, 33–42.

64 On Epicurean pleasure, defined as 'freedom from trouble' (*ataraxia*) rather than the carnal pleasures imputed to the sect by its critics, see Rist 1972, 100–26; O'Keefe 2010, 111–27; Woolf in Warren 2009, 158–78.

65 Mizera 1982, 367–8.

66 See, e.g. Coleman 1977, 172; Hubbard 1998, 89–95.

67 For 'correction', see Thomas 1986 on modes of allusion in Virgil's *Georgics*.

68 Smith (1970, 500 n. 11) shows that *DRN* 5.1383 is the first use of 'hemlock' as a musical term in hexameter poetry; cf. Lipka 2001, 157.

69 Traina 1965; Frischer 1975 treats Epicurean issues in *B.* 7; Davis 2012 offers detailed treatment of *Buc.* 1, 2, 4, 5, 6, 8, 9, and 10.

70 Davis 2012, 99–111.

71 Nussbaum 1994, 149–91.

72 Rosenmeyer 1969, 81–2.

73 Davis 2012, 135–6.

74 Davis 2012, 128–9.

75 Davis 2012, 131. On the Epicurean appropriation of Platonic names and characteristics, see Sider 1997, 23–4.

76 *exordia* is the reading of Rω and Macrobius (*Sat.* 6.2.22) as against *ex omnia* in P, which Mynors (1969, 15) prints. Lipka (2001, 74 n.212) notes that whether Virgil wrote *exordia* or *ex omnia*, 'in either case Virgil is adapting Lucretius'.

77 On the Epicurean details and Lucretian language, see Coleman 1977, 183–6; Lipka 2001, 73–5; Davis 2012, 132–3.

78 For Lucretian diction elsewhere in *B.* 6, see Lipka 2001, 66–7, 73, 75. For the dismissal of Epicurean elements in the poem, even within Silenus' cosmogony, see, e.g. Clausen 1994.

79 Conte 1992.

80 On the programme of *B.* 6, see Ross 1975, 18–38 (= Volk 2008a, 189–215).

81 See, e.g. Coleman 1977, 190.

82 On Parthenios, see Lightfoot 1999.

83 On the hellenistic literary antecedents of these themes, see Hubbard 1998, 104–6.

84 Conte in Volk 2008a, 216–44.

85 On Virgil's Arcadia, see Snell 1945 (= Hardie 1999, 1.44–67); Schmidt 1975 (= Volk 2008a, 16–47); Jenkyns 1989; Alpers 1996.

86 Call. *Hymn* 2.19; cf. Euphorion, fr. 80.3 Powell.

87 Ross 1975, 69; cf. Clausen 1994, 300.

88 Breed 2006.

89 Brown 1963; Otis 1964; Skutsch 1969; Van Sickle 2004. Hardie (1998, 22–5) has a sensible and sympathetic treatment of the issues.

Chapter 3

1   On Hesiod as the 'model' for the *Georgics*, see Farrell 1991, 27–77 and 131–63.

2   On Nikander, commonly dated to the second century BCE, see Gow 1953.

3   On Cicero's *Aratea*, see most recently Gee 2014, with further bibliography.

4   On the tradition of Latin didactic verse, see Volk 2002; Gale 2004.

5   On continuity in diction, theme, setting and imagery between the *Bucolics* and *Georgics*, see Kettemann 1977.

6   Thibodeau 2011.

7   On Virgil's 'gods of the land' in *B.* and *G.*, see Fantham 2009, 34–62.

8   This interpretation of the opening and closing prayers of the first *Georgic*, as an expression of the poet-*praeceptor*'s philosophically informed political principles (or his politically informed philosophical principles), may help to assuage contemporary readers' discomfort with the panegyric note unabashedly sounded at the outset of Virgil's new poetic project, most acutely expressed in Powell 2008, 227–81; cf. Thomas 1988a, 1.73 on *G.* 1.24–42, who notes the model of Alexandrian court literature.

9   The passage is replete with allusions to the final eclogue, which is the only one in which *labor*, in the sense of poem, appears (*B.* 10.1, Ch. 3.3). The didactic reminder that the shade of trees may be harmful (*G.* 1.121) also recalls the final lines of the last eclogue (*B.* 10.75–6).

10 On combinatorial allusion, in which a classical poet alludes simultaneously to two distinct models, see Thomas 1986, with special reference to Virgil.

11 In his presentation of the importance of *labor* ('work has conquered all') to *G.* here, Virgil revises his adaptation of the Gallan motto 'love conquers all' in the last eclogue (*B.* 10.69), where it emblematizes the programmatic significance of the theme of love to both Gallan elegy and Virgilian pastoral.

12 Following Hinds 1998, 41–2, I use the term 'code' model.

13 Thomas 1988a, 1.114.

14 Farrell 1991, 27–60.

15 The title of Putnam 1979.

16 Virgil draws on many other didactic poems in *G.* 1, including (in addition to Hesiod and Aratus) Callimachus' *Aetia* (1.24–42), Eratosthenes' *Hermes* (1.231–56), Cicero's *Aratea* (1.244–6) and Lucretius' *De rerum natura* (Ch. 3.2). Elsewhere he draws on Nicander's *Theriaka* (4.414–39) and Varius' *De morte* (2.506–7, Ch. 3.2), among many others.

17 Farrell 1991, 141 and 148.

18 Thomas 1988a, 1.127 on *G.* 1.351–463. 'Weather-signs' were a traditional focus of discussion by the natural philosophers.

19 Thomas 1988a, 1.140 on *G.* 1.432.

20 On 'self-reflexive' or 'annotated' allusion, see Hinds 1998, 1–10.

21 Farrell 1991, 79–83. On Virgil's interest in Aratus, see also Gee 2013, 39–48, with further bibliography.

22 On the interplay of Lucretian *ratio* and Virgilian *miratio* in this passage, and elsewhere in the *Georgics*, see Gale 2000, 196–231.

23 On Virgil's use of prose sources, with a special focus on Varro, see Salvatore 1977; and Thomas [1997] in Volk 2008b, 43–80.

24 Kronenberg 2009, 108–29; Nelsestuen 2015.

25 For the analogy between property management and civic rule in classical philosophy, cf. Pl. *Plt.* 258e–9d, *Prt.* 318e–19a; Arist. [*Oec.*] 1.1343a, 2.1345b–6a; the analogy is rejected at Arist. *Pol.* 1.1252a. On *oeconomia* in this sense, see Kronenberg 2009, *passim*, esp. 21 n.78; Tsouna 2012; Nelsestuen 2015.

26 Tsouna 2007, 163–94, and *ead.* 2012.

27 On the tradition, in which both Philodemos and Virgil write, as also Xenophon, Theophrastos and Varro, see Kronenberg 2009; Tsouna 2012, xiii–xxxvii.

28 Translations of Philodemos' *De oeconomia* are from Tsouna 2012.

29 Tsouna 2012, 96.

30 The following paragraph rehearses Tsouna 2012, xxvi.

31 Tsouna 2012, xxvi.

32 See, e.g. Phld. *De oec.* col. 11: 'That it is appropriate to have to distribute the tasks so as not to endanger all the possessions at once is, of course, good advice for an ordinary person. But the philosopher, properly speaking, does not work, nor, if he ever works, does he seem to put everything at risk

so as [to need exhortation] not to do it'. Cf. Epicurus, *Ep. Men.* 128; Lucr. *DRN* 3.59–64, 5.1430–3; and see further Gale 2000, 147–52.

33 E.g. Miles 1980; Morgan 1999.

34 See, e.g. Farrell 1991; Schäfer 1996; Gale 2000, with further bibliography.

35 Mynors 1990, 169 on *G.* 2.490; *contra* Thomas 1988a, 1.253 on *G.* 2.490.

36 Lucretius' phrase 'farming folk' (*DRN* 4.586) surely drew Virgil's attention.

37 Epicurus' treatise, reported in Diogenes Laertius (10.27), does not survive. On Philodemos' treatise, see Obbink 1996.

38 Thibodeau 2011, esp. 17–37 and 74–115.

39 On Virgil's wealth, see also Thibodeau 2011, 245–7.

40 Cod. Par. Lat. 7530 fol. 28^r. 1–5, on which see Hollis 1996, 28–9.

41 Yona 2018, 238–43.

42 Bowditch 2001, 235.

43 Tsouna (2012, xl) suggests that we should think of the landowner as 'a gracious host who offers his country property as a peaceful retreat where philosophy flourishes and true enjoyment is attained'.

44 See the commentaries of Thomas 1988a and Mynors 1990 on the passage.

45 On Epicurean philosophy in *G.* 4.559–66, see Freer 2019.

46 Cf. Mynors 1990, 166 on *G.* 2.475. For another example of Virgil's idealization of the farming life, cf. the Corycian farmer of *G.* 4.116–46, whose 'Garden' evokes Epicurus' philosophical school and whose happy life exemplifies Epicurean felicity: see La Penna 1977, 57; Johnson 2004.

47 Cf. Epicurus, *On theories of disease and death* (D.L. 10.28; cf. *P.Herc.* 1012 col. 38); Lucr. *DRN* 3; and Philodemos, *On death*. On Varius, see Hollis 1996 and 2007, 263–7.

48 On the plague at Noricum see Harrison 1979; Farrell 1991, 84–94; Gale 1991 and 2000.

49 Thomas 1988a, 2.131 on *G.* 3.478–566.

50 Cf. the title of Seneca's *De beneficiis*.

51 Farrell 1991, 196–7.

52 On the Lucretian valence of the line, see Thomas 1988a, 1.78, and Mynors 1990, 14, on *G.* 1.60.

53 Farrell 1991, 191–5.

54 Virgil's physics are discussed by Ross 1987; Farrell 1991, 196–7; and Gale 2000, 201–20.

55 On metapoetic *labor* in *G.*, see Henkel 2014.

56 On *labor* in Lucretius and Virgil, see Gale (2000, 143–95), who notes (2000, 153 n.29) that 'surviving fragments of Epicurus and Philodemus tend to imply that it is not desirable to devote too much effort to poetic composition'.

57 Thomas (1988a, 1.7) sets out general principles; specific examples are recorded in his index (printed in both volumes of his commentary), s.v. 'Callimachus, Callimacheanism'. See also Thomas 1999.

58 Thomas 1988a, 1.39 ad *G.* 3.7–8, suggests that the subject 'must have appealed to Callimachus'.

59 On Virgil's adaptation of Callimachus' *Victoria Berenices* (*Aet.* 3, frr. 54–60j Harder) in the proem to *G.* 3, see Thomas 1988a, ad loc.

60 Cf. e.g. Hor. *Carm.* 1.2, *Epist.* 2.1, both addressed to Augustus. On Virgil's adaptation of Egyptian court panegyric, see Thomas 1988a, 1.73 on *G.* 1.24–42.

61 Harder considers the case for the supplement at 2012, 2.108 on Callim. *Aet.* 2b.1–3, and 2.110–11 on 2.4.

62 Meban 2008.

63 On Virgil's union of the style and themes of didactic and natural philosophy, see Farrell 1991, 207–53 and 272.

64 The allusion was identified by Scaliger in 1561: see Ross 1987, 48–54; Thomas 1988a, 2.84–5; Farrell 1991, 211–12.

65 On military imagery in the *Georgics*, see Gale 2000, 243–69.

66 On *G.* 4, see Griffin 1979 (= Volk 2008b, 225–48); Farrell 1991, 238–72; Thomas 1988a; Mynors 1990.

67 On Virgil's preference for *miratio*, by contrast to Lucretius' for *ratio*, see Gale 2000, 196–231, esp. 208–20.

68 There may be an Epicurean distaste for their excessive industry in the poet's observation that bees have 'an innate love of acquisition' (4.177).

69 On the passage, see Thomas 1988a, 2.158–62, who shows how closely Virgil here reworks Varro's account of swarming (*Rust.* 3.16.29–31).

70 Mynors 1990, 270 on *G.* 4.86–7.

71 Harder 2012, 1.8–11.

72 The phrase 'as the story goes' (*ut fama*) has been called 'a virtual footnote, suggesting a prior version' (Thomas 1988a, 2.203 on *G.* 4.318); Mynors 1990, 300 on *G.* 4.318, compares Callim. frr. 510 Pf. and 612 Pf. The device was a favourite among the Alexandrian poets and their Roman followers,

who took ostentatious pleasure in flaunting their book-learning: Hinds 1998, 1–5.

73 Farrell 1991, 207–72; Morgan 1999, index s.v. 'Homer'.

74 Thomas 1988a, 2.202–3 on *G.* 4.315; cf. Mynors 1990, 300 on *G.* 4.315–16.

75 Cf. Sarpedon's statement to Glaucus of the 'heroic code' in the *Iliad* (12.310–28).

76 Scheid and Svenbro 1996; Rosati 1999.

77 On Clymene's song, see Rosati 1999.

78 On Virgil's debt to Callimachus' treatise 'On Rivers' in this passage, see Thomas 1988a, 2.213 on *G.* 4.367.

79 On Gallus' line, see Courtney 1993, 263; Hollis 2007, 240–1. On the 'Gallus papyrus', see Anderson, Parsons and Nisbet 1979; Courtney 1993, 263–8; Hollis 2007, 241–52. Virgil annotates his allusion to Gallus' line on the Hypanis in his application of the epithet 're-sounding' to the river here.

80 'We must remember, as I said before, that the last part of this book has been changed: for Gallus' praises were contained in that place which now holds the story of Orpheus, itself inserted after Gallus died, a victim of Augustus' anger'.

81 On the practical limitations on the printing and circulation of books in classical Rome, see Kenney 1982, 15–23.

82 On the controversy, see Griffin 1979 (= Volk 2008b, 225–48); *contra* Jocelyn 1984. Nisbet 1987, 189, suggests that Servius misreports a reception tradition that interpreted the Aristaeus passage as allegorical praise of Gallus.

83 The standard history of classical epyllion is that of Crump 1931.

84 For *Maeonius* of Homer, cf. Hor. *Carm.* 1.6.2; Prop. 2.28.29; Ov. *Rem.* 373, *Pont.* 3.3.31; Mart. 7.46.2; Sil. 4.525. For *Maeonides* of Homer, cf. Ov. *Am.* 1.15.9, *Tr.* 4.10.22; Pers. 6.11; Stat. *Silv.* 5.3.130; Mart. 5.10.8.

85 Coleman 1977, 197 on *B.* 6.71; see also Ross 1975, 23–38.

86 Clausen 1982, 4–13.

87 Cf. Lucretius' hymn to Venus (1.1–20); on Virgil's debt to Lucretius, see Thomas 1988a, 1.86 on *G.* 3.242–3; Gale 2000, 221–3.

88 On the *bugonia* see Griffin 1979 (= Volk 2008b, 225–48); Perkell 1989, 74–80; Morgan 1999; Volk 2008b, 9–10; Keith 2018, 122–6.

Chapter 4

1 Standard discussions include Anderson 1957; Otis 1964; Gransden 1984. The traditional account of the epic's two discrete 'halves' has always been complicated by Virgil's use of 'local' models from both Homeric poems across all twelve books of the *Aeneid*, even as his Homeric narrative unfolds within this overarching scheme: see Knauer 1964. Cairns 1989, 177–214, discusses the importance of the *Odyssey* as a model for the *Aeneid* in its entirety; Dekel (2012, 2) argues that 'Virgil uses the *Odyssey* both as a conceptual model for writing an intertextual epic and as a powerful refracting lens for the specific interpretation of the *Iliad* and its consequences'.

2 On Virgil's interest in aetiology, and his literary debt to Callimachus' *Aetia* in the *Aeneid*, see George 1974; Clausen 1987 and 2002; Horsfall 1991; Bleisch 1994.

3 On Virgil's ambition to write an epic that was 'Homeric in form, Callimachean in style' (Clausen 1987, 14), see Clausen 2002.

4 The 'cyclic epics' were a series of poems composed in the seventh and sixth centuries BCE, and put into chronological order by the scholars of the Alexandrian Library. The Trojan cycle comprised eight poems, including Homer's *Iliad* and *Odyssey*, and an *Ilioupersis* ('Fall of Troy') attributed to Arctinus of Miletus: see *VE* s.v. 'Epic cycle'.

5 Knauer 1964; English summary in Knauer 1965. Nelis 2001 is an equally comprehensive treatment of Virgil's debts to the model of Apollonius of Rhodes' *Argonautica* for both his condensation of Homeric epic in his plot and his refinement of Alexandrian artistry in his poetics.

6 Barchiesi 2015[1984], 71–3.

7 On Virgil's complex of allusions to the Homeric *Hymn to Aphrodite* here, see Gladhill 2012.

8 In addition to Knauer 1964, see Cairns 1989, 129–35. The model of Apollonius of Rhodes' Medea is also important in Virgil's characterization of Dido: see Nelis 2001, 186–226. Servius notes (on *A.* 4.1) that *A.* 4 is entirely taken from *Arg.* 3.

9 Cairns 1989, 136–50.

10 On *militia amoris*, see Murgatroyd 1975; Kennedy 1993.

11 On the conventional tropes of love elegy, see Cairns 1989, 147–9; Kennedy 1993, 46–63.

12 Harrison 1972/73.

13 Clausen (1987, 42) heard a double-entendre here, with *succumbere* carrying a sexual connotation, and *uni* referring to Aeneas, a sense (of syntax completed) only dispelled by enjambed *culpae.*

14 Rudd 1976, 32–53 (= Harrison 1990, 145–66); Moles 1984 (= McAuslan and Walcot 1990, 142–8), and 1987. On the influence of tragedy in the Dido episode, see De Witt 1907; Pease 1935, 8–11; Quinn 1963, 29–58, and 1968, 323–49; Wlosok 1976 (translated in Hardie 1999); Muecke 1983; Clausen 1987, 40–60; Schiesaro 2008; Mac Góráin 2018.

15 Loraux 1987.

16 Sophocles (fifth century BCE) wrote a *Laocoon* and *Sinon*; the Latin tragedian Naevius (third century BCE) an *Equus Troianus*; and Accius (early first century BCE) a *Deiphobus.* On tragedy in the *Aeneid*, see Stabryła 1970; Wigodsky 1972, 18–21, 76–97; Hardie 1997; Conte 2007, 150–69; Panoussi 2009.

17 Gowers 2011 offers a compelling reading of Aeneas' 'systematic extirpation of the House of Priam' in *A*.

18 The 'Helen episode' (*A*. 2.567–88) is not preserved in the late antique manuscripts of *A*., but reported by Servius in his note on *A*. 2.566, where the omission is explained as the result of a decision to excise the passage taken by Virgil's literary executors after his death. Scholars have not universally accepted Virgilian authorship because of the peculiarities of the episode's textual transmission: see Horsfall 2008, 553–86, arguing against authenticity; Conte 2006, arguing for it.

19 Perkell 1981; cf. Keith 2000, 117–18.

20 For the parallels, cf. *pone* of the women following 'behind' their respective husbands (*G*. 4.487, *A*. 2.725), and the near success of both men (*G*. 4.485, *A*. 2.730–1).

21 Heinze 1993[1903], 68–70.

22 On Apollo in the *Aeneid*, see Heinze 1993; Paschalis 1986; Miller 2009.

23 On *Aeneid* 3, see Lloyd 1957a and 1957b.

24 On tree violation in the *Aeneid*, see Thomas 1988b; Dyson 2001; cf. Gowers 2011.

25 On Virgil's Harpies, see Keith 2000, 70–2.

26 On Virgil's intertextual relations with Apollonius' Harpies, see Nelis 2001, 32–8; Miller 2009, 122–5.

27 On the episode, see Horsfall 2006, 233–51; Keith 2016.

28 In addition to her eponymous tragedies by Euripides (extant) and Ennius (lost), Andromache appears in Euripides' *Troades* and Seneca's tragedy of the same name.

29 Quint 1991; cf. Quint 1993, 53–63.

30 On Achaemenides in Virgil (and Ovid), see Hinds 1998, 111–15.

31 Burgess 2015, 124–30.

32 Perkell in Ganiban 2012, 309.

33 On pathos in *A.*, see Conte 2007.

34 Lyne 1989, 48–51; Keith 2000, 24.

35 On the temporal problem, see Giusti 2018.

36 Farrell in Ganiban 2012, 367.

37 On the games in *Aeneid* 5, see Cairns 1989, 215–48.

38 Nelis 2001, 8–21.

39 Farrell in Ganiban 2012, 379.

40 On Ascanius' role in *A.*, see Rogerson 2017.

41 On ecphrasis in *A.*, see Putnam 1998.

42 The passage is well discussed by Horsfall 2000, 67–76, at 69.

43 Cairns 1989, 151–76, discusses Virgil's use of lyric topoi in connection with Lavinia.

44 On the gendered dichotomy of female war-mongers and male peacemakers in *A.*, see Keith 2000, 65–81.

45 On Pandarus and Bitias, see Hardie 1994, 213–34.

46 On Nisus and Euryalus as lovers, on the model of Achilles and Patroclus, see Hardie 1994, 32–4.

47 Barchiesi 2015[1984], 41–52, esp. 41–3.

48 On Camilla, see Arrigoni 1982; Boyd 1992; Keith 2000, 27–31; Boyd 2014.

49 Pöschl 1962[1950], 13–33; on the gendered nature of this dichotomy, see Keith 2000.

50 On the multiple erotic undercurrents in the following scene (12.54–80), see Lyne 1983; Tarrant 2012, 102–9.

51 Loraux 1987, 7–30.

52 Pöschl 1962[1950], 131.

53 On Virgil's similes, and their relation to the simile of Apollonius of Rhodes, see Nelis 2001; on his reuse of *G.* in *A.*, see Briggs 1980; Niehl 2002, 185–201.

54 On Ennius' *Annales*, see Elliott 2013; on Virgil's Ennius, see Goldschmidt 2013.

55 Elliott 2010.

56 On Jupiter's prophecy, see O'Hara 1990, 132–63.

57 Powell 2008 argues for Virgil as a partisan of Octavian/Augustus in all his poetry.

58 On the 'Parade of Heroes', see Feeney 1986; O'Hara 1990, 163–72; Hardie 1998, 96–7.

59 Aeneas wins the *spolia opima* in personal combat with Mezentius in *A*. 10. On the *spolia opima* at Rome, see Harrison 1989; Flower 2000.

60 On the shield of Aeneas, see Hardie 1986, 336–76; O'Hara 1990, 173–5; Putnam 1998.

61 On 'orientalism' in Virgil's depiction of the Battle of Actium, see Wyke 2002[1992], 196–243; Quint 1993, 21–31.

62 On Carthage in *A*., see Harrison 1984; Giusti 2018.

63 Toll 1991 and 1997.

64 Horsfall 2000, 360 on *A*. 7.545, citing Clausen 1994, 58 on *B*. 1.71.

65 For the instability of Juno's reconciliation, see Feeney 1984.

66 Buffière 1956; Lamberton 1986; Feeney 1991, 5–56.

67 On these issues see Feeney 1986; Hardie 1986; Braund 1997.

68 The interpretation is as old as Seneca, and has enjoyed particular currency in German scholarship: see, e.g. Heinze 1993[1915], 227[279], 374[475]; Wlosok 1983; *contra* O'Hara 1990.

69 Heinze 1993[1915], 227[278]; Bowra 1933.

70 Nelis 2015.

71 Nussbaum 1994, 402–38.

72 On anger in *A*., see Galinsky 1988 and 1994; Putnam 1990; Erler 1992; Fowler 1997; Wright 1997; Nelis 2015. Mellinghof-Bourgerie 1990 and Gill 2006, 435–61, argue for the importance of Hellenistic philosophy, especially Epicureanism, in *A*.

73 Asmis 1991.

74 On the philosophical undertones of Iopas' song, and its relation to the songs of Demodocus on Scheria, see Hardie 1986, 52–66; Farrell 1991, 258–62; Nelis 2001, 96–112; Adler 2003, 9–16.

75 On Dido as negative exemplum of Epicurean doctrine, see Dyson 1996; Gordon 1998 and 2012, 60–71.

76 On Virgil's extensive engagement with Lucretius and Philodemos in *A*., see Hardie 1986 and 2009; Adler 2003; Freer 2014.

77 Gill 2006, 460, even-handedly concludes that 'the *Aeneid* is written from a Stoic or an Epicurean standpoint (perspectives which often, if not always, converge on each other)'.

78 Feeney 1991, 173; Dyson 1996.

79 Gordon 2012, 68–71.

80 Bremmer 2009.

81 On the Orphic hues of Elysium, see Horsfall 2013, 1.xx–xxi, 2.437–508.

82 Lamacchia 1964.

83 Horsfall 2013, 609.

84 On the twin gates, see Tarrant 1982; Horsfall 2013, 2.612–18.

85 Gotoff 1985.

Chapter 5

1 On the reception of Virgil, especially *A.*, see Hardie 2014.

2 On 'frigidity' in ancient criticism, see Jocelyn 1979.

3 Krevans 2010.

4 Kidd 1977; Rumpf 2009.

5 Franklin 1997; Milnor 2009.

6 Zanker 1988, 179–83.

7 Franklin 1997; Richardson 2000.

8 Farrell 2002.

9 On Nemesianus' pastoral poetry, see Green in Rees 2004, 17–32.

10 On Virgil in early modern pastoral, see Alpers 1996.

11 On the reception history of *G.* in antiquity, see Thibodeau 2011; Goodfellow 2015.

12 Connors 1998, 100–46.

13 On Virgil and his Latin epic successors, see Feeney 1991, 128–391; Hardie 1993; Quint 1993; Keith 2000.

14 On Probus and his methods, see Jocelyn 1984, 1985a and 1985b.

15 Joseph 2012.

16 On Augustine's interest in Virgil, see MacCormack 1998; Wills in Farrell and Putnam 2010, 123–32; Clark 2019.

17 Modern scholars are sceptical of the use of the *sortes Vergilianae* in antiquity, and have viewed their appearance in *HA* as an emulative

response to the contemporary usage of the *sortes biblicae* among Christians and/or the established tradition of using Homer for prophecy (Dio *Cass*. 79.8.5–6): see Den Hengst in Rees 2004, 172–88.

18 On the late antique cento see Pollmann in Rees 2004, 79–96; McGill 2005; Sandness 2011.

19 On late antique biblical epic, see Roberts 1985; Green 2006.

20 Jacoff in Farrell and Putnam 2010, 155.

21 On the impact of Virgil and the Virgilian commentary tradition on these Latin epics, see Haynes 2014. On Virgil in the middle ages, see Comparetti 1997[1885]; Ziolkowski and Putnam 2008.

22 Jacoff in Farrell and Putnam 2010, 153.

23 On Vegio's *Supplement*, see Putnam 2004.

24 On the reception of Virgil in early modern Europe, see Martindale 1984; Kallendorf 1989, 2007a and 2007b; Wilson-Okamura 2010; Houghton and Sgarbi 2018. On Virgil in: French art and literature, see A. Pop in *VE* 890–1, and P.J. Usher in *VE* 2, 503–10; German art and literature, see D.B. Joyner in *VE* 2.539–41 and A. Classen, G. Atherton and T. Ziolkowski in *VE* 2.542–50; Italian art and literature, see I.D. Rowland in *VE* 2.671–4 and L. Pertile in *VE* 2.674–80; and American literature, see W. Briggs in *VE* 1.61–6. On the fascist reception of Virgil, see Thomas 2001, 222–59; on Virgil and Joyce, see Pogorzelski 2016.

25 Baswell 1995, 220–69; Gransden 1996, 1–4. Dido's appeal has endured through the ages: English highlights include Chaucer's 'Legend of Dido' in *The Legend of Good Women* (*c.* 1372–1380), Marlowe's *Tragedy of Dido, Queen of Carthage* (1594), and Henry Purcell's opera *Dido and Aeneas* (1680). On the reception of Dido in European art, literature, music and translation, see, e.g. Semrau 1930; Martin 1990; Reid 1993, I.48–58, 346–7; Desmond 1994; Kailuweit 2005. On Dido in Dryden and the Massachusetts' translation of John D. Long, see Thomas 2001, 154–89.

26 Keith 2018. On Virgil and his translators, see Braund and Torlone 2018.

27 Burrow 1997, 24.

28 On Milton and Virgil, see Quint 1993, 41–6; Du Rocher 2001; Martindale 2002.

29 On the politics of Dryden's translation of Virgil, see Thomas 2001, 122–53.

30 Harrison 1967, 91.

31 We may note, however, that the mid-eighteenth century had already seen the first prose translation of the *Aeneid*, by Joseph Davidson (1743; repr. 1754, 1790).

32 Ziolkowski 1993, 111, ascribes Day Lewis' 'lifelong preoccupation with Virgil' to *pietas*.

33 See Jamison 2017, on Robert Traill Spence Lowell IV – Poet Laureate Consultant in Poetry to the Library of Congress (1947–1948) and winner of the Pulitzer Prize for Poetry (1947, 1974), National Institute of Arts and Letters Award (1947), and National Book Critics Circle Award (1977).

34 Keith 2000 explores the gendered dynamics of the *Aeneid*. On 'Virgil's presence in contemporary women's writing', see Cox 2011.

35 Ruden 2008; Johnston 2012. For another recent literary translation of a single book of the *Aeneid*, see Heaney 2016.

Abbreviations

Names of classical authors and titles of their works are abbreviated following the conventions of the *Oxford Classical Dictionary*.

EV   *Enciclopedia Virgiliana*, 5 vols. Rome: Instituto della Enciclopedia italiana.

RE   Pauly-Wissowa (ed.), *Real-Encylopädie*.

Suppl. Hell.   H. Lloyd-Jones and P. Parsons (eds), *Supplementum Hellenisticum*. Berlin, 1983.

VE   R.F. Thomas and J.M. Ziolkowski (eds), *The Virgil Encyclopedia*, 3 vols. Malden MA and Oxford: Wiley-Blackwell.

Bibliography

Adler, E. 2003. *Vergil's Empire: Political Thought in the Aeneid*. Lanham.

Alpers, P. 1979. *The Singer of the* Eclogues: *A Study of Virgilian Pastoral*. Berkeley.

Alpers, P.J. 1996. *What is Pastoral?* Chicago.

Anderson, R.D., Parsons, P.J., and Nisbet, R.G.M. 1979. 'Elegiacs by Gallus from Qasr Ibrîm', *JRS* 69, 125–55.

Anderson, W.S. 1957. 'Vergil's Second *Iliad*', *TAPA* 88, 17–30.

André, J.-M. 1949. *La vie et l'œuvre d'Asinius Pollion*. Paris.

Arena, V. 2013. Libertas *and the Practice of Politics in the Late Roman Republic*. Cambridge.

Armstrong, D., Fish, J., Johnston, P.A., and Skinner, M.B. (eds) 2004. *Vergil, Philodemus and the Augustans*. Austin, TX.

Arrigoni, G. 1982. *Camilla amazzone e sacerdotessa di Diana*. Milan.

Asmis, E. 1991. 'Philodemus's Poetic Theory and "On the Good King According to Homer"', *CA* 10.1, 1–45.

Barchiesi, A. 2015. *Homeric Effects in Vergil's Narrative* tr. I. Marchesi and M. Fox. Princeton. [Originally published in Italian as *Traccia del modello*. Pisa: Giardini, 1984.]

Baswell, C. 1995. *Virgil in Medieval England: Figuring the* Aeneid *from the twelfth century to Chaucer*. Cambridge.

Benferhat, Y. 2005. Ciues Epicurei. *Les épicuriens et l'idée de monarchie à Rome et en Italie de Sylla à Octave*. Brussels.

Benko, S. 1980. 'Virgil's Fourth Eclogue in Christian Interpretation', *ANRW* II.31.1, 646–705.

Bing, P. 2016. 'Epicurus and the *Iuvenis* at Virgil's *Eclogue* 1.42', *CQ* 66.1, 172–9.

Bleisch, P. 1994. 'The Aetiological Tradition in Vergil's "Aeneid" Books 1–6'. PhD Dissertation, UCLA. Los Angeles.

Blum, R. 1991. *Kallimachos: the Alexandrian Library and the Origins of Bibliography*. Madison, WI.

Bowditch, P.L. 2001. *Horace and the Gift Economy of Patronage*. Berkeley.

Bowra, C.M. 1933. 'Aeneas and the Stoic ideal', *G&R* 3, 8–21 (= Harrison 1990, 363–77; Hardie 1999, 3.204–17).

Boyd, B.W. 1992. 'Virgil's Camilla and the Tradition of Catalogue and Ecphrasis (*Aeneid* 7.803–17)', *AJP* 113, 213–34.

Boyd, B.W. 2014. 'Camilla', *VE* 1, 224–5.

Braund, S. 1997. 'Virgil and the Cosmos: Religious and Philosophical Ideas', in Martindale 1997, 204–21.

Braund, S., and Torlone, Z. (eds) 2018. *Virgil and His Translators*. Oxford.

Breed, B.W. 2006. *Pastoral Inscriptions: Reading and Writing Virgil's Eclogues*. London.

Bremmer, J.N. 2009. 'The Golden Bough: Orphic, Eleusinian, and Hellenistic-Jewish Sources of Virgil's Underworld in *Aeneid* VI', *Kernos* 22, 183–208.

Briggs, W.W. 1980. *Narrative and Simile from the* Georgics *in the* Aeneid. Leiden.

Brown, E.L. 1963. Numeri Vergiliani: *Studies in* Eclogues *and* Georgics. Brussels.

Buffière, F. 1956. *Les mythes d'Homère et la pensée grecque*. Paris.

Burgess, J.S. 2015. *Homer*. London.

Burrow, C. 1997. 'Virgil in English Translation', in Martindale 1997, 21–37.

Buxton, J.B. 1995. *Theocritus's Urban Mimes: Mobility, Gender, Patronage*. Berkeley.

Cairns, F. 1989. *Virgil's Augustan Epic*. Cambridge.

Cairns, F. 2008. 'C. Asinius Pollio and the *Eclogues*', *PCPS* 54, 49–79.

Castner, C.J. 1988. *Prosopography of Roman Epicureans from the Second Century B.C. to the Second Century A.D.* Frankfurt am Main.

Cavallo, G. 1983. *Libri scritture scribe a Ercolano*. 1st suppl. to *CErc* 13. Naples.

Chillet, C. 2016. *De l'Étrurie à Rome: Mécène et la foundation de l'empire*. Rome.

Clark, G. 2019. 'Augustine's Virgil', in Martindale and Mac Góráin 2019, 77–87.

Clausen, W. 1982. 'The New Direction in Poetry', in E.J. Kenney (ed.), *The Cambridge History of Classical Literature: The Early Republic*, Vol. 2.2, 4–32. Cambridge.

Clausen, W. 1987. *Virgil's* Aeneid *and the Tradition of Hellenistic Poetry*. Berkeley.

Clausen, W. (ed.) 1994. *A Commentary on Virgil*, Eclogues. Oxford.

Clausen, W. 2002. *Virgil's* Aeneid: *Decorum, Allusion, and Ideology*. Munich and Leipzig.

Clay, D. 2009. 'The Athenian Garden', in Warren 2009, 9–28.

Coleman, R. (ed.) 1977. *Vergil, Eclogues.* Cambridge.

Comparetti, D. 1997[1885]. *Vergil in the Middle Ages*, tr. E.F.M. Benecke. Princeton.

Conte, G.B. 1992. 'Proems in the Middle', *YCS* 29, 147–59.

Conte, G.B. 2006. 'Questioni di metodo e critica dell'autenticità: discutendo ancora l'episodio di Elena', MD 56, 157–74.

Conte, G.B. 2007. *The Poetry of Pathos.* Oxford.

Connolly, J. 2001. 'Picture Arcadia: The politics of representation in Vergil's *Eclogues*', *Vergilius* 74, 89–116.

Connors, C. 1998. *Petronius the Poet.* Cambridge.

Courtney, E. 1981. 'The Formation of the Text of Vergil', *BICS* 28, 13–29.

Courtney, E. (ed.) 1993. *The Fragmentary Latin Poets.* Oxford.

Cova, P.V. 1989. *Il poeta Vario.* Milan.

Cox, F. 2011. *Sibylline Sisters: Virgil's Presence in Contemporary Women's Writing.* Oxford.

Crump, M.M. 1931. *The Epyllion from Theocritus to Ovid.* Oxford.

Currie, H. MacL. 1976. 'The Third Eclogue and the Roman Comic Spirit', *Mnem.* 29.4, 411–20.

Daintree, D. 1990. 'The Virgil Commentary of Aelius Donatus', *G&R* 37, 65–79.

Davis, N.G.G. 2012. *Parthenope: The Interplay of Ideas in Vergil's* Eclogues. Leiden.

De Witt, N.W. 1907. 'The Dido Episode as Tragedy', *CJ* 2, 283–8.

Dekel, E. 2012. *Virgil's Homeric Lens.* New York and London.

Desmond, M. 1994. *Reading Dido: Gender, Textuality, and the Medieval* Aeneid. Minneapolis.

Deufert, M. 2013. 'Vergilische Prosa? Überlegungen zu Macr. Sat. 1, 24, 11', *Hermes* 141, 331–50.

Du Rocher, R.J. 2001. *Milton among the Romans.* Pittsburgh.

Dyson, J. 1996. 'Dido the Epicurean', *CA* 15, 203–21.

Dyson, J. 2001. *King of the Wood: The Sacrificial Victor in Virgil's* Aeneid. Norman, OK.

Eck, W. 2007. *The Age of Augustus*, 2nd edition, tr. D.L. Schneider. Malden, MA.

Elliott, J. 2010. 'Ennius as Universal Historian: The Case of the *Annales*', in P. Liddel and A. Fear (eds), *Historiae Mundi: Studies in Universal History*, 148–61. London.

Elliott, J. 2013. *Ennius and the Architecture of the* Annales. Cambridge.

Erler, M. 1992. 'Der Zorn des Helden: Philodemus *De Ira* und Vergils Konzept des Zorns in der *Aeneis*', *GB* 18, 103–26.

Fairweather, J. 1974. 'Biographies of Ancient Writers', *Anc Soc* 5, 231–75.

Fairweather, J. 1981. *Seneca the Elder*. Cambridge.

Fairweather, J. 1984. 'Traditional Narrative, Inference and Truth in the *Lives* of Greek Poets', *PLLS* 4, 315–69.

Fantham, R.E. 2006. Julia Augusti, *the Emperor's Daughter*. London and New York.

Fantham, R.E. 2009. *Latin Poets & Italian Gods*. Toronto.

Farrell, J. 1991. *Vergil's* Georgics *and the Traditions of Ancient Epic*. Oxford.

Farrell, J. 2002. 'Greek Lives and Roman Careers in the Classical *Vita* Tradition', in P. Cheney and F. de Armas (eds), *European Literary Careers: The Author from Antiquity to the Renaissance*, 24–46. Toronto.

Farrell, J., and Putnam, M.C.J. 2010. *A Companion to Vergil's* Aeneid *and Its Tradition*. Chichester, UK and Malden, MA.

Fears, J.R. 1981. 'The Cult of Virtues and Roman Imperial Ideology', *ANRW* II.17.2, 827–948.

Feeney, D.C. 1984. 'The Reconciliations of Juno', *CQ* 34, 179–94.

Feeney, D.C. 1986. 'History and Revelation in Vergil's Underworld', *PCPS* 32, 1–24.

Feeney, D.C. 1991. *The Gods in Epic*. Oxford.

Fish, J. 2011. 'Not All Politicians Are Sisyphus: What Roman Epicureans Were Taught About Politics', in J. Fish and K.R. Sanders (eds), *Epicurus and the Epicurean Tradition*, 72–104. Cambridge.

Flower, H.I. 2000. 'The Tradition of the Spolia Opima: M. Claudius Marcellus and Augustus', *CA* 19.1, 34–64.

Fowler, D.P. 1997. 'Epicurean Anger', in S.M. Braund and C. Gill (eds), *The Passions in Roman Thought and Literature*, 16–35. Cambridge.

Franklin, J.L., Jr. 1997. 'Vergil at Pompei: A Teacher's Aid', *CJ* 92, 175–84.

Freer, N.W. 2014. *Vergil and Philodemus*. Ph.D. Dissertation, University College London. London.

Freer, N.W. 2019. 'Virgil's *Georgics* and the Epicurean Sirens of Poetry', in Xinyue and Freer 2019, 79–90.

Frischer, B. 1975. *At tu aureus esto. Eine Interpretation von Vergils 7. Ekloge.* Bonn.

Gale, M.R. 1991. 'Man and Beast in Lucretius and the *Georgics*', *CQ* 41, 414–26.

Gale, M.R. 2000. *Virgil on the Nature of Things: The* Georgics, Lucretius *and the Didactic Tradition*. Cambridge.

Gale, M.R. (ed.) 2004. *Latin Epic and Didactic Poetry.* Swansea.

Galinsky, G.K. 1988. 'The Anger of Aeneas', *AJP* 109, 321–48.

Galinsky, G.K. 1994. 'How to be Philosophical About the End of the *Aeneid*', *ICS* 19, 191–201.

Ganiban, R.T. (gen. ed.) 2012. *Vergil, Aeneid Books 1-6.* Newburyport, MA.

Gee, E. 2013. *Aratus and the Astronomical Tradition.* Oxford.

Gelzer, M. 1982. 'Die drei Briefe des C. Asinius Pollio', *Chiron* 2, 297–312.

George, E.V. 1974. Aeneid *8 and the* Aitia *of Callimachus.* Leiden.

Gigante, M. 1990. 'I frammenti di Sirone', *Paedeia* 45, 175–98.

Gigante, M., and Capasso, M. 1989. 'Il ritorno di Virgilio a Ercolano', *SIFC* 7, 3–6.

Gilbert, N. 2015. *Among Friends: Cicero and the Epicureans.* PhD Thesis, University of Toronto. Toronto.

Gill, C. 2006. *The Structured Self in Hellenistic and Roman Thought.* Oxford.

Giusti, E. 2018. *Carthage in Virgil's Aeneid.* Cambridge.

Gladhill, C.W. 2012. 'Sons, Mothers, and Sex: *Aeneid* 1.314–20 and the *Hymn to Aphrodite* Reconsidered', *Vergilius* 58, 159–68.

Goldschmidt, N. 2013. *Shaggy Crowns: Ennius' Annales and Virgil's Aeneid.* Oxford.

Goodfellow, M.S. 2015. 'Early Reception of Vergil's *Georgics: Protinus Italiam Concepit'*, *Vergilius* 61, 43–76.

Gordon, M.L. 1934. 'The Family of Vergil', *JRS* 24, 1–12.

Gordon, P. 1998. 'Phaeacian Dido: Lost Pleasures of an Epicurean Intertext', *CA* 17, 188–211.

Gordon, P. 2012. *The Invention and Gendering of Epicurus.* Ann Arbor, MI.

Gotoff, H. 1985. 'The Difficulty of the Ascent from Avernus', *CP* 80, 35–40.

Gow, A.S.F. (ed.) 1950. *Theocritus, with Translation and Commentary*, 2 vols. Cambridge.

Gow, A.S.F. 1953. *Nicander of Colophon, Poems and Poetical Fragments.* Cambridge.

Gowers, E. 2011. 'Trees and Family Trees in the *Aeneid*', *CA* 30.1, 87–118.

Gransden, K.W. 1984. *Virgil's* Iliad: *an Essay on Epic Narrative.* Cambridge.

Gransden, K.W. (ed.) 1996. *Virgil in English.* London: Penguin.

Graziosi, B. 2009. 'Horace, Suetonius, and the *Lives* of the Greek Poets', in L.B.T. Houghton and M. Wyke (eds), *Perceptions of Horace: A Roman Poet and his Readers*, 140–60. Cambridge.

Green, R.P.H. 2006. *Latin Epics of the New Testament.* Oxford.

Griffin, J. 1979. 'The Fourth *Georgic*, Virgil and Rome', *G&R* 26, 61–80 (= Volk 2008b, 225–48).

Griffin, M. 1989. 'Philosophy, Politics, and Politicians at Rome', in M. Griffin and J. Barnes (eds), *Philosophia Togata: Essays on Philosophy and Roman Society*, 1–37. Oxford.

Gruen, E. 1967. 'Cicero and Licinius Calvus', *HSCP* 71, 215–33.

Gutzwiller, K. 1996. 'The Evidence for Theocritean Poetry Books', in M.A. Harder, R.F. Regtuit, and G.C. Wakker (eds), *Theocritus* (Hellenistica Groningana 2), 119–48. Groningen.

Gutzwiller, K. 1998. *Poetic Garlands: Hellenistic Epigrams in Context.* Berkeley.

Hadas, M. 1966. *Sextus Pompey.* New York.

Harder, A. (ed.) 2012. Aetia: *Introduction, Text, Translation, and Commentary*, 2 vols. Oxford.

Hardie, P. 1986. *Cosmos and Imperium.* Oxford.

Hardie, P. 1993. *The Epic Successors of Virgil.* Cambridge.

Hardie, P. (ed.) 1994. Aeneid. *Book IX.* Cambridge.

Hardie, P. 1997. 'Virgil and Tragedy', in Martindale 1997, 312–26.

Hardie, P. 1998. *Virgil.* Greece & Rome New Surveys in the Classics No. 28. Cambridge.

Hardie, P. (ed.) 1999. *Virgil: Critical Assessments of Classical Authors*, 4 vols. London.

Hardie, P. 2009. *Lucretian Receptions: History, the Sublime, Knowledge.* Cambridge.

Hardie, P. 2014. *The Last Trojan Hero.* London.

Harrison, E.L. 1972/73. 'Why Did Venus Wear Boots? Some Reflections on *Aeneid* 1.314 f', *PVS* 12, 10–25.

Harrison, E.L. 1979. 'The Noric Plague in Virgil's Third *Georgic*', *PLLS* 2, 1–65.

Harrison, E.L. 1984. 'The *Aeneid* and Carthage', in T. Woodman and D. West (eds), *Poetry and Politics in the Age of Augustus*, 95–115. Cambridge.

Harrison, S.J. 1989. 'Augustus, the Poets, and the Spolia Opima', *CQ* 39.2, 408–14.

Harrison, S.J. (ed.) 1990. *Oxford Readings in Vergil's* Aeneid. Oxford and New York.

Harrison, T.W. 1967. 'English Virgil: The *Aeneid* in the XVIII Century', *Philologica Pragensia* 10, 1–11, 80–91.

Haynes, J. 2014. *Recovering the Classic: Twelfth-Century Epic and the Virgilian Tradition.* PhD Dissertation, University of Toronto. Toronto.

Heaney, S. 2016. Aeneid, *Book VI.* London.

Heinze, R. 1993. *Virgil's Epic Technique*, tr. H. Harvey, D. Harvey, and F. Robertson. Berkeley.

Henderson, J. 1998. 'Virgil's Third *Eclogue*: How Do You Keep an Idiot in Suspense?', *CQ* 48, 213–28 (= Volk 2008a, 125–54).

Henkel, H. 2014. 'Vergil Talks Technique: Metapoetic Arboriculture in *Georgics 2*', *Vergilius* 60, 33–66.

Highet, G. 1974. 'Performances of Vergil's *Bucolics*', *Vergilius* 20, 24–5.

Hinds, S. 1998. *Allusion and Intertext: Dynamics of Appropriation in Roman Poetry*. Cambridge.

Höschele, R. 2013. 'From Ecloga to Mime to Vergil's *Eclogues* as Mimes: *ein Gedankenspiel*', *Vergilius* 59, 37–60.

Hollander, J. 1981. *The Figure of Echo: A Mode of Allusion in Milton and After*. Berkeley.

Hollis, A.S. 1996. 'Virgil's Friend Varius Rufus', *PVS* 22, 19–33.

Hollis, A.S. (ed.) 2007. *Fragments of Roman Poetry c. 60 BC – AD 20*. Oxford.

Horsfall, N. 1981. 'Some Problems of Titulature in Roman Literary History', *BICS* 28, 103–14.

Horsfall, N. 1991. 'Virgil and the Poetry of Explanations', *G&R* 38, 203–11.

Horsfall, N. (ed.) 1995. *A Companion to the Study of Virgil*. Leiden.

Horsfall, N. 2000. *Virgil, Aeneid 7: A Commentary*. Leiden.

Horsfall, N. 2006. *Virgil, Aeneid 3: A Commentary*. Leiden.

Horsfall, N. 2008. *Virgil, Aeneid 2: A Commentary*. Leiden.

Horsfall, N. 2013. *Virgil, Aeneid 6: A Commentary*. Berlin.

Houghton, L.B.T., and Sgarbi, M. (eds) 2018. *Virgil and Renaissance Culture*. Tempe, AZ.

Hubbard, T.K. 1998. *The Pipes of Pan: Intertextuality and Literary Filiation in the Pastoral Tradition from Theocritus to Milton*. Ann Arbor, MI.

Hubaux, J. 1927. 'Le vers initial des Eglogues. Contribution a l'histoire du texte des *Bucolicque* latins', *RBPh* 6, 603–16.

Hunter, R. 1996. *Theocritus and the Archaeology of Greek Poetry*. Cambridge.

Hunter, R. 1999. *Theocritus: A Selection*. Cambridge.

Inwood, B., and Gerson, L. 1997. *Hellenistic Philosophy: Introductory Readings*, 2nd edition. Indianapolis and Cambridge.

Jamison, K.R. 2017. *Robert Lowell: Setting the River on Fire*. New York.

Jenkyns, R. 1989. 'Virgil and Arcadia', *JRS* 79, 26–39.

Jocelyn, H.D. 1979. 'Vergilius Cacozelus (Donatus "Vita Vergilii" 44)', *PLLS* 3, 67–104.

Jocelyn, H.D. 1984. 'The Annotations of M. Valerius Probus', *CQ* 34, 464–72.

Jocelyn, H.D. 1985a. 'The Annotations of M. Valerius Probus, ii: Some Virgilian Scholia', *CQ* 35, 149–61.

Jocelyn, H.D. 1985b. 'The Annotations of M. Valerius Probus, iii: Some Virgilian Scholia', *CQ* 35, 466–74.

Johnson, W.R. 2004. 'A Secret Garden: *Georgics* 4.116–148', in Armstrong et al. 2004, 75–83.

Johnston, P.A. 2012. *The Aeneid of Vergil.* Norman OK.

Jones, F. 2011. *Virgil's Garden: The Nature of Bucolic Space.* London.

Joseph, T.A. 2012. *Tacitus the Epic Successor: Virgil, Lucan, and the Narrative of Civil War in the* Histories. Leiden.

Kailuweit, T. 2005. *Dido—Didon—Didone: Eine kommentierte Bibliographie zum Dido-Mythos in Literatur und Musik.* Frankfurt am Main.

Kallendorf, C. 1989. *In Praise of Aeneas: Virgil and Epideictic Rhetoric in the Early Italian Renaissance.* Hanover, NH.

Kallendorf, C. 2007a. *The Virgilian Tradition: Book History and the History of Reading in Early Modern Europe.* Aldershot.

Kallendorf, C. 2007b. *The Other Virgil: 'Pessimistic' Readings of the Aeneid in Early Modern Culture.* Oxford.

Kania, R. 2016. *Virgil's* Eclogues *and the Art of Fiction: A Study of the Poetic Imagination.* Cambridge.

Karakasis, E. 2011. *Song Exchange in Roman Pastoral.* Berlin.

Kaster, R.A. 1988. *Guardians of Language: The Grammarian and Society in Late Antiquity.* Berkeley.

Kaster, R.A. 2014. 'Suetonius', *VE* 3, 1224–5.

Keith, A.M. 2000. *Engendering Rome: Women in Latin Epic.* Cambridge.

Keith, A.M. 2016. 'City Lament in Republican Latin Epic: Antitypes of Rome from Troy to Alba Longa', in M.R. Bachvarova, D. Dutsch, and A. Suter (eds), *The Fall of Cities in the Mediterranean,* 156–82. Cambridge.

Keith, A.M. 2018. 'Love and War: Translations of *Aeneid* 7 into English', in Braund and Torlone 2018, 63–79. Oxford.

Kennedy, D.F. 1993. *The Arts of Love: Five Studies in the Discourse of Roman Love Elegy.* Cambridge.

Kenney, E.J. 1982. 'Books and Readers in the Roman World', in E.J. Kenney (ed.), *The Cambridge History of Classical Literature,* 2.1.3–32. Cambridge.

Keppie, L. 1983. *Colonisation and Veteran Settlement in Italy 47–14 BC.* Rome.

Kettemann, R. 1977. *Bukolik und Georgik: Studien zu ihrer Affinität bei Vergil u. spatter.* Heidelberg.

Kidd, D.A. 1977. 'Virgil's Voyage', *Prudentia* 9, 97–103.

Knauer, G.N. 1964. *Die Aeneis und Homer.* Göttingen.

Knauer, G.N. 1965. 'Vergil's *Aeneid* and Homer', *GRBS* 5, 61–84 (= Harrison 1990, 390–412).

Körte, A. 1890. 'Augusteer bei Philodem', *RhM* 45, 112–17.

Krevans, N. 2010. 'Bookburning and the Poetic Deathbed: The Legacy of Virgil', in P.R. Hardie and H. Moore (eds), *Classical Literary Careers and Their Reception*, 197–208. Cambridge.

Kroll, W. 1927. 'Siro', *RE* 2.3, 353–4.

Kronenberg, L. 2009. *Allegories of Farming from Greece and Rome: Philosophical Satire in Xenophon, Varro, and Virgil*. Cambridge.

Kronenberg, L. 2016. 'Epicurean Pastoral: Daphnis as an Allegory for Lucretius in Vergil's *Eclogues*', *Vergilius* 62, 25–56.

La Penna, A. 1977. '*Senex Corycius*', in *Atti del Convegno Virgiliano sul Bimillenario delle Georgiche*, 37–66. Naples.

Lamacchia, R. 1964. 'Ciceros Somnium Scipionis und das sechste Buch der Aeneis', *RhM* 107, 261–78.

Lamberton, R. 1986. *Homer the Theologian: Neoplatonist Allegorical Reading and the Growth of the Epic Tradition*. Berkeley.

Le Doze, P. 2014. *Mécène: Ombres et flamboyances*. Paris.

Le Guin, U. 2008. *Lavinia*. New York.

Leach, E.W. 1978. 'Vergil, Horace, Tibullus: Three Collections of Ten', *Ramus* 7, 79–105.

Lefkowitz, M.R. 2012. *The Lives of the Greek* Poets, 2nd edition. Baltimore, MD.

Lightfoot, J.L (ed.) 1999. *Parthenius of Nicaea*. Oxford.

Lipka 2001. *Language in Vergil's Eclogues*. Berlin.

Lloyd, R.B. 1957a. '*Aeneid* III: A new approach', *AJP* 78, 133–51.

Lloyd, R.B. 1957b. '*Aeneid* III and the Aeneas Legend', *AJP* 78, 382–400.

Loraux, N. 1987. *Tragic Ways of Killing a Woman*, tr. A. Forster. Cambridge, MA.

Lyne, R.O.A.M. 1983. 'Lavinia's Blush: Vergil, *Aeneid* 12.64–70', *G&R* 30, 55–64.

Lyne, R.O.A.M. 1989. *Words and the Poet: Characteristic Techniques of Style in Vergil's* Aeneid. Oxford.

Mac Góráin, F. 2018. 'Vergil's Sophoclean Thebans', *Vergilius* 64, 131–56.

MacCormack, S. 1998. *The Shadows of Poetry: Vergil in the Mind of Augustine.* Berkeley.

Maltby, R. 1991. *A Lexicon of Ancient Latin Etymologies.* Leeds.

Martin, R. (ed.) 1990. *Énée et Didon: Naissance, fonctionnement et survie d'un myth.* Paris.

Martindale, C. (ed.) 1984. *Virgil and His Influence: Bimillennial Studies.* Bristol.

Martindale, C. (ed.) 1997. *The Cambridge Companion to Virgil.* Cambridge.

Martindale, C. 2002. *John Milton and the Transformation of Ancient Epic*, 2nd edition. London.

Martindale, C., and Mac Góráin, F. (eds) 2019. *The Cambridge Companion to Virgil*, 2nd edition. Cambridge.

Mayer, R. 1983. 'Missing Persons in the *Eclogues*', *BICS* 30, 17–30.

McAuslan, I., and Walcot, P. 1990. *Greece & Rome Studies: Virgil.* Oxford.

McGill, S. 2005. *Virgil Recomposed: The Mythological and Secular Centos in Antiquity.* Oxford.

Meban, D. 2008. 'Temple Building, Primus Language, and the Proem to Virgil's Third *Georgic*', *CP* 103, 150–74.

Mellinghof-Bourgerie, V. 1990. *Les incertitudes de Virgile: contributions épicuriennes à la théologie de l'Enéide.* Brussels.

Miles, G.B. 1980. *Virgil's* Georgics: *A New Interpretation.* Berkeley.

Miller, J.F. 2009. *Apollo, Augustus and the Poets.* Cambridge.

Milnor, K. 2009. 'Literacy in Roman Pompeii: the Case of Vergil's *Aeneid*', in W.A. Johnson (ed.), *Ancient Literacies: The Culture of Reading in Greece and Rome*, 288–319. Oxford.

Mizera, S.M. 1982. 'Lucretian Elements in Menalcas' Song, "Eclogue" 5', *Hermes* 110, 367–71.

Moles, J.L. 1984. 'Aristotle and Dido's *hamartia*', *G&R* 31, 48–54 (= McAuslan and Walcot 1990, 142–8).

Moles, J.L. 1987. 'The Tragedy and Guilt of Dido', in M. Whitby et al. (eds), Homo Viator: *Classical Essays for John Bramble*, 153–61. Bristol.

Momigliano, A. 1941. 'Epicureans in Revolt', *JRS* 31, 149–57.

Morgan, L. 1999. *Patterns of Redemption in Virgil's* Georgics. Cambridge.

Muecke, F. 1983. 'Foreshadowing and Dramatic Irony in the Story of Dido', *AJP* 104, 134–55.

Murgatroyd, P. 1975. '*Militia amoris* in the Roman Elegists', *Latomus* 34, 59–79.

Murgia, C.E. 2003. 'The Dating of Servius Revisited', *CP* 98, 45–69.

Mynors, R.A.B. (ed.) 1969. Vergili Maronis Opera. Oxford: Clarendon Press.

Mynors, R.A.B. (ed.) 1990. *Virgil,* Georgics. Oxford: Clarendon Press.

Naumann, H. 1981. 'Suetonius' Life of Virgil', *HSCP* 85, 185–7.

Nelis, D.P. 2001. *Vergil's* Aeneid *and the* Argonautica *of Apollonius Rhodius.* Leeds.

Nelis, D.P. 2015. 'Juno, Sea-storm and Emotion in Virgil, *Aeneid* 1.1–156: Homeric and Epicurean contexts', in D. Cairns (ed.), *Emotions between Greece and Rome*, 149–61. London.

Nelsestuen, G.A. 2015. *Varro the Agronomist: Political Philosophy, Satire, and Agriculture in the Late Republic.* Columbus, OH.

Néraudau, J.-P. 1983. 'Asinius Pollion et la poésie', *ANRW* II.30.3, 1732–50.

Niehl, R. 2002. *Vergils Vergil: Selbstzitat und Selbstdeutung in der* Aeneis. *Ein Kommentar und Interpretationen.* Frankfurt am Main.

Nisbet, R.G.M. 1987. 'Pyrrha among Roses: Real Life and Poetic Imagination in Augustan Rome', review of J. Griffin, *Latin Poets and Roman Life* (London 1985), *JRS* 77, 184–90.

Nisbet, R.G.M., and Hubbard, M. 1970. *A Commentary on Horace,* Odes, *Book I.* Oxford.

Nussbaum, M.C. 1994. *The Therapy of Desire: Theory and Practice in Hellenistic ethics.* Princeton.

O'Hara, J.J. 1990. *Death and the Optimistic Prophecy in Vergil's* Aeneid. Princeton.

O'Hara, J.J. 1996. *True Names: Vergil and the Alexandrian Tradition of Etymological Wordplay.* Ann Arbor MI.

O'Keefe, T. 2010. *Epicureanism.* Berkeley.

Obbink, D. (ed.) 1996. *Philodemus,* On Piety Part 1: Critical Text with Commentary. Oxford.

Otis, B. 1964. *Virgil: A Study in Civilized Poetry.* Oxford.

Panayotakis, C. 2008. 'Virgil on the Popular Stage', in E. Hall and R. Wyles (eds), *New Directions in Ancient Pantomime*, 186–97. Oxford.

Pandey, N. 2013. 'Caesar's Comet, the Julian Star, and the Invention of Augustus', *TAPA* 143.2, 405–49.

Panoussi, V. 2009. *Greek Tragedy in Vergil's* Aeneid: Ritual, Empire, and Intertext. Cambridge.

Paschalis, M. 1986. 'Virgil and the Delphic Oracle', *Philologus* 130, 44–68.

Paturzo, F. 1999. *Mecenate, il ministro d'Augusto: politica, filosofia, letteratura nel period augusteo.* Cortona.

Pease, A.S. (ed.) 1935. Aeneidos liber quartus. Cambridge MA.

Peirano, I. 2012. *The Rhetoric of the Roman Fake: Latin Pseudepigrapha in Context.* Cambridge.

Perkell, C. 1981. 'On Creusa, Dido, and the Quality of Victory in Virgil's *Aeneid*', *Women's Studies* 8, 201–23.

Perkell, C. 1989. *The Poet's Truth: A Study of the Poet in Virgil's* Georgics. Berkeley.

Perutelli, A. 1995. 'Bucolics', in Horsfall 1995, 27–62.

Pogorzelski, R.J. 2016. *Virgil and Joyce: Nationalism and Imperialism in the* Aeneid *and* Ulysses. Madison, WI.

Pöschl, V. 1962. *The Art of Vergil*, tr. G. Seligson. Ann Arbor, MI.

Posch, S. 1969. *Beobachtungen zur Theokritnachwirkung bei Vergil.* Commentationes Aenipontanae 19. Innsbruck.

Powell, A. 2008. *Virgil the Partisan: A Study in the Re-integration of Classics.* Swansea.

Powell, A., and Welch, T. (eds) 2002. *Sextus Pompeius.* Swansea.

Powell, A., and Hardie, P. (eds) 2017. *The Ancient Lives of Virgil: Literary and Historical Studies.* Swansea.

Putnam, M.C.J. 1970. *Virgil's Pastoral Art: Studies in the* Eclogues. Princeton.

Putnam, M.C.J. 1979. *Virgil's Poem of the Earth: Studies in the* Georgics. Princeton.

Putnam, M.C.J. 1990. 'Anger, Blindness and Insight in Virgil's *Aeneid*', *Apeiron* 23.4, 7–39.

Putnam, M.C.J. 1998. *Virgil's Epic Designs: Ekphrasis in the* Aeneid. New Haven CT.

Putnam, M.C.J. (ed.) 2004. *Short Epics: Maffeo Vegio.* Cambridge MA.

Quinn, K. 1963. *Latin Explorations: Critical Studies in Roman Literature.* London.

Quinn, K. 1968. *Virgil's* Aeneid: *A Critical Description.* London.

Quint, D. 1991. 'Repetition and Ideology in the *Aeneid*', *MD* 23, 9–54.

Quint, D. 1993. *Epic and Empire.* Princeton.

Rees, R. (ed.) 2004. Romane Memento: *Vergil in the Fourth Century.* London.

Reid, J.D. 1993. *The Oxford Guide to Classical Mythology in the Arts, 1300–1990*, 2 vols. Oxford.

Reynolds, L.D. (ed.) 1983. *Texts and Transmission: A Survey of the Latin Classics.* Oxford.

Richardson, L. 2000. *A Catalog of Identifiable Figure Painters of Ancient Pompeii, Herulaneum, and Stabiae.* Baltimore, MD.

Rist, J. 1972. *Epicurus: An Introduction.* Cambridge.

Roberts, M. 1985. *Biblical Epic and Rhetorical Paraphrase in Late Antiquity.* Liverpool.

Rogerson, A. 2017. *Virgil's Ascanius: Imagining the Future.* Cambridge.

Rosati, G. 1999. 'Form in Motion: Weaving the Text in the *Metamorphoses*', in P. Hardie, A. Barchiesi and S. Hinds (eds), *Ovidian Transformations: Essays on the* Metamorphoses *and its Reception*: 240–53. Cambridge.

Rosenmeyer, T.G. 1969. *The Green Cabinet: Theocritus and the European Pastoral Lyric.* Berkeley.

Roskam, G. 2007. 'Live Unnoticed' (Λάϑε βιώσας): On the Vicissitudes of an Epicurean Doctrine. Leiden.

Ross, D.O., Jr. 1975. *Backgrounds to Augustan Poetry: Gallus, Elegy and Rome.* Princeton.

Ross, D.O., Jr. 1987. *Virgil's Elements: Physics and Poetry in the Georgics.* Princeton.

Rudd, N. 1976. *Lines of Inquiry.* Cambridge.

Ruden, S. 2008. *The* Aeneid. New Haven CT.

Rumpf, L. 2009. '*Caelum ipsum petimus stultitia.* Zur poetologischen Deutung von Horaz' c. 1.3', *RhM* 152, 292–311.

Salvatore, A. 1977. '*Georgiche* di Virgilio e *De Re Rustica* di Varrone', in *Atti del Convegno Virgiliano sul Bimillenario delle Georgiche*, 67–111. Naples.

Sandness, K.O. 2011. *The Gospel 'According to Homer and Virgil': Cento and Canon.* Leiden.

Saunders, T. 2008. *Bucolic Elegy: Virgil's* Eclogues *and the Environmental Literary Tradition.* London.

Schäfer, S. 1996. *Das Weltbild der Vergilischen* Georgika *in seinem Verhältnis zu* De rerum natura *des Lukrez.* Frankfurt am Main.

Scheid, J., and Svenbro, J. 1996. *The Craft of Zeus: Myths of Weaving and Fabric.* Cambridge MA.

Schiesaro, A. 2008. 'Furthest Voices in Virgil's Dido', *SIFC* 6, 60–109, 194–245.

Schmidt, E.A. 1975. 'Arkadien: Abendland und Antike', *A&A* 21, 36–57 (tr. = Volk 2008a, 16–47).

Scullard, H.H. 1981. *Festivals and Ceremonies of the Roman Republic.* Ithaca NY.

Sedley, D.N. 2009. 'Epicureanism in the Roman Republic', in Warren 2009, 29–45.

Segal, C.P. 1967. 'Vergil's *caelatum opus*: An Interpretation of the Third Eclogue', *AJP* 88, 279–308.

Semrau, E. 1930. *Dido in der deutschen Dichtung.* Berlin.

Sider, D. 1997. *The Epigrams of Philodemus.* Oxford.

Skutsch, O. 1969. 'Symmetry and Sense in the *Eclogues*', *HSCP* 73, 153–68.

Smith, P.L. 1970. 'Vergil's *Avena* and the Pipes of Pastoral Poetry', *TAPA* 101, 497–510.

Snell, B. 1945. 'Arkadien: Die Entdeckung einer geistigen Landschaft', *A&A* 1, 26–41 (tr. = Hardie 1999, 1.44–67).

Stabryła, A. 1970. *Latin Tragedy in Virgil's Poetry.* Wroclaw.

Starr, R.J. 1995. 'Vergil's Seventh *Eclogue* and its Readers: Biographical Allegory as an Interpretative Strategy in Antiquity and Late Antiquity', *CP* 90, 129–38.

Syme, R. 1939. *The Roman Revolution*. Oxford.

Tarrant, R.J. 1982. 'Aeneas and the Gates of Sleep', *CP* 77, 51–5.

Tarrant, R.J. 2012. *Virgil, Aeneid Book XII*. Cambridge.

Thibodeau, P.J. 2011. *Playing the Farmer: Representations of Rural Life in Vergil's Georgics*. Berkeley.

Thill, A. 1979. *Alter ab illo: recherches sur l'imitation dans la poésie personnelle à l'époque augustéenne*. Paris.

Thomas, R.F. 1986. 'Vergil and the Art of Reference', *HSCP* 90, 171–98.

Thomas, R.F. 1988a. *Virgil. Georgics*, 2 vols. Cambridge.

Thomas, R.F. 1988b. 'Tree Violation and Ambivalence in Virgil', *TAPA* 118, 261–73.

Thomas, R.F. 1999. *Reading Virgil and His Texts: Studies in Intertextuality*. Ann Arbor, MI.

Thomas, R.F. 2001. *Virgil and the Augustan Reception*. Cambridge.

Toll, K. 1991. 'The *Aeneid* as an Epic of National Identity', *Helios* 18, 3–14.

Toll, K. 1997. 'Making Roman-ness and the *Aeneid*', *CA* 16, 35–56.

Traina, A. 1965. 'Si numquam fallit imago': Riflessioni sulle *Bucoliche* e l'epicureismo', in *Poeti latini (e neolatini): note e saggi filologici*, 2nd edition, 163–74. Bologna.

Tsouna, V. 2007. *The Ethics of Philodemus*. Oxford.

Tsouna, V. (ed.) 2012. *Philodemus, On Property Management*. Atlanta.

Van Sickle, J. 2004. *The Design of Virgil's Bucolics*, 2nd edition. London.

Vaughn, J.W. 1981. 'Theocritus Vergilianus and Liber Bucolicon', *Aevum* 55, 47–68.

Volk, K. 2002. *The Poetics of Latin Didactic*. Oxford.

Volk, K. (ed.) 2008a. *Vergil's Eclogues. Oxford Readings in Classical Studies*. Oxford.

Volk, K. (ed.) 2008b. *Vergil's Georgics. Oxford Readings in Classical Studies*. Oxford.

Warren, J. (ed.) 2009. *The Cambridge Companion to Epicureanism*. Cambridge.

Weinstock, S. 1971. *Divus Julius*. Oxford.

White, P. 1993. *Promised Verse: Poets in the Society of Augustan Rome*. Cambridge MA.

Wigodsky, M. 1972. *Vergil and Early Latin Poetry*. Wiesbaden.

Wilson-Okamura, D.S. 2010. *Virgil in the Renaissance*. Cambridge.

Winterbottom, M. 1976. 'Virgil and the Confiscations', in McAuslan and Walcot 1990, 65–8.

Wirszubski, C. 1950. *Libertas as a Political Idea at Rome During the Late Republic and Early Principate*. Cambridge.

Wiseman, T.P. 1974. *Cinna the Poet, and other Roman Essays*. Leicester.

Wlosok, A. 1976. 'Vergils Didotragödie. Ein Beitrag zum Problem des Tragischen in der Aeneis', in H. Görgemanns and E.A. Schmidt (eds), *Studien zum antiken Epos*, 228–50. Meisenheim.

Wlosok, A. 1983. 'Vergil als Theologe: Iuppiter-pater omnipotens', *Gymn.* 90, 187–202.

Wright, J.E.G. 1983. 'Virgil's Pastoral Programme: Theocritus, Callimachus and *Eclogue* 1', *PCPS* 29, 107–60.

Wright, M.R. 1997. '*Ferox uirtus*: Anger in Virgil's *Aeneid*', in S.M. Braund and C. Gill (eds), *The Passions in Roman Thought and Literature*, 169–84. Cambridge.

Wyke, M. 2002. *The Roman Mistress*. Oxford.

Xinyue, B., and Freer, N. 2019. *Reflections and New Perspectives on Virgil's Georgics*. London.

Yona, S. 2018. *Epicurean Ethics in Horace. The Psychology of Satire*. Oxford.

Zanker, P. 1988. *The Power of Images in the Age of Augustus*, tr. H.A. Shapiro. Ann Arbor MI.

Zecchini, G. 1982. 'Asinio Pollione: dall'attività politica alla riflessione storiografica', *ANRW* II.30.2, 1265–96.

Zetzel, J.E.G. 1973. '*Emendaui ad Tironem*', *HSCP* 77, 227–45.

Ziolkowski, J.M. 1993. *Virgil and the Moderns*. Princeton.

Ziolkowski, J.M., and Putnam, M.C.J. 2008. *The Virgilian Tradition: The First Fifteen Hundred Years*. New Haven CT.

Index Locorum

General Index